THE OTHER SIDE OF THE GOOD NEWS

universalism | annihilationism | postmortem conversion | eternal punishment

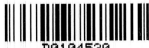

"Dr. Larry Dixon capably defends the church's historic position on hell, responsibly handles the Scriptures, respectfully interacts with opponents and writes in a manner that is at once attractive, passionate and accessible to ordinary believers."

Robert A. Peterson, Covenant Theological Seminary
Author, *Hell on Trial* and
***Two Views on Hell* (Co-authored with Edward Fudge)**

"Larry Dixon has addressed a topic which is of great current importance . . . This is a book which every serious student of the Bible and theology must read."

Millard J. Erickson, Professor at Truett Divinity School,
Baylor University

"Larry Dixon is refreshing! His courage in dealing with the 'hard truth' of the much ignored doctrine of hell is to be commended – a 'must read' for every believer."

Steve Brown, KeyLife Network

"In a climate where universalism is very fashionable in churches and seminaries, Dr. Dixon stands forthrightly in support of the traditional orthodox doctrine of endless conscious punishment."

Roger Nicole, Reformed Theological Seminary,
Orlando Campus

"A thoughtful, provocative, and fair-minded treatment of a controversial theme in Christian doctrine."

Thomas Oden,
Drew University Graduate and Theological School

"This outstanding book is a comprehensive treatment of a vitally important topic and it is characterized by top level scholarship and eminent readability."

Ajith Fernando,
Author; National Director, Youth for Christ, Sri Lanka
Author, *Crucial Questions about Hell.*

THE OTHER SIDE OF THE GOOD NEWS

universalism | annihilationism | postmortem conversion | eternal punishment

CONFRONTING THE CONTEMPORARY CHALLENGES TO JESUS' TEACHING ON HELL

LARRY DIXON

Christian Focus

For further works by Larry Dixon, please check out his website at: www.docdevos.com

ISBN1-85792-804-0

Published in 2003
by
Christian Focus Publications, Ltd.
Geanies House, Fearn, Tain,
Ross-shire, IV20 1TW, Great Britain.

www.christianfocus.com

Cover Design by Alister MacInnes

Printed and bound by
Mackays of Chatham

Contents

Dedication

This work is fondly dedicated to my first theology teacher, Mr. Bill Anderson. I thank the Lord for your encouragement to me to pursue the truth of God — wherever it may lead.

Foreword

"To die," said Barrie's Peter Pan, "would be an awfully big adventure." The biblical statement, "man is destined to die once, and after that to face judgment" (Heb. 9:27), might prompt the comment that he was more right than he knew; and certainly dying is not an adventure to which the modern Westerner looks forward. This is partly because modern Westerners love this present world so strongly. The law of fallen human nature, that the more you have the more you want, is operating. Modern medicine and affluence give most of us a longer, more comfortable, more varied and more pleasant life than our grandfathers thought possible, and as a result we want it to go on for ever, and cling to it with a passion that is sometimes positively degrading. But another factor operates too. The sense that death is to be feared because it is in some way retribution for wrongdoing is ineradicable, however much we try to rationalize it away with the filmmakers' secular mythology of ultimate happiness after death and the New Age mythology of reincarnation. Deep down, everybody feels uneasy about death and with good reason. After death, we face judgment.

To believe what the Bible appears to say about human destiny apart from the grace of God is a bitter pill indeed, and no one should wonder that attempts are made to explore alternative understandings of God's revelation on this topic. It is suggested that the Bible is unclear, or incoherent, or inconsistent, or untrustworthy, when it speaks of the outcome of judgment after death, or alternatively that virtually the whole church has for two thousand years misunderstood the texts. Are any of these suggestions plausible? I do not think so, nor does Dr. Dixon. He has mounted an argument that, however disconcerting, must be reckoned with in any future discussion of Bible teaching on human destiny. I for one am grateful for his work, and commend it to all who are willing to be biblically rational on this somber subject.

J.I. Packer
Board of Governors' Professor of Theology,
Regent College

Introduction

The Thinker, Rodin's famous statue, sits in mute amazement, contemplating lost souls entering hell. Most of us certainly prefer to think about something other than the eternal destiny of those who reject Jesus Christ, but that's what this book is about.

One motivation for this book is personal. A faithful youth worker forty years ago challenged a small, insecure, pimpled group of adolescents with a simple question: "If you were to die tonight, where would you spend eternity?" It's the kind of question we see brightly painted on large rocks on interstate highways. But like only a few of the many questions which we hear in life, this one sunk deep into my heart on that Friday night so long ago.

I knew the Gospel, but had not yet come to know the Person of that good news. The question of eternity burned in my mind all the way home that night, and I barely made it to my room before dropping to my knees beside my bed and receiving Christ. It was a teenager's sense of guilt — and rightfully deserved judgment in hell — but I'm not ashamed to acknowledge that the Holy Spirit used fear to bring me to Christ.

Many youth groups since that night have come and gone. How many have been (or are being) asked that same question about eternity?

Today's "kinder and gentler" evangelicalism seems to question such a motivation for salvation. "People should respond to the love of God, not to His wrath," we are told. More than fifty years ago the evangelist Billy Sunday declared, "If there is no Hell, a good many preachers are obtaining money under false pretenses!" His assumption was that preachers were proclaiming the doctrine of perdition. Today's sermons, however, seldom include any reference to hell and seem as if they were inspired by a kind of Miltonian collection entitled "Perdition Lost."

In a world which has lost its ability to blush (Jer. 6:15; 8:12), people who come to Christ out of the fear of judgment and hell are looked at as a bit old-fashioned and perhaps theologically uninformed. But if the biblical doctrine of hell is true, there is indeed something to fear! To paraphrase songwriter Stevie Wonder: "When you don't believe in things you don't understand, then you suffer!"

But is the biblical doctrine of hell true? A more basic question might be "Is there a biblical doctrine of hell?" or are Christians free to hold a variety of viewpoints on this issue?

The traditional doctrine of eternal conscious punishment has always been attacked by the cults. Charles Taze Russell, the founder of the Jehovah's Witnesses, once believed fervently in the doctrine of hell. In fact, he was so fearful of hell that he would write a warning about it on the sidewalks of Pittsburgh, urging people to go to church and get right with God. One day he met a skeptic whose questions he could not answer, and he gave up his belief in hell.

Evangelical Christians have the same challenge today, except the questions are coming from fellow evangelicals. One theologian writes:

> How can Christians possibly project a deity of such cruelty and vindictiveness whose ways include inflicting

> everlasting torture upon his creatures, however sinful they may have been? Surely a God who would do such a thing is more nearly like Satan than like God, at least by any ordinary moral standards, and by the Gospel itself.[1]

Hell in the Headlines

Magazine articles on the end times, especially the doctrine of eternal lostness, continue to multiply. *Time* magazine's July 1, 2002, cover story was entitled "The Bible and the Apocalypse: Why More Americans Are Reading and Talking about the End of the World." That article focused on the literary phenomenon of the *Left Behind* novels, ten of which at the time of that article had sold almost *36 million* copies!

Newsweek's August 12, 2002, cover story was entitled "Visions of Heaven: How Views of Paradise Inspire — And Inflame — Christians, Muslims, and Jews." The concluding article in that discussion was Kenneth L. Woodward's "Why We Need Hell, Too."

The public's interest and belief has seldom in recent history been higher in what one writer calls "the fantasy of the fanatical." Over a decade ago articles in secular magazines sported titles and cover stories such as "The Rekindling of Hell" (*U.S. News and World Report*, March 25, 1991), "Heaven" (including a survey on and a history about hell, *Newsweek*, March 27, 1991), and "Soft Selling Hell" (subtitled, "Don't Worry, Says a Catholic Theologian, It's Really No Worse Than a Three-Star Motel," *Western Report*, July 8, 1991). One wonders when *Life* magazine will provide a photo layout.

The April 24, 1991 issue of *Newsweek*, for example, included a letter to the editor which read:

> I noticed that your article on heaven and hell credits unspecified Newsweek bureau reports. Do you have correspondents filing dispatches from one or both of those places?

Bill Faris, pastor of Crown Valley Vineyard Christian Fellowship in Orange County, California, says that he never mentions hell to his congregation. "It isn't sexy enough anymore," Faris said. ("Hell Hath . . . No Fury," *The State* newspaper, July 12, 2002). Harvey Cox Jr., an eminent author and professor at Harvard Divinity School, said, "There has been a shift in religion from focusing on what happens in the next life to asking, 'What is the quality of this life we're leading now?' You can go to a whole lot of churches week after week and you'd be startled even to hear a mention of hell." ("Hell Hath . . . No Fury," *The State* newspaper, July 12, 2002).

Christians have responded to the disappearance of hell. Ten years ago articles such as "Heaven and Hell," subtitled "Who Will Go Where and Why" (*Christianity Today*, May 27, 1991) and "Evangelicals and the Annihilation of Hell" (*Christian Research Journal*, Spring and Summer, 1991) discussed the destiny of the damned. Robert Peterson's book, *Hell on Trial: The Case for Eternal Punishment* (Phillipsburg, N.J.: P&R Publishing, 1995), provides a helpful summary of various attacks on the traditional view of hell. The *Evangelical Quarterly*'s October 1995 issue published an article entitled "Jonathan Edwards on Hell." *The Journal of Religion* published an article with the strange title "The Beauty of Hell" in its July 1993 issue.

The 2001 Gallup poll of adults nationwide found that 71 percent believe in hell, but they just don't want to hear about it. A previous Gallup poll determined that more Americans believe in hell today than did in the generally more wholesome and pious 1950s. "Three out of five Americans believe in Hades," proclaimed *U.S. News and World Report's* article "Hell's Sober Comeback" over ten years ago. (March 25, 1991). Belief in hell is stronger among those between the ages of eighteen and twenty-nine, the Gallup organization's 1990 survey reveals. A whopping 78 percent of Americans surveyed felt they had an excellent or good chance of going to heaven when they died; only 4 percent thought their destiny would be the fiery pit. Even those who claim no religious belief expect life to go on after death (46 percent believe in heaven, 34 percent in hell).

A Christian Decline

Yet with the increasing belief of those not committed to biblical Christianity, there is a corresponding unbelief (or uncertainty) of those who profess to be committed Christians. Evangelicals were, perhaps, not surprised to hear Pope John Paul II state in 1999 that hell should be seen not as a fiery underworld but as "the state of those who freely and definitively separate themselves from God, the source of all life and joy. So eternal judgment is not God's work but is actually our own doing."[2] But Bruce Shelley, a senior professor of church history at Denver Theological Seminary, honestly speaks of many evangelicals when he says that preaching on hell "is just too negative. Churches are under enormous pressure to be consumer-oriented. Churches today feel the need to be appealing rather than demanding."[3]

In an article in *World* magazine, David Wells, author of *No Place for Truth* and *God in the Wasteland*, speaks about the issue of Christian "core beliefs." He laments the fact, borne out by a recent survey by George Barna, that supposedly born-again people make up half of the American population. But they are simply *consumers*, says Wells.

> For a one-time admission of weakness and failure they got eternal peace with God. That was the deal. They took it and went on with their lives as before. The result is that there is no significant difference between the way born-againers live at an ethical level as compared with those who are nonreligious . . . . Clearly, the evangelical church is not building the kind of steel-like character that can resist the temptations modern life brings along with its many benefits.[4]

Consumerism may well be the problem. A 1998 poll by Barna Research Group discovered that church-hopping has become a way of life for many Christians. One in seven adults changes churches *each year*; one in six regularly rotates among congregations.[5] Martin Marty, professor emeritus of religion and culture at the University of Chicago Divinity School, comments: "Once pop evangelism went into market analysis, hell was just dropped."[6]

Over ten years ago James Davison Hunter wrote in his *Evangelicalism: The Coming Generation* that several surveys reflect "a softening of doctrinal certainties" among undergraduate and seminary students who describe themselves as fundamentalist Christians. There is, especially, "a measurable degree of uneasiness within this generation of Evangelicals with the notion of an eternal damnation."[7]

When asked what would be their first step in seeking to influence non-Christians to convert to Christ, only one out of ten said that that first step would be to warn them of the wrath of God and eternal damnation. Sixty-seven percent claimed that the first reason they would give a nonbeliever would be either the "sense of meaning and purpose in life" coming from being a Christian or a personal testimony that "God has made a difference in my life." Virtually half (46 percent) of the seminarians surveyed "felt that under most circumstances or even all circumstances, to emphasize to nonbelievers that 'they will be eternally damned in hell if they do not repent of their sins' was in 'poor taste.'"[8]

Later Hunter points out that "the symbolic boundaries of Protestant orthodoxy are not being maintained or reinforced." He continues:

> Evangelicals generally and the coming generation particularly have adopted to various degrees an ethical code of political civility. This compels them not only to be tolerant of others' beliefs, opinions, and lifestyles, but more importantly, to be tolerable to others. The critical dogma is not to offend but to be genteel and civil in social relations .... [Such] a religious style ... entails a de-emphasis of Evangelicalism's more offensive aspects, such as accusations of heresy, sin, immorality, and paganism, and themes of judgment, divine wrath, damnation, and hell.[9]

To the question "why the comeback of hell?" among non-Christians, Martin Marty sees it as the return of American baby boomers to traditional religion. Such nostalgia, he argues, may be simply an attempt to recover the beliefs of their childhood. "If people really believed in hell," he said, "they wouldn't be watching basketball or even the TV preachers. They'd be out rescuing people."[10]

C.S. Lewis asks the same question: "How is it right . . . for creatures who are every moment advancing either to Heaven or hell to spend any fraction of the little time allowed them in this world on such comparative trivialities [as the ordinary pursuits of life]?" Kenneth Kantzer rightly responds by saying that "we dare not forget that God has given other commands: we are to care for the widows; to bind up the wounds of the injured in our society; to seek justice; to celebrate our joys. Our Lord," he continues, "attended a merry wedding in Galilee. The Apostle Paul urged the Thessalonians to stick to their ordinary jobs. He even provided instruction about going to dinner parties held by pagans. 'Christianity,' as Lewis sums up, 'does not exclude any of the ordinary human activities.'"[11]

Several years ago *Time* magazine had an article entitled "Evil" which suggested that perhaps "evil is a problem that is more intelligently addressed outside the religious context of God and Satan."[12] The biblical fact is that Christ came to solve the problem of evil — personal and universal. The good news of the Gospel is that God's work through Christ is the only solution to the dilemma of evil.

The Bad News of the Good News

But what about those who reject God's solution? For them the good news becomes very bad news. The story is told of C.S. Lewis hearing a young man's sermon on judgment. He concluded his Gospel message with the statement: "If you do not receive Christ as your Savior, you will suffer grave eschatological ramifications!" Lewis asked the young preacher after the service: "Do you mean that a person who doesn't believe in Christ will go to hell?" "Precisely," said the young man. "Then say so," Lewis advised.[13]

We not only need to understand what those "grave eschatological ramifications" are, but we need to "say so," to clearly warn our lost world. Some today suggest that all without exception will be saved, whether they want to be or not (universalism, discussed in chapter 2). Others argue that hell is God's consuming of the wicked (annihilationism, addressed in chapter 3), not His eternally tormenting them. Still others hold forth the hope that death is not the end of opportunity for redemption, but perhaps a door to future chances for salvation (postmortem conversion, the subject of chapter 4). Each of these three alternative views to hell are discussed in this book.

The Good Shepherd, if He has spoken out clearly on the fate of the wicked, should be our final source for our view of that bad news (the focus of chapter 5). Our last chapter will ask, "Does it make any difference what view Christians hold about the Other Side?" Can there be alternative positions within the church?

In the final analysis, we must seek to be biblical Christians who aren't afraid to speak of that bad news. A brave journalist who was in Baghdad when the bombs landed during the Gulf War, cried out in his television report, "I have been *in hell!*" As horrible as war is we would have to say to him, "No, you haven't. If we understand Jesus correctly, war is only a small foreshadowing of that final condition of the forsaken."

Certainly there could be no less winsome topic than this one. But if hell is a reality, if it is in fact the reality for all who reject Christ, we must challenge people not only to flee from the wrath to come, but to flee to the One who bore that wrath for sinners. Frederick Buechner reminds Christians that there is indeed a price to pay for faithfully proclaiming biblical truth:

> To tell the story of who we really are, and of the battle between light and dark, between belief and unbelief, between sin and grace that is waged within us all, costs

> plenty and may not gain us anything, we're afraid, but an uneasy silence and fishy stare.[14]

May we be ready to pay that price to bring lost people to Christ so that they won't spend eternity on The Other Side of the Good News.

1

Must We Even *Discuss* the Other Side?

"Imagine there's no heaven; it's easy if you try. No hell below us — above us only sky." (John Lennon)

"Today, hell is theology's H-word, a subject too trite for serious scholarship." (*Newsweek*)

"[The doctrine of hell] seems to be relegated at present to the far-off corners of the Christian mind, and there to sleep in deep shadow." (William Gladstone)

"Therefore, let us leave the elementary teachings about Christ . . . [such as] eternal judgment." (Heb. 6:1-2)

"Hell is Manhattan at rush hour," proclaims the noted "theologian" Woody Allen. He astutely points out: "There's no question that there's an unseen world. The question is, how far is it from midtown and how late does it stay open?"[1]

The American church historian Martin Marty observes that "hell disappeared and no one noticed." While preparing a Harvard University lecture on the vanishing of hell, Marty consulted the indices of several scholarly journals, including one dating back to 1889, but failed to find a single article on hell. *Newsweek*'s Kenneth Woodward states that for many heaven and hell are no longer to be "thought of as different locations, with separate ZIP codes," while Harvard professor Gordon Kaufman says, "I don't think there can be any future for heaven and hell."[2] Robert Schuller says he hasn't preached on hell in 40 years. Schuller says that he wants his theology to "emphasize that we're 'saved' not just to avoid 'hell' (whatever that means and wherever that is), but to become positive thinkers inspired to seek God's will for our lives and dream the divine dreams that God has planned for us."[3]

The discussion of the Other Side of the Good News, that is, the fate of those who reject Christ, appears to be a theological topic which polite people don't bring up in mixed company. In a society which values tolerance above truth, the doctrine of hell is a theological unmentionable.

However, when one is conditioned to be tolerant of all viewpoints, he or she is drained of a passion for truth. For the Christian, a passion for truth ought to lead to a passion for souls. One article acknowledges that the doctrine of hell "no longer gets its float in the church parade; it has become a museum piece at best, stored in the shadows of a far corner."[4]

The Other Side in History

There have been times when the Other Side's "float" led the doctrinal parade. The fate of the wicked has been the subject of grotesque speculation and extended publicity during several periods of church history. Certain writers focused on the Other Side from the perspective of retributive punishment. For example, the noncanonical *Apocalypse of Peter*, written early in church history, singles out blasphemy and murder as meriting horrendous judgment. Blasphemers are seen "hanging by their tongues, while the flaming fire torments them from beneath." Murderers are thrown into "a pit full of evil reptiles by which they were smitten and tormented while their victims stood by them and cried forth: 'O God, righteous is thy judgment.'"[5]

The Apocalypse of Paul, another extrabiblical book written within the first several hundred years of the church, graphically describes "a river of fire in which the wicked are sunk to their knees, stomach, lips, or eyelids depending on which member of their bodies committed sin."[6]

Other literature delights with lurid curiosity in the torturous side of the Other Side. The book *The Eleven Pains of Hell* illustrates one example of such speculation:

> There are more pains there than there are birds flying under heaven; There are burning trees upon which are hanged the souls of those who would never go to church in this life, Thicker they hang than do the bees in their hive. There is an oven heated, at which stand seven devils who shovel the guilty souls into the furnace. There is snow, ice, clotted blood, snakes, adders that fiercely sting: No rest have the guilty souls.[7]

The *Koran* describes the miseries of the damned with what one writer calls "thoughtful care." It teaches that not only are the skins of the tormented burnt away; the condemned are then provided with new ones so that the burning can continue forever.[8] The sixth-century English historian Bede imagined a man in torments in which "the flames of fire gushed out from his ears and eyes and nostrils and at every pore." Such graphic depictions of the fate of the wicked would make even the horror writer Stephen King wake up in a cold sweat.

Medieval writers, however, did not have a monopoly on discussing the destiny of the condemned. Jonathan Edwards, one of the Great Awakening's most scholarly preachers, agonizingly concentrates upon the image of fire in his sermon

"Sinners in the Hands of an Angry God."[9] Emphasizing the urgency of repentance, Edwards uses a variety of expressions to point out the certainty of God's judgment on the sinner. He declares that "there is nothing that keeps wicked men at any one moment out of hell, but the mere pleasure of God." Combining several word pictures, he says of the wicked that "the wrath of God burns against them, their damnation does not slumber; the pit is prepared, the fire is made ready, the furnace is now hot, ready to receive them; the flames do now rage and glow. The glittering sword is whet, and held over them, and the pit hath opened its mouth under them."

In fact, Edwards describes the state of the man without Christ as liable to *self*-combustion: "There are in the souls of wicked men those hellish principles reigning, that would presently kindle and flame out into hell fire, if it were not for God's restraints. There is laid in the very nature of carnal men, a foundation for the torments of hell." Man's own nature is composed of "the seeds of hell fire." Edwards mixes this concept of the wicked's virtual combustibility with the scene of a satanic welcoming party: "the devil is waiting for them, hell is gaping for them, the flames gather and flash about them, and would fain lay hold on them, and swallow them up; the fire bent up in their own hearts is struggling to break out."

Later in his sermon Edwards focuses upon the sheer gravity of man's own sin: "Your wickedness makes you as it were heavy as lead, and to tend downwards with great weight and pressure towards hell; and if God should let you go, you would immediately sink and swiftly descend and plunge into the bottomless gulf."

"You cannot save yourself," Edwards warns, "your own care and all your righteousness, would have no more influence to uphold you and keep you out of hell, than a spider's web would have to stop a fallen rock." There is some evidence, by the way, that Edwards might have done a Master's thesis on spiders!

Describing God's wrath as a dreadful storm, as dam waters that can no longer be held back, and as a flood of God's vengeance, he then takes up a hunting image: "The bow of

God's wrath is bent," he says, "and the arrow made ready on the string, and justice bends the arrow at your heart, and strains the bow, and it is nothing but the mere pleasure of God, and that of an angry God, without any promise or obligation at all, that keeps the arrow one moment from being made drunk with your blood."

Edwards goes so far as to describe the Christless sinner as an object of God's hatred: "The God who holds you over the pit of hell, much as one holds a spider, or some loathsome insect over the fire, abhors you, and is dreadfully provoked . . . . you are ten thousand times more abominable in His eyes, than the most hateful venomous serpent is in ours."

Returning to the idea of God's "mere" mercy, Edwards says to this Connecticut congregation in 1741: "It is to be ascribed to nothing else, that you did not go to hell the last night; that you was [*sic*] suffered to awake again in this world, after you closed your eyes to sleep. And there is no other reason to be given, why you have not dropped into hell since you arose in the morning, but that God's hand has held you up."

The wicked without Christ have no support in themselves. "You hang by a slender thread," says Edwards, "with the flames of divine wrath flashing about it, and ready every moment to singe it, and burn it asunder."

Lest one think that this preacher provides no good news, he invites his listeners to repent: "Now you have an extraordinary opportunity, a day wherein Christ has thrown the door of mercy wide open, and stands in calling and crying with a loud voice to poor sinners; a day wherein many are flocking to him, and pressing into the kingdom of God." His sermon concludes with the invitation: "Therefore, let every one that is out of Christ, now awake and fly from the wrath to come."

Although early periods of church history seemed to glorify speculation about the Other Side in terms of detailed suffering or retributive punishment, Edwards uses certain images to plead with this congregation (which he was only visiting) to bring them to faith. Certainly the nineteenth-century preacher C.H. Spurgeon borrowed some of Edwards' language when he declared to one church: "Many of you are hanging over the mouth of hell by a solitary plank, and that plank is rotten!"

A Figment of the Theological Imagination?

Today's treatment of the Other Side, however, seems to have excised the doctrine of hell. The term "hell" itself has degenerated into an overused expletive of exasperation. The contemporary attitude might well be thought of as a Bart Simpson T-shirt with the caption: "I'm bored with hell . . . and proud of it, man!" The issue of what happens to those who reject Christ is a topic either ridiculed or rejected.[10]

Sir Arthur Conan Doyle, the author of the Sherlock Holmes novels, considered hell nothing less than theological slander. "This odious conception, so blasphemous in its view of the Creator," says Doyle, "may perhaps have been of service in a coarse age when men were frightened by fires, as wild beasts are scared by the travelers. Hell as a permanent place does not exist."[11] Another writer categorically declares that "the doctrine of hell has no place in a religion of love!"[12]

Other theological writers, appearing to defend God's character, protest the doctrine of hell. A leading churchman of the nineteenth century said that "the doctrine of eternal torment is . . . the most terrific blasphemy, the most audacious and unmitigated libel ever uttered against a God of love!"[13] Nels Ferré, a professor of theology, said that "no worthy faith can ever attribute eternal hell to God . . . . To attribute eternal hell to God," he continues, "is literally blasphemy, the attributing of the worst to the best. From such blasphemy may God deliver everyone."[14] The doctrine of eternal conscious punishment cannot be linked with the God of the Bible, argue numerous theologians. One liberal theologian asks: "Is it possible that any human being can practically believe such a horrible collection of revolting absurdities to be the truth sent us by a loving and merciful God?"[15]

Other theologians also claim that the church suffers at the hands of its speculators. "Hell is only a figment of the theological imagination," said one such commentator.[16]

Reinhold Niebuhr was dispensing his best advice, some would say, when he stated that "it is unwise for Christians to claim any knowledge of either the furniture of heaven or the temperature of hell."

Neither delight in morbid speculation nor dismissal of biblical truth will receive God's approval. Stanley Hauerwas argues that "when we lose the cosmic character of our faith, the saints are reduced to being merely saintly — that is, to people who are eternally nice."[17] The highest effect of the Gospel is not to make believers eternally nice or piously polite, but personally faithful to God's truth, whatever its effect upon the surrounding culture's sensibilities. In his excellent book, *No More Mr. Nice Guy! Saying Goodbye to "Doormat" Christianity*, Stephen Brown reminds believers that "God don't make no wimps!" In other words, we are to take the truth of God's Word and speak it forth, whatever our prevailing society may think.

Some Christians seem to have the attitude that if the subject of hell is not brought up, perhaps it will burn out on its own. Other evangelical leaders have taken an aggressive stance to advance the disappearance (or at least the overhaul) of hell. One such leader caricatured Jonathan Edwards' view of hell by quipping: "just as one can imagine certain people watching a cat trapped in a microwave oven squirming in agony and taking delight in it, so the saints in heaven will, according to Edwards, experience the torments of the damned with pleasure and satisfaction!"[18]

Why We Must Discuss the Other Side

As much as the church might prefer not to discuss the Other Side, especially in the light of sometimes excessive and perhaps embarrassing historical speculation, the subject must be addressed for at least three reasons.

First, we must discuss the Other Side of the Good News because the fate of the wicked is already being discussed, debated, and supposedly debunked. We dare not stand on the sidelines of that discussion. One evangelical writer says that

"The reality of hell . . . demands we haul the monstrous thing out again and study it until it changes us."[19] It may be more comfortable to sit on the sidelines, watching the action. But such a posture is disobedience to the Savior who wants us to warn others to "flee from the coming wrath" (Matt. 3:7; cf. John 3:36).

Followers of Christ need to realize that the public's awareness of spiritual matters is largely based on talk shows with New Age divas and reruns of *Highway to Heaven* or *Touched by an Angel.* Films such as *What Dreams May Come*, *Flatliners*, and *Always* provide a doctrinal diet for moviegoers which, if accepted as final truth, will spiritually starve them. Do we honestly think that people learn their theology only from the Bible and church sermons? How can the church compete against a Bill Cosby who in earthly life (*The Cosby Show*) is successful with little reference to God and in the next life (*Ghost Dad*) becomes a good-deed-doing angel with no fear of judgment after death? The entertainment media powerfully conveys concepts incompatible with biblical teaching. How dare we Christians be silent about what the Bible teaches on this exceedingly important issue?

Chuck Colson's challenge to the church applies to this area of doctrinal debate: "The battle is raging today all around, but many are perishing because we Christians have failed to engage the enemy at the point of attack. We not only flinch; for the most part we are not even looking in the right direction."[20]

Second, we must discuss the Other Side of the Good News because of the nature of the Gospel. The word Gospel may mean "good news" in Greek, but in English it communicates little more than a sober and somber, "alternative" life-style. Our world needs to hear not so much nice news, as rescue-from-judgment news. People need to know that the Gospel is not solely good news; there is very bad news to the good news of the Gospel. Negative consequences will follow a rejection of Christ as surely as positive consequences follow a reception of the Savior and His work. A shoulder-shrugging, so-what society must hear that the Good News is neither received without personal faith nor rejected without eternal consequences.

The Gospel presented by many Christians today has no teeth. When the message about Jesus Christ is expressed only in terms of providing a superior joy or peace to that which the world offers, already joyful and peaceful pagans patronize the messenger and ignore the message. Rather than trying to convince non-Christians that they really aren't that happy, Christians need to faithfully proclaim the complete Gospel. That complete Gospel says, for example, that happiness without holiness is counterfeit Christianity, that self-fulfillment and a positive self-image do not bring eternal forgiveness. Such a complete Gospel proclaims that sins must either be pardoned or punished.

Jude 23 pictures people you and I know, people with whom we should share the Gospel, as already experiencing God's judgment. Jude urges us to "snatch others from the fire and save them." Those people you and I rub shoulders with every day will not be snatched from that judgment by a message whittled away to only peace, joy, and happiness. Even though our world is "going to hell in a hand basket," only 4 percent of people surveyed believed that they had a good or excellent chance of going to that place according to a 1990 Gallup poll. Apparently, the church is not persuasively communicating the bad news of the Good News.

Modern man needs to see the exceeding sinfulness of sin. In a world which blames God for the brokenness brought about by man's own rebellion, the bad news of the Good News must be announced. Someone has said that if Jonathan Edwards were to preach his famous sermon to audiences today, it would have to be renamed "God in the Hands of Angry Sinners."

The theme of God's wrath and announced judgment is an essential element of the Gospel. H. Richard Niebuhr caustically indicted nineteenth-century American liberalism because, as he said, it believed in "a God without wrath [who] brought men without sin into a kingdom without judgment through the ministrations of a Christ without a cross."[21] To water down the penalty of rejecting Christ or by silence to fail to warn the unbeliever of the fact that "God is a righteous judge, a God who expresses His wrath every day" (Ps. 7:11), is to betray the truth which Christ paid for with His life. A doctor who comforts a dying, but curable, patient with words which deny the illness and ignore the cure would be unworthy of his or her profession. If Christians misdiagnose the disease of sin and fail to warn others of its awful consequences, they are guilty of spiritual malpractice.

The warning to "flee from the coming wrath" (Matt. 3:7) is desperately needed by a sin-numbed and self-deceived world. The teaching of God's judgment of those who ignore or reject Christ is not a matter of personal, speculative religious opinion, but revealed truth. As Mrs. Billy Graham puts it, "If God does not one day judge America, He will have to apologize to Sodom and Gomorrah!"

The Gospel message is responded to by many today with the same ho-hum attentiveness paid to an airline flight attendant's instructions before takeoff. Imagine being seated on an airplane, seatbelt buckled, awaiting departure. An immaculately-attired flight attendant stands before you, microphone in hand, and says "Ladies and Gentlemen, you are all going to die! But, it doesn't have to happen today, while I'm on duty, on my flight! (She grabs a magazine out of the hands of a weary businessman in first class, looks into his bloodshot eyes and whispers, "You'd better listen to me, mister! What I've got to say in the next few moments could save your life!")

She continues to the passengers: "Now that I have your attention, folks, I want to tell you about this aircraft you're strapped to. Don't miss a word of what I'm going to say because this incredibly heavier-than-air machine might very well drop from the sky like a rock, crash and burn, and kill us all! Although the chances of that happening are rather slim, what I'm going to tell you in these two minutes will maximize the possibility of your safely walking away from this flying gas tank!"

This flight attendant would, of course, lose her job. Not because she told people the truth, but because she frightened them into listening to what she had to say. But one thing is for sure, they listened to her every word! The world needs spiritual flight attendants who refuse to sugarcoat the truth.

Third, we must discuss the Other Side of the Good News because our Savior discussed it. Had Jesus been silent about this issue we would have no right to speculate about what happens to the wicked. The Christian ought to speak clearly where the Bible speaks clearly, and he or she ought to be silent where the Bible is silent.

It is often pointed out that Jesus spoke more about hell than about heaven. Do the four Gospels, however, support that assertion? If one looks at several key terms statistically, Jesus uses the term "heaven" many more times than He uses the term "hell." It's interesting that the common term for hell is Gehenna and of its twelve uses in the Gospels, eleven are from the lips of the Savior. However, simply counting the number of times terms are used does not necessarily establish the relative importance of the subject. A more reliable measure of Jesus' emphasis would be the teaching or didactic sections of the four Gospels. As will be shown in a later chapter, Jesus Christ taught more on the need to escape hell than He did on the joy of entering heaven.

The fact is that the four Gospels are abridged accounts of the words and works of Christ (John 21:25). Because their purpose appears to be evangelistic (proving that Jesus is the Messiah, the Servant of Jehovah, the Son of Man, and the Son of God respectively), the reporting of Jesus' warnings of judgment reflects the conviction that Jesus knew that men and women need more to be warned of the judgment of hell than wooed by the pleasures of heaven.

Jesus not only discussed the Other Side, He has provided the church with clear and frightening information about the fate of those who reject Him. Chapter 5 ("The Other Side According to Jesus") will explore in detail the teaching and warnings of the Savior about the Other Side. Here we will only point out that Jesus was not the least bit reluctant to "frighten" people into faith. Some might describe Jesus as a "scare theologian." His warnings about that Other Side do seem designed to produce a godly fear which leads to a confident faith.

But, must there even be an Other Side? Perhaps hell will be unpopulated. Several prominent theologians argue that all without exception will be brought into God's family. Chapter 2 will discuss the popular doctrine of universalism, sometimes referred to as the doctrine of a finally empty hell.

2

The Other Side: Will It Have **Any** Occupants?

"Heaven can be heaven only when it has emptied hell." (Nels F.S. Ferré)

"The vague and tenuous hope that God is too kind to punish the ungodly has become a deadly opiate for the consciences of millions." (A.W. Tozer)

"There is no doctrine which I would more willingly remove from Christianity than [hell], if it lay in my power ... I would pay any price to be able to say truthfully: 'All will be saved.'" (C.S. Lewis)

"For it pleased the Father ... to reconcile all things to Himself ... whether things on earth or things in heaven." (Col. 1:19-20, NKJV)

"Hell exists," says the convert to Roman Catholicism Richard John Neuhaus, "but no one is in it." Some theologians today acknowledge that there may indeed be a place of perdition, but believe it will be unoccupied. Claiming to base their conviction upon the nature of God, or upon the concept of a cleansed universe, or upon what they consider the conclusive teaching of Scripture, these writers have, at least in their minds, emptied hell.

The liberal scholar John A.T. Robinson, agreeing with the sentiments of the second century Alexandrian theologian Origen, pointedly charges in the article "Universalism – Is It Heretical?" that "Christ . . . remains on the Cross as long as one sinner remains in hell. This is not speculation: it is a statement grounded in the very necessity of God's nature. In a universe of love there can be no heaven which tolerates a chamber of horrors, no hell for any which does not at the same time make it hell for God. He cannot endure that — for that would be the final mockery of his nature — and He will not."[1]

The appeal of universalism, the doctrine which says that all without exception will be redeemed, is powerful. Such a theological position appears to reflect the self-declared desire of God as One who "is not willing that any should perish" (2 Peter 3:9, NKJV).

Some argue that universal salvation is the only theological option which makes sense in the new heavens and the new earth. If one day God "may be all in all" (1 Cor. 15:28), then must not all human beings be brought into God's family?

Annihilationism (which we will consider in chapter 3), the concept that the wicked will be put out of existence at the end of time, is, in one sense, a form of universalism. That is, if an everlasting hell constitutes what Seventh-Day Adventism calls "a plague spot in the universe of God throughout eternity,"[2] then the wicked must be extinguished (so that only one class of human beings – the redeemed – remains). Annihilationism does posit a temporary double destiny for humans. However, the wicked will simply cease to exist; nothingness can hardly be considered an eternal, conscious destiny.

Universalism, also known as the doctrine of *apokatastasis* (restoration), emphasizes that one day the bad dream of sin will be over and we shall all rise and go back to our Father and home. Sin's rebellion shall be done away, says one universalist, for "the grace of God shall triumph in the end and break down all resistance."[3]

Is universalism solely a twentieth-century heresy, advocated by a few obscure liberal theologians? Hardly. Although one could quote Satan's words to that original pair in the garden – "You will not surely die!" (Gen. 3:4) – as the earliest expression of universalism, Clement of Alexandria (ca. 155-ca. 220), appears to have held this viewpoint. He states, for example, in *The Stromata*:

> Wherefore also all men are His; some through knowledge, others not yet so; and some as friends, some as faithful servants, some as servants merely . . . For either the Lord does not care for all men; and this is the case either because He is unable (which is not to be thought, for it would be a proof of weakness), or because He is unwilling, which is not the attribute of a good being . . . Or He does care for all, which is befitting for Him who has become Lord of all. For He is Savior; not [the Savior] of some, and of others not . . . And how is He Savior and Lord, if not the Savior and Lord of all? But He is the Savior of those who have believed, because of their wishing to know; and the Lord of those who have not believed, till, being enabled to confess Him, they obtain the peculiar and appropriate boon which comes by Him.[4]

God's attributes of love and power can only be shown by universalism, according to Clement. The statement "If Christ is not Lord of all, He is not Lord at all," often heard at revival meetings, has certainly taken on a new meaning!

Origen: The Father of Universalism

The Alexandrian theologian Origen (ca. 185-ca. 254) suffered several setbacks in his illustrious career. His efforts to be martyred as a teenager with his father in the Severian persecution of 202 were thwarted, we are told, by his mother who hid his clothes! He subsequently devoted his life to study, his academic pursuits being subsidized by a wealthy widow. For twenty-eight years he headed the Catechetical School in Alexandria and has been described by scholars as a "philosopher, philologist, critic, exegete, dogmatician, apologist, [and] polemicist."[5]

Origen's work, *De Principiis*, the church's first systematic theology and manual of dogma, sets forth such matters as his view of the Heavenly Hierarchy of the Father, the Word, and the Spirit (Book 1); the creation and redemption of man (Book 2); the freedom of the will in struggling against the forces of good and evil (Book 3); and his biblical hermeneutics (Book 4).

His book *Contra Celsum* demonstrates Origen's philosophical skills as he endeavored to reconcile Greek philosophy with Christian doctrine. The church decided that Origen went too far and had departed from orthodox Christianity. Justinian, for example, published his ten *Anathematisms Against Origen* (540), stating in the ninth anathema that "If any one says or thinks that the punishment of demons and impious men is only temporary and will have an end, and that a restoration [*apokatastasis*] will take place of demons and impious men, let him be anathema."[6]

Accused of subordinationism by Jerome and Epiphanius, he was condemned for that teaching by some synods, such as the Synod of Constantinople of 543. "Perhaps one should not take these rejections too seriously," writes one biographer, "since he was the first of the systematic theologians and a seminal thinker."[7]

On the other hand, "Origen," writes another scholar, "is the foundation upon which practically all subsequent forms of universalism have been based."[8] His doctrine of *apokatastasis* colors much of his writings. He saw the threats of hell only as remedial, not retributive. Origen's allegorical method of interpretation (which he may have developed after taking Matthew 19:12 too literally) allowed him to fit God's wrath and the concept of future punishment into his system of universal salvation, leaving no room for the retributive wrath of God.

God As a Consuming Fire

In Origen's thought, "gehenna," says one writer, "stands for the torments that cleanse the soul . . . God is indeed a consuming fire, but that which He consumes is the evil that is in the souls of men, not the souls themselves . . . The hope of Origen colors even his view of the guilt of Judas, and he sees in his suicide the act of one who wished to meet his Master in the world of the dead, and there to implore forgiveness."[9]

In his work *Contra Celsum*, Origen writes:

> The sacred Scripture does, indeed, call "our God a consuming fire," (Deut. 4:24) and says that "rivers of fire go before his face," (Dan. 7:10) and that "he shall come as a refiner's fire, and purify the people" (Mal. 3:2). As, therefore, God is a consuming fire, what is it that is to be consumed by him? We say that it is wickedness, and whatever proceeds from it, such as is figuratively called "wood, hay, stubble," (1 Cor. 3) which denote the evil works of man. Our God is a consuming fire in this sense; and he shall come as a refiner's fire to purify rational nature from the alloy of wickedness, and other impure matter which has adulterated the intellectual gold and silver; consuming whatever of evil is admixed in all the soul.[10]

Origen taught that the threats of eternal punishment were only hortatory. One scholar writes that Origen "admits that the grammatical sense of the scriptural terms teaches an everlasting and inextinguishable fire; but considers this an intentional and gracious deceit on the part of God to deter men from sinning."[11]

Hell is understood by Origen as purification, not punishment. Eternal punishment is not necessary because the wicked will come around at some point, and all things will be restored to their original condition (*apokatastasis*).

Hell As Internal Anguish

He argues in *De Principiis* that the wicked will suffer internal anguish brought about by their separation from God. Commenting upon Isaiah 50:11 ("Look, all you who kindle a fire, who encircle yourselves with sparks: walk in the light of your fire and in the sparks you have kindled."), Origen suggests that there will be a kind of self-generated purgatory:

> By these words it seems to be indicated that every sinner kindles for himself the flame of his own fire, and is not plunged into some fire which has been already kindled by another, or was in existence before himself. Of this fire the fuel and food are our sins, which are called by the Apostle Paul wood, and hay, and stubble . . . When the soul has gathered together a multitude of evil works, and an abundance of sins against itself, at a suitable time all that assembly of evils boils up to punishment, and is set on fire to chastisements; when the mind itself, or conscience, receiving by divine power into the memory all those things of which it had stamped on itself certain signs and forms at the moment of sinning, will see a kind of history, as it were, of all the foul, and shameful, and unholy deeds which it has done, exposed before its eyes: then is the conscience itself harassed, and, pierced by its own goads becomes an accuser and a witness against itself.[12]

Hell As School

Origen, one writer declares, teaches that "The whole universe is one vast school system in which nobody is 'flunked out.' The rod is applied skillfully according to the need of each pupil. All are assured of final graduation. Each pupil learns at his own pace. There is no need to hurry. Eternity is available. Even the 'dunce' of them all, the devil, will some day graduate, and school then be declared officially over."[13] Nels F.S. Ferré, a twentieth-century liberal theologian, holds this same view of hell as remedial education, as we shall see later.

The anguish which the wicked will experience will bring about purification, eventuating in the restoration of all creatures (including Satan) to their original condition. Sounding like the Roman Catholic doctrine of purgatory, Origen's view is broader in that hell is not limited to the burning away of the sins of those who possess explicit or implicit faith (as in Roman Catholicism). Rather, Origen's hope includes those who expressed themselves as enemies of God (such as the Sodomites, Pharaoh, and even Satan himself).[14]

Origen clearly expresses his hope of universal restoration by saying that there will be:

> a time which God alone knows, when He will bestow on each one what he deserves. We think, indeed, that the goodness of God, through His Christ, may recall all His creatures to one end, even His enemies being conquered and subdued. For thus says holy Scripture . . . "For all things must be put under Him." What, then, is this, "putting under" by which all things must be made subject to Christ? I am of the opinion that it is this very subjection by which we also wish to be subject to Him, by which the apostles also were subject, and all the saints who have been followers of Christ. For the name "subjection," by which we are subject to Christ, indicates that the salvation which proceeds from Him belongs to His subjects . . .[15]

Other texts used by Origen to support his *apokatastasis* include: Philippians 2:10-11's prediction that all will bow and confess Christ's Lordship, John 17:20-21's teaching of promised unity, and Ephesians 4:13's imagery of the perfect man. However, as one writer summarizes Origen's use of these passages, "[T]hese verses are more in context when interpreted as referring to the ruin of the enemies in the final subjugation. They are removed from the possibility of further resistance. These Scriptural passages are certainly slender threads upon which to suspend so vast a weight as the reconciliation of the entire universe!"[16]

Future Falls?

Origen's view of the perpetual freedom of human will presents him with a serious difficulty. What is to prevent man from asserting his free will against God and experiencing another fall? And then another? Although Origen's supporters reply that he held to a time when the cycle would be complete, one writer states that "so far did [Origen] carry his idea of the freedom and mutability of the will that he appears to have held to the possibility of renewed falls hereafter, and of worlds to take the place of the present for the recovery, once more, of inconstant souls."[17]

Origen's perspective on hell as a purifying process is not limited to his time period. Some theologians today hold out the hope that, although hell may be very real, it will not be particularly permanent. One of my friends (who professes to be an evangelical) gives evidence of being what Packer calls a "wishful universalist" and suggested to me that a long time may be needed by God to persuade the unbeliever to accept his redemption in Christ, but accept it he will! Another theologian argues that, given an eternity of opportunity, God can demonstrate His wisdom with such force that continued resistance is impossible. That process may involve much time and suffering, but just as irresistible logic brings us to conclusions which we may not like but nevertheless accept, so also the appeals of God after death may bring even the most stubborn souls to yield to divine mercy, without the sinner's personality being overridden in the process.[18]

As we shall emphasize in chapter 6, the choices we make in this life have abiding consequences in the next life. Dorothy Sayers captures the biblical picture of the Other Side and the permanent nature of the sinner's choosing against Christ when she writes:

> It is the deliberate choosing to remain in illusion and to see God and the universe as hostile to one's ego that is of the very essence of Hell: The dreadful moods when we hug our hatred and misery and are too proud to let them

> go are foretastes in time of what Hell eternally is . . . But if, seeing God, the soul rejects Him in hatred and horror, then there is nothing more that God can do for it. God, who has toiled to win it for Himself, and borne for its sake to know death, and suffer the shame of sin, and set His feet in Hell, will nevertheless, if it insists, give it what it desires . . . He cannot, against our own will, force us into Heaven.[19]

Sayers aptly points out that "it is of the essence of heaven and hell that one must abide forever with that which one has chosen."[20]

Other Advocates of Universalism

Other theologians such as Karl Barth, C.H. Dodd, John A.T. Robinson, and Nels F.S. Ferré either imply or argue on behalf of universalism. We will also look at several contemporary examples.

Karl Barth (1886-1968)

Barth, described as "one of the theological giants of all time – not just of this century,"[21] was born in Basel, Switzerland. He is probably best known for his commentary on Romans which one writer characterized as a "bomb on the playground of the theologians."[22]

Barth's numerous theological writings (his thirteen-volume *Church Dogmatics* contains 15,000 Scriptural citations) overwhelm many who wish to grasp his thought. But a survey of Barth's writings demonstrates that this formative neo-orthodox theologian sets forth a view of triumphal divine election which appears to lead to universalism. As one writer points out, "[T]here runs through the whole of Barth's dogmatics a strong universalistic strain which comes to expression in a variety of connections."[23] Barth taught that Jesus Christ "is God's Word, God's decree, and God's beginning. He is so all-inclusively, comprehending absolutely within

Himself all things and everything, enclosing within Himself the autonomy of all other words, decrees, and beginnings."[24]

Barth's "Christomonism" sees Christ as the Elect Man and emphasizes the fact that we are elected in Him collectively — not as separate individuals.[25] "God has ascribed to man . . . election, salvation, and life; and to Himself He has ascribed . . . reprobation, perdition, and death."[26] He emphasizes that "predestination is the non-rejection of man. It is so because it is the rejection of the Son of God."[27]

His Perspective on Predestination

Barth viewed redemption from a double predestination perspective in that Christ is both the reprobate and the elect for all (what he termed a "purified Supralapsarianism"). He states:

> Jesus Christ is the atonement. But that means that He is the maintaining and accomplishing and fulfilling of the divine covenant as executed by God Himself. He is the eschatological realisation of the will of God for Israel and therefore for the whole race. And as such He is also the revelation of this divine will and therefore of the covenant. He is the One for whose sake and towards whom all men from the very beginning are preserved from their youth up by the long-suffering of God, notwithstanding their evil heart.[28]

God's covenant "does seriously apply to all men and is made for all men . . . it is the destiny of all men to become and to be members of this covenant."[29] Barth allows no competing views to the one he sets forth concerning God's covenant. He says that "according to the revelation accomplished in Jesus Christ . . . for all men of all times and places . . . this was and is the critical point of all faith in God and knowledge of God and service of God. This God," says Barth, "or none at all."[30]

Barth characterizes Calvin's concept of predestination as a "grim doctrine" (because it portrays Christ as dying not for all men, but only for the elect), but finds some affinity with Zwingli's view of God's covenant. Zwingli's view, says Barth, "stood for something which cannot be surrendered, the character of the covenant as the true light which lighteth every man (John 1:9) and for which, therefore, every man is claimed."[31] But Barth concludes his evaluation of these other views of God's covenant by charging them with "the abandonment of an original universalism in the conception of the atonement."[32]

Man's Response

Barth's doctrine of election appears to minimize man's response to the Gospel. He says that "Jesus Christ is God's mighty command to open our eyes and to realise that this place is all around us, that we are already in this kingdom, that we have no alternative but to adjust ourselves to it, that we have our being and continuance here and nowhere else. In Him we are already there, we already belong to it. To enter at His command is to realise that in Him we are already inside."[33]

Man's responsibility is to live out his election in Christ. It appears in Barth that God makes the choice, not only of man, but for him. "Man has already been put in the place and kingdom of peace with God," says Barth. "His decision and act, therefore, can consist only in obedience to the fact that he begins and does not cease to breathe in this place and kingdom, that he follows the decision already made and the act already accomplished by God, confirming them in his own human decision and act; that he, for his part, chooses what has already been chosen and actualized for him."[34]

Man's choice either for or against God seems irrelevant. For example, Barth says that "If man has forfeited his salvation, what do we have to grasp in this event but the inconceivable fact that all the same it is given to him?"[35] How does Barth view unbelief, then? He states that "With the divine No and Yes spoken in Jesus Christ the root of human unbelief, the man of sin, is pulled out. In its place there is put the root of faith, the new man of obedience. For this reason unbelief has become an objective, real and ontological impossibility and faith an objective, real and ontological necessity for all men and for every man. In the justification of the sinner which has taken place in Jesus Christ these have both become an event which comprehends all men."[36]

Does this mean that God acts against man's will? Yes, according to Barth. He states that "we are those whose place has been taken by another, who lives and suffers and acts for them, who for them makes good that which they have spoiled, who – for them, but also without them and even against them – is their salvation."[37] As Berkouwer points out, "The new situation exists independently of the proclamation or non-proclamation of it. It also exists independently of belief or nonbelief in it. The Kingdom of God 'has its truth in itself, not in that which in pursuance of it happens or does not happen on the earth.'"[38]

Berkouwer concludes his evaluation of this aspect of Barth's theology by stating that "The error of universalism does not lie in glorying in God's grace, but in integrating grace into a system of conclusions which is in conflict with grace as a sovereign gift. The gripping element in all universalism is that at the moment when this integration takes place the seriousness of calling, of responsibility, and of the human decision of faith, is eliminated."[39]

An Objectivistic Bent

Donald G. Bloesch, whose view of the Other Side is evaluated in chapter 4, finds difficulty with Barth's soteriology. Bloesch states that "there is an unmistakable objectivistic bent in Barth's theology that tends to undercut the necessity for personal faith and repentance."[40] According to Bloesch, Barth's position teaches that "it is not the mandate of the church to call people to a decision for salvation, since salvation already extends to them because of Christ's redemptive work on the cross; instead, we should call our hearers to a decision for obedience. The response that is expected of those who hear the Gospel is basically ethical rather than soteriological in significance."[41]

"But," asks Bloesch, "does not Scripture plainly teach that only those who believe are justified and sanctified, that apart from personal faith and repentance we stand condemned in our sins (cf. Luke 13:3; John 3:18; 12:35-36; Rom. 3:22-26; 4:24-25; 10:9-11; Heb. 10:38-39)?"[42]

Berkouwer agrees that Barth underemphasizes man's acceptance of grace. He says that "The normal course of things for the New Testament man is that grace is not only offered to him but that he also accepts it. The situation has been changed. It is now an objective factuality manifested in the faithfulness of God to Himself and to His will as Creator."[43]

Brunner's "Nein"

Although no friend of evangelical Christianity, another universalist, Emil Brunner, criticizes Barth for his position that man cannot "cancel" God's decision,[44] and that the judgment which has once struck Jesus Christ can strike no one again.[45] Barth states, for example, that "God has acted in His grace . . . He has acted, therefore, without us and against us and for us, as a free subject in Jesus Christ. He has by Himself posited a new beginning. But He has really acted. What He has done is not just something which applies to us and is intended for us, a proffered opportunity and possibility. In it He has actually taken us, embraced us, as it were surrounded us, seized us from behind and turned us back again to Himself."[46]

Brunner believes that Barth underplays the subjective decision of faith; Brunner emphasizes that grace is for all "in so far as they believe" and that "whoever excludes himself is excluded." Brunner opposes Barth's doctrine of election as a "fundamental alteration of the Christian message of salvation."[47]

Brunner criticizes Barth's view of election by means of an illustration of men who are threatened with shipwreck at sea. "In reality, however, they are not at all on a sea where they can founder, but in shallow water in which they cannot drown. They just do not know it."[48]

Barth's Irrevocable "Yes"

Berkouwer says that Brunner does not give an unfair picture of Barth's doctrine of election by means of this illustration. "The already taken and no longer nullifiable decision is indeed the fundamental thesis of Barth's view of election."[49] For example, Barth says that "This alteration in the human situation has already taken place. This being is self-contained. It does not have to be reached or created. It has already come and cannot be removed. It is indestructible, it can never be superseded, it is in force, it is directly present."[50]

Ontologically, Barth stresses that in Christ "a new human subject was introduced, the true man beside and outside whom God does not know any other, beside and outside whom there is no other."[51] Barth's definition of man ties in with his universalism: "To be a man is to be in the sphere where the first and merciful will of God toward His creatures, His will to save and keep them from the power of nothingness, is revealed in action."[52]

Barth's Universal "Yes"

With a series of questions Barth drives home his conviction that the reality of the entire world's reconciliation to God is certain:

> But is it so inconceivable, does it need such a great imagination to realise, is it not the simplest thing in the world, that if the history of Jesus is the event of atonement, if the atonement is real and effective because God Himself became man to be the subject of this event, if this is not concealed but revealed, if it is the factor which calls us irresistibly to faith and obedience, then how can it be otherwise than that in this factor, and therefore in the history of Jesus, we have to do with the reality which underlies and precedes all other reality as the first and eternal Word of God, that in this history we have actually to do with the ground and sphere, the atmosphere of the being of every man, whether they lived thousands of years before or after Jesus?[53]

Emphasizing the unity of the human race in Christ's reconciling work, Barth says, "We died: the totality of all sinful men, those living, those long dead, and those still to be born, Christians who necessarily know and proclaim it, but also Jews and heathen, whether they hear and receive the news or whether they tried and still try to escape it. His death was the death of all: quite independently of their attitude or response to this event."[54]

Connecting the nature of God Himself with the exclusive character of the covenant, Barth says, that "We are therefore prevented from thinking otherwise about ourselves . . . than as being engaged and covenanted to God . . . Just as there is no God but the God of the covenant, there is no man but the man of the covenant."[55]

Berkouwer compares Barth's view to the liberation of a city from an occupying enemy. "The armies of liberation have already entered the occupied city and the capitulation has taken place, but the wonderful news has not yet penetrated into all the streets and suburbs of the city. Not everyone 'knows' that the liberating event has taken place. This detracts nothing, however, from the fact of the objective liberation. The subjective knowledge of it does not yet correspond to the objective situation."[56]

The Impossibility of "No"

Barth utilizes several images to convey his belief in universalism. For example, he speaks of man's response to the Gospel as "a kind of silhouette of the elective, free and total activity of God."[57] The old man who continues to break God's covenant can only be a lie, says Barth. He is "a shadow moving on the wall."[58] Although man is reconciled to God in Jesus Christ, "he can still rebel and lie and fear, but only in conflict, in impotent conflict, with his own most proper being . . . All his mistakes and confusions and sins are only like waves beating against the immovable rock of his own most proper being and to his sorrow necessarily breaking and dashing themselves to pieces against this rock."[59]

"Human trespasses," Barth says, "can still be committed, but they no longer count, they can no longer be entered up – like items in a well-kept statement or account. What counts now," says Barth, "what is reckoned to men, is the righteousness of God which they are made in Jesus Christ. That and that alone is their true yesterday and today and tomorrow."[60] Man's decision to act in obedience to his position in Christ "is not a loud and stern and foreign thing, but the quiet and gentle and intimate awakening of children in the Father's house to life in that house."[61]

The Eternal Verdict of "Yes"

Changing the image to a courtroom scene, Barth declares that the eternal verdict of God's Yes has been pronounced. He states that, "With all the truth and validity and force of a sentence which has not only been pronounced but executed, and therefore pronounced once and for all, it declares that man is no longer the transgressor, the sinner, the covenant-breaker that God has found him and he must confess himself to be, that as such he has died and perished from the earth, that he cannot be dealt with as such, that as such he has no future."[62]

Barth particularly revolts against the idea of dividing God's grace into two graces:

> We cannot . . . split [grace] up into an objective grace which is not as such strong and effective for man but simply comes before him as a possibility, and a subjective grace which, occasioned and prepared by the former, is the corresponding reality as it actually comes to man. But the grace of the one God and the one Christ, and therefore the objective grace which never comes to man except from God, must always be understood as the one complete grace, which is subjectively strong and effective in its divine objectivity, the grace which does actually reconcile man with God.[63]

A Matter of Knowledge

What, then, is the difference between the Christian and the non-Christian in Barth's understanding? Let us make no mistake here, the non-Christian *is* in God's family. Barth states that Christian love is to be shown toward each person, "because in his Christian and also in his non-Christian form he is a member of the people of which Jesus Christ is the king."[64] The difference is that those who are part of the visible church understand and seek to be obedient to their reconciliation through Christ. Barth states that:

> the love of God in Jesus Christ brings together Himself with all men and all men with Himself. But at the same time it is obviously the coming together of all men one with another. And as that communion is known it is once and necessarily evident that there is a solidarity of all men in that fellowship with God in which they have all been placed in Jesus Christ, and a special solidarity of those who are aware of the fact, the fellowship of those who believe in Him, the Christian community.[65]

The church's responsibility, says Barth, is not to speculate about the consequences of rejected grace. "To reflect today with unseemly seriousness about the possibility of the eternal damnation of this one or that one," says Barth, "and tomorrow with an equally unseemly cheerfulness about the ultimate reconciliation of one and all is *one* thing; *another* (and that is the charge that has been given to the Christian Church) is to regard oneself obliged to witness with Christian word and deed to Jesus Christ not only as Lord but as the Redeemer of the world and, as such, its future."[66]

As forcefully as Barth shouted *Nein* to Brunner's concept of natural theology, he shouts *Ja* to the universal intention (and accomplishment) of the reconciling work of God in Christ. In his commentary upon the Apostles' Creed, Barth says that "We do not have to believe in hell and in eternal death. I may only believe in the resurrection and the judgment of Christ, the judge and advocate, who has loved me and defended my cause . . . We cannot 'believe' in sin, in the devil, in our death sentence. We can only believe in the Christ who has overcome the devil, borne sin and removed eternal death."[67]

Concerning the question of Christ's "descent into hell" (a doctrine which we discuss in chapter 4), Barth writes, "As soon as the body is buried, the soul goes to hell, that is, into remoteness from God, into that place where God can only be the Adversary, the enemy. In our place the Christ suffered that situation which ought to have been ours. Our lives too know despair. But it is not, it is no longer, that total despair suffered by Jesus Christ alone . . . we now know that Jesus Christ has destroyed the power of hell, however great it may be."[68]

An Admitted Universalist?

Barth specifically denied teaching the idea of a universal homecoming (*apokatastasis*), because he saw such a position as tying God to a principle. Universal salvation cannot be formally declared, not because of man's freedom to say no, but because of *God's* freedom in giving grace:

> To the man who persistently tries to change the truth into untruth, God does not owe eternal patience and therefore deliverance . . . We should be denying or disarming that evil attempt and our own participation in it if, in relation to ourselves or others or all men, we were to permit ourselves to postulate a withdrawal of that threat and in this sense expect or maintain an *apokatastasis* or universal reconciliation as the goal and end of all things. Even though theological consistency might seem to lead our thoughts and utterances most clearly in this direction, we must not arrogate to ourselves that which can be given and received only as a free gift . . . But universal salvation remains an open possibility for which we may hope.[69]

Bloesch agrees that there is much in Barth's writings which suggests universalism, but he adds that "there is another side to

Barth's theology . . . [that] he explicitly declares that God is under no obligation to continue to favor those who spurn his mercy."[70]

An interesting anecdote about Barth is related by Eberhard Busch, Barth's personal secretary from 1965 until Barth's death in 1968. Busch recalls that one day he came to Barth,

> and he was very nervous. I saw this and asked him what had happened. Then, as was typical for him, he said, "I had an awful dream." And Barth had a very great sense of dreams. I asked him, "What have you dreamt?" He said, "I was dreaming that a voice asked me, 'Would you like to see hell?' And I replied, 'Oh, I am very interested to see it once.'" Then a window was opened and he saw an immense desert. It was very cold, not hot. In this desert there was only one person sitting, very alone. Barth was depressed to see the loneliness. Then the window was closed and the voice said to him, "And that threatens you." So Barth was very depressed by this dream. Then he said to me, "There are people who say I have forgotten this region. I have not forgotten. I know about it more than others do. But because I know of this, therefore I must speak about Christ. I cannot speak enough about the gospel of Christ."[71]

From the *Letters* of Barth it is evident that he tired of being badgered about universalism. But, as Bernard Ramm says, "the question will not go away." Although we don't agree with the wag who said, "Christianity ain't important unless somebody around here can get damned!", Barth says very little about eternity without God. Ramm says that "Barth has not taught universalism in so many words and cannot be charged formally with teaching it . . . [However,] the very fact that the charge persists indicates that Barth shows a strong bent toward the doctrine."[72] We would respond to Ramm by saying that it seems that Barth uses many words to drive readers to his view. To the end of his life, in spite of all his statements indicating otherwise, Barth refused to identify himself as a universalist.

C.H. Dodd (1884-1973)

Dodd, a British Congregational minister and New Testament scholar, reacted to the evangelical concept which to him appeared to say that the great bulk of humanity had been created only to perish. He responded to this idea by teaching that in the end God would relent and forgive everyone, treating all persons as if they had believed.[73]

Paul's "Development"

The Apostle Paul held to what Dodd calls "the Jewish concept" (expressed in the Apocryphal book of 2 Esdras) concerning the fate of the wicked. Paul "steels his heart," says Dodd, "to accept this inflexible and gloomy eschatology in which at most but an elect handful of Jews inherits the Age to Come, while the rest of mankind perish in inconceivable misery."[74]

Dodd sees a progression in Paul's thought from 1 Thessalonians and Galatians (which seem to proclaim the final and irrevocable rejection of the Jews) to his argument in Romans 11 that Israel's rejection *cannot* be final. He says that for Paul, "the coming of Christ in fact marks a crisis in God's dealings with the human race, in that down to that time His purpose proceeded by successive stages of exclusion (Ishmael, Esau, the unrepentant Israel of prophetic times, and the Jews who rejected Christ), but since His resurrection it proceeds by way of inclusion, until in the end no member of the human race is left outside the scope of salvation."[75]

Dodd believes that Paul meant exactly what he said in Romans 11:32 that "God has shut up all in disobedience that He might show mercy to *all*" (NASB, emphasis mine). "In other words," Dodd says, "it is the will of God that all mankind shall ultimately be saved."[76]

In his treatment of Romans 11, Dodd states that "the arguments by which Paul asserts the final salvation of Israel are equally valid (in fact are valid only) if they are applied to mankind at large."[77] "Whether or not, therefore, Paul himself drew the 'universalist' conclusion," Dodd argues, "it seems that we must draw it from his premises."[78]

Commenting on Romans 8:21 (Paul's teaching that creation will be finally delivered), Dodd says that what that text "really expresses is a religious conviction or intuition that, if God is what we believe Him to be, then all the evil in the world must in the end be worked out."[79] Dodd argues that "If there is but one God, and He wholly good, then all mankind must be His care."[80] "As every human being lies under God's judgment, so every human being is ultimately destined, in His mercy, to eternal life."[81] "The entire created universe is to be 'redeemed' and 'reconciled' to its Creator, 'that God may be all in all.' This is the final meaning of the entire process in time."[82]

Dodd sees development in the epistles in that, for example, 2 Thessalonians 1:6-10 indicates that the "bulk of mankind . . . will be destroyed at the coming of Christ to judgment. [However,] in the later epistles [Rom. 11:32; 8:18-23; Col. 1:20; Eph. 3:6-10; 1:10] the Church is truly universal, for by an inward necessity it must ultimately include all mankind, and form the centre of a reconciled universe."[83]

Referring to this apparent development of Paul's thought, illustrated by Ephesians 1:10 (that God will sum up all things in Christ, things in heaven and things on earth), Dodd states:

> The ultimate unity of all things in God is secured not by the mere suppression or destruction of hostile elements, human, sub-human, or super-human, but by bringing them all into harmony with the will of God as expressed in Christ . . . But though we may have to confess that we cannot have any certainty on these points, it does at least seem clear that after the period represented by Galatians and by 2 Corinthians as a whole, there is a growing emphasis on the idea of reconciliation, and a growingly clear expression of a belief in the ultimate universality of salvation in Christ.[84]

According to Dodd, Paul outgrew his harsh, dualistic *Weltanschauung* (worldview) with which he began. He forsook his two categories of the "elect" and the rest of humanity and "matured" in his view of final things. He states that, "It is no accident that from this time . . . we find in his epistles a revised eschatology combined with a generous recognition of the natural goodness of men and of human institutions, a willingness to claim all sides of human life as potentially Christian, and a larger hope for mankind and the whole universe."[85]

Dodd then concludes, that if his understanding of Paul's developing eschatology is correct, "the interpreter of Paul's thought should have regard to the changes which it underwent, and judge it finally not from stages which he outgrew, but in the light of its maturity."[86]

Obviously, Dodd's view of inspiration leaves a great deal to be desired! Perhaps God's thought also underwent changes as He inspired Paul in his writings. The implication is simple: we also should "grow up" in our understanding and hold to universalism rather than the final and eternal loss of those who reject the Gospel. Dodd issues the further challenge that, "If we really believe in One God, and believe that Jesus Christ, in what He was and what He did, truly shows us what God's character and His attitude to men are like, then it is very difficult to think ourselves out of the belief that somehow His love will find a way of bringing all men into unity with Him."[87]

In discussing Israel's "ethical monotheism," Dodd says that "Holding firmly to this belief [Israel was] also convinced that His righteous will is the sole finally effective force in the universe."[88] Dodd sees both a universalistic as well as a nationalistic bent in the Old Testament. "Yet there can be no going back upon the prophetic discovery that God is the God of all men. The Old Testament wrestles with the problem and hands it on unsolved to the New."[89] Of course, Dodd feels the problem is solved in the "maturing" of Paul's theology!

The Problem of Evil

Dodd also believes that the problem of evil is better dealt with by a universalistic position. He states that:

> There is another way of confronting the problem of evil. It is to believe that although there is evil in the world,

> yet it is God's world, and the sphere of His Kingdom. His purpose is becoming effective in every part of it, though with varying degrees of intensity. Its inhabitants are all His children, and it is His will to save them all. In all our contacts with the world, we are in touch, in one way or another, with His purpose.[90]

As we shall demonstrate in our final chapter, universalism does not solve the thorny problem of evil. If anything, universalism takes human sin far too lightly.

John A.T. Robinson (1919-1985)

Bishop Robinson, the infamous author of *Honest to God*, also argues that "the very necessity of God's nature" demands that not one sinner be left in hell.

A War Over God's Nature

Robinson expresses his conviction that the issue is really a battle for the nature of God: "there must be a war to the death . . . We are here in the presence of two doctrines of God, and between them there can be no peace."[91] For example, he says that "the truth of universalism is not the peripheral topic of speculation for which it has often been taken. If God is what ultimately He asserts Himself to be, then how He vindicates Himself as God and the nature of His final lordship is at the same time the answer to what He essentially is. The truth or falsity of the universalistic assertion, that in the end He is Lord entirely of a world wanting His lordship, is consequently decisive for the whole Christian doctrine of God."[92]

Robinson makes it clear that any Scriptural pronouncement about the future of the wicked or the righteous is not primarily a "guess about the turn of future events . . . [but] they are statements rather of conviction about the eternal nature of a God whose last word could not be one of destruction. They represent . . . insight rather than foresight."[93] "False ideas of the last things," argues Robinson, "are direct reflections of inadequate views of the nature of God."[94]

Misunderstanding Myths

Some of those false ideas stem from a misunderstanding of the purpose of myth in the Bible, Robinson believes. As a kind of working picture, myth in the Bible is not to be pressed in a literal fashion. Concerning these myths, Robinson says that

> their truth does not depend on the mythical representations themselves being scientifically or historically accurate. Neither the myths of Genesis nor of Revelation set out to be historical reconstructions, i.e., literal accounts of what did, or what will, happen. As history they may be entirely imaginary, and yet remain theologically true. The only test of a myth is whether it adequately represents the scientific facts to be translated . . . . The eschatological statements of the Bible are of this "mythical" nature, in precisely the same way as its narratives of the Creation and Fall . . . The form of the myth is governed by the current presuppositions of a particular age and place, and is not integral to its truth. But the truth itself is not speculative, it is scientific.[95]

So, Robinson is clear that we are not able to trust the accuracy of either the beginning or the end of the biblical description of life.

Like fellow universalists, Robinson emphasizes that love is God's basic attribute, and declares that "it is most important to hold to the fact that justice is in no sense a substitute for love, which comes into operation when the other has failed to be effective . . . [God] has no purpose but the purpose of love and no nature but the nature of love."[96]

T.F. Torrance challenges Robinson's out-of-hand rejection of the total witness of Scripture to the nature of God:

> The whole argument presupposes that what I can think is, and what I cannot think is not . . . The extraordinary fact is that Dr. Robinson claims to be able to assert now by his own logic the truth of a doctrine which even he admits rests ultimately upon the final action of God . . .

> Is the love of God to be understood abstractly in terms of what we can think about it on a human analogy, such as human love raised to the nth degree, or are we to understand the love of God in terms of what God has actually manifested of His love, that is Biblically?[97]

Nels F.S. Ferré (1908-1971)

Ferré also built his theology on the central thought of divine love, not on God's justice. He describes God's "Agape" love as "unconditional, uncaused, unmotivated, groundless, uncalculating, spontaneous Love, creative of fellowship . . . Love for enemies, if need be, is an intrinsic, inseparable part of Agape, universally, unconditionally and eternally."[98]

All-Encompassing Agape

Such a definition of love, however, rules out any divine enmity toward God's enemies as well as any concept of retributive justice. Such a presupposition concerning the nature of God, if found to be incompatible with the biblical data, flaws his theology. Discussing his theological starting point, Ferré acknowledges that "if the starting point is correct and meaningful, we have both the right and the need for basic theological revision in order to let the Christian faith become rightly understood and properly effective. If this starting point is wrong, on the other hand, our whole theology needs redoing."[99]

One's starting point must be carefully examined, and Ferré's (which he calls the "new wine of the centrality of the love of God") dispels the dark clouds of the wrath of God from all those who stand under its umbrella.

God's justice, Ferré argues, is completely in the service of His love. With appropriate ridicule, one critic of universalism says that universalists have fallen in love with an imaginary deity of their own creation:

> This is wonderful because it means that we have evolved in our religious thinking beyond the men of the Bible,

> who were supposed to be inspired by the Lord. They thought that God was a God who not only could love but also judge. The prophets were wrong when they spoke about judgment. Jesus did not really mean it when He said something about some "shall go away into everlasting punishment, but the righteous unto life eternal." As for the others, Paul with his "the wages of sin is death," and John with his "wrath of God" and "lake of fire," and all those others, they were merely deluded. They believed in a God who loved so much that He was just. But that day is past. Today, we have created another God, One who is compatible with the latest thinking, up-to-date, and He doesn't have to worry us.[100]

Much as Robinson declared, so Ferré sees the theological battlefield to be the nature of God. "Traditional orthodoxy," Ferré says, "has to be challenged, fought and slain."[101]

Heaven Rules Out Hell

Ferré assumes that love and punishment, heaven and hell are mutually exclusive categories:

> Some have never really seen how completely contradictory are heaven and hell as eternal realities. Their eyes have never been opened to this truth. If eternal hell is real, love is eternally frustrated and heaven is a place of mourning and concern for the lost. Such joy and such grief cannot go together. There can be no psychiatric split personality for the real lovers of God and surely not for God himself. That is the reason that heaven can be heaven only when it has emptied hell, as surely as love is love and God is God. God cannot be faithless to Himself no matter how faithless we are; and His is the power, the kingdom and the glory.[102]

Sounding much like some recent evangelicals who have rejected the traditional doctrine of hell as a "moral outrage," Ferré says that:

> The very conception of an eternal hell is monstrous and an insult to the conception of last things in other religions, not to mention the Christian doctrine of God's sovereign love. Such a doctrine would either make God a tyrant, where any human Hitler would be a third degree saint, and the concentration camps of human torture, the king's picnic grounds. That such a doctrine could be conceived, not to mention believed, shows how far from any understanding of the love of God many people once were and, alas, still are.[103]

Ferré makes it quite clear that the very character and nature of God is at stake. "Not to believe in full consummation insults the character of God or sells the power of Christ short."[104] In another place he says that "The logic of the situation is simple. Either God could not or would not save all. If He could not He is not sovereign; then not all things are possible with God. If He would not, again the New Testament is wrong, for it openly claims that He would have all to be saved. Nor would He be totally good."[105]

Ferré is overlooking the biblical teaching that all things are *not* possible with God! For example, Scripture declares that it is "impossible for God to lie" (Heb. 6:18). We are also told that "He cannot deny Himself" (2 Tim. 2:13, KJV). Christ has promised that the one who comes to Me I will never drive away" (John 6:37, NIV); He has *not* promised that those who *don't* come will be forced into His family. God has committed Himself to His program of salvation for humans, which some, to their own eternal peril, can ultimately reject.

Love Never Fails

God's particular attribute of love is at stake, says Ferré. "The total logic of the deepest message of the New Testament, namely, that God both can and wants to save all, is unanswerable. On the grounds of our total analysis of truth, moreover, our existential ultimate requires that all be saved, or else Agape is not ultimate."[106]

"Christ is love," declares Ferré, "and Love never fails. To say that Love fails is to insult God." The biblical doctrine of Christ rests upon a proper view of the restoration of all things, insists Ferré. "The final resurrection can mean nothing less than the victory of Christ over all his enemies; the final victory of universal Love is universal salvation . . . Christology is deceit except it end in a hallelujah chorus."[107]

Ferré overlooks Jesus' teaching that the wicked will be cast out to a place where "there will be weeping and gnashing of teeth" (Matt. 8:12; 22:13; 24:51; 25:30; Luke 13:28). In Matthew 13:42 and 50, Jesus uses the phrase "wailing and gnashing of teeth" (NKJV) to describe the emotional and physical condition of the rejected. This hardly sounds like a hallelujah chorus!

An Empty Hell

No one shall go to a place called hell forever, declares Ferré. "The wonder of Christology is the waiting for the final victory by scorned Love and the transfigured glory of accepted Love where none shall stand outside it."[108] Again, Ferré ignores Christ's authoritative declaration in Matthew 7:21-23:

> Not everyone who says to Me, "Lord, Lord," shall enter the kingdom of heaven, but only he who does the will of My Father who is in heaven. Many will say to Me on that day, "Lord, Lord, did we not prophesy in Your name, and in Your name drive out demons and perform many miracles?" Then I will tell them plainly, "I never knew you. Away from Me, you evildoers!"

Jesus is clearly saying that some in the day of judgment will vigorously defend their right to enter the kingdom of heaven. They will use orthodox language, doubly appealing to Jesus as "Lord!" There will be "many," Jesus says, who will make this desperate plea for admission. In fact, some will list the deeds which they did *in Christ's name.* Jesus does not say that He will deny that such deeds were done; He will deny their doers entrance because He never *knew* them. His words to those on that day, contrary to Ferré, will be words of woe, not of welcome, and they will be told to "depart"! Obviously, there will be "many" (v. 22) who *will indeed* "stand outside the transfigured glory of accepted Love."

Similar language is used by Jesus in Luke 13:23-28 in response to the question "Lord, are there few who are saved?" Jesus replies:

> Strive to enter through the narrow gate, for many, I say to you, will seek to enter and will not be able. When once the Master of the house has risen up and shut the door, and you begin to stand outside and knock at the door, saying, "Lord, Lord, open for us," and He will answer and say to you, "I do not know you, where you are from," then you will begin to say, "We ate and drank in Your presence, and You taught in our streets." But He will say, "I tell you I do not know you, where you are from. Depart from Me, all you workers of iniquity." There will be weeping and gnashing of teeth, when you see Abraham and Isaac and Jacob and all the prophets in the kingdom of God, and you your selves thrust out (NKJV).

In this passage, Jesus again emphasizes that there will be "many" (v. 24) who will attempt to enter heaven, but will be prevented from doing so! Using the imagery of a homeowner awakened in the night, Jesus states that the homeowner has a perfect right to shut his own door to outsiders.

How are we to understand verse 25 which indicates that many *want* to enter in, but are denied? Doesn't God desire to save all who come to Him? The answer to this question occurs in the next verse where these outsiders begin to present their arguments as to why they should be allowed entrance. To paraphrase their defense, they say "Jesus, we partied together! Don't You remember the great times we had at so-and-so's place? And, Jesus, You gave some stirring religious lectures right on *our* block. Look — we have notes, the outlines of Your very inspiring sermons, to prove that we were there, listening to Your every word!"

The fact is that these outsiders demand to be escorted into heaven on their own basis (an earthly association with Jesus), rather than on God's basis, and the Savior's sole response to such a self-righteous demand is "go away!" Rather than agreeing with Ferré that heaven will be an inclusive place "where none shall stand outside it," Jesus categorically teaches that heaven will be an *exclusive* home where only redeemed children will find entrance. All others will be "thrust out" to where there "will be weeping and gnashing of teeth" (v. 28, NKJV).

Hell As School

But God has "no permanent problem children," Ferré says. "He will make our way so self-punishing that at last we come to our better selves and see how good for us is His way. By our own choices and experiences we shall become willing and loving children of God."[109]

"This life," he confidently declares, "is no final examination at the end of life's full story."[110] "He who thinks that not God but death settles our fate, believes more in human life than in God."[111] Apparently, Hebrews 9:27's truth that "man is destined to die once, and after that to face judgment" has escaped Ferré's attention.

Ferré sees hell, like Origen, as an educational institution. "Beyond earthly life lies the larger school where we are expected to mature according to new conditions."[112] Matt Groening, the creator of *The Simpsons* TV show, has produced a comic book trilogy entitled *Full of Hell: Love, Work, and School Is Hell.* Apparently, according to Ferré, we can turn that sentence around and declare that hell is school!

If we are indeed to "preach hell as having also a school and a door in it,"[113] how long will that program of study be? Ferré emphasizes that, "There may be many hells. There may be enough freedom even in the life of hell for man to keep rejecting God for a very long time. Hell may be not only unto the end of the age, but also unto the end of several ages. It cannot be eternal, but it can be longer than we think, depending upon the depth and stubbornness of our actual freedom now and whether or not God will give us fuller freedom in the life to come, and how much."[114]

Hell cannot be eternal, Ferré argues, because "the only way to live in eternity beyond conditional time is within love's fellowship. An eternal hell is incongruous, a false mixing of categories. Evil never reaches eternal status. Eternal hell confuses the two orders of time."[115]

Man's Freedom?

But what if one does not wish to believe? Regarding the issue of man's freedom, Ferré emphasizes that "ultimately God's freedom and man's belong together; and man's freedom to be over-against God is not the freedom to remain an eternal problem child. God's creation and pedagogy are both too good for that!"[116]

Man cannot ultimately or eternally respond negatively to God; in fact, says Ferré, "[F]reedom can be real [only] if God finally controls it . . . Freedom is real and serious precisely because it is God who gives it, who cannot be escaped for our own good."[117] The issue is really one of finiteness verses infinity: "Finality is never of finitude, but of eternity. Finality belongs to God and His purpose, and not to man and his temporal choices."[118]

However, as has been frequently pointed out:

> The advocates of universal restoration are commonly the most strenuous defenders of the inalienable freedom of the human will to make choices contrary to its past character and to all the motives which are or can be brought to bear upon it. As a matter of fact, we find in this world that men choose sin in spite of infinite motives to the contrary. Upon the theory of human freedom just mentioned, no motives which God can use will certainly accomplish the salvation of all moral creatures. The soul which resists Christ here may resist him forever.[119]

William Barclay (although himself a universalist; see chapter 3, note 76) aptly concludes that "It is a great fact of life that God will never fail the man who has tried to be true to Him, but not even God can help the man who has refused to have anything to do with God."[120]

"God will not give up on man!" retorts Ferré. "A terrible thing is hell . . . in the long run, beyond our understanding, but the God who loves us will never be mocked by our stubborn depth of freedom, but for our sakes will put on the screws tighter and tighter until we come to ourselves and are willing to consider the good which He has prepared for us.[121]

An Answer to Evil

There is no place in Ferré's system for the finality of evil in any form. Referring to the belief in Satan, he says that "there is no totally evil fact. There is no single, unrelated, permanently satanic fact. We know of no static structure permanently contradicting the good. The evil that we know is adjectival. It is a minor, never a major, premise; a subordinate, never a coordinate, clause . . . We know of no permanent or final negation."[122]

In his book *God without Thunder*, John Crowe Ransom ridicules the God of liberal theology (which Ferré represents):

> The new religionists, however, would like to eat their cake and have it too. They want One great God, yet they want him to be wholly benevolent, and ethical after the humane definition. What will they do about evil? They will do nothing about it. They will pretend that it is not there. They are not necessarily Christian Scientists in the technical sense, for they do acknowledge some evil, of a kind which is now or prospectively curable by the secular sciences. But they are virtually Christian Scientists so far as they gloze the existence of incurable evil. They represent evil in general as a temporary, incidental, negligible, and slightly uncomfortable phenomenon, which hardly deserves an entry in the theological ledger.[123]

Ferré does not hedge in his view that universalism is the only viable position for Christians: "Those who worship the sovereign Lord are proclaiming nothing less than the total victory of His love. No other position can be consistently Christian. All other positions limit either God's goodness or His power, in which case both fundamentalism and modern liberalism have their own varieties of the finite God."[124]

Regarding "Bible Thumpers"

Conservatives who hold to the traditional doctrine of hell are objects of Ferré's ridicule. He especially attacks the concept of an infallible Bible. "We idolize the relative and freeze history into perversion and impotence. Or 'the book' becomes perfect! Even the words become considered inerrant. Fearful human beings, claiming a liberating Gospel, barricade themselves behind a book. God's historic help in the Bible becomes frustrating Biblicism. God's good means is thus defiled through its perversion. The false use becomes demonic and destructive; and faith flees."[125]

As an "umbrella"[126] which "cloaks the spirit and implications of the Gospel,"[127] the Bible is only "a first century museum."[128] It "handicaps"[129] the church and "thwarts"[130] the Holy Spirit. The Bible is not the final authority, only the concept of God as Agape love. "It is still Christ who constitutes the authority of the Bible. Is it anything less than the full picture of the universal love of God the Father in the face of Jesus Christ that is the authority of the Bible?"[131]

One is reminded of the famed author of *Alice in Wonderland*, Lewis Carroll (the pen name of Charles Lutwidge Dodgson, the son of an Anglican minister). Dodgson said that if the Bible really taught the doctrine of everlasting punishment, "I would give up the Bible."[132]

However, the Christ to which Ferré refers is not the Christ of the Bible. Ferré states that "it is not the biblical Christ of the past that is the standard but the living Christ who bids us look less back to Jesus than up to God."[133] Because there is "no such thing as a frozen final revelation to the Universalist,"[134] truth is dynamic and revelation continues. Ferré states that "instead of trying to prove . . . that Christianity has a closed and final revelation, we are convinced, rather, that the true revelation of the absolute makes knowledge an infinite adventure."[135]

One theologian evaluates Ferré's view by stating "If Scripture is not accepted as an objective authority then the true meaning and intent of revelation is lost in subjectivism."[136] Ferré emphasizes that "the total logic of the deepest message of the New Testament, namely, that God both can and wants to save all is unanswerable."[137] He later states that we should not "base the conclusion, however, solely on New Testament grounds. The witness of the New Testament is inconclusive."[138] One evangelical theologian responds: "If the Biblical evidences are inconclusive, then the 'deepest message' of the Bible must also be."[139]

Venting his self-righteous indignation at those who cite Jesus as their final authority for the doctrine of eternal conscious punishment, Ferré says that such believers hold to "a narrow, literalistic Biblicism . . . that the New Testament teaches eternal hell and that it even was taught by their Lord and Savior, which is enough for them. To question the morality of eternal hell is for them to question God Himself and the only way by which they know, authoritatively, about Him."[140]

Mixed Motives

Ferré also says that some hold to an eternal hell out of an insecurity as to the reality of the Gospel or out of a professional lust for power. "[Preachers don't give up eternal hell because they know] that people are more driven by what they fear than drawn by what they love, and for that reason they feel that to give up the preaching of eternal hell is to give up the most powerful hold that they exercise over people."[141]

Ferré concludes his evaluation as to why some hold to the concept of eternal hell by stating that "professional insecurity and longing for power join with Biblicism, personal success and historic heritage to confirm this doctrine of eternal hell."[142]

Continuing his criticism of evangelicalism, Ferré argues that this branch of Christendom can be described as "the historic main line of theology which has condemned God and crucified Christ afresh by condemning the full Gospel itself that God is sovereign love."[143] Ferré frankly admits that by condemning Origen at this point the church judged itself the proclaimer of another than the Christian Gospel.[144] So it is the church, not Origen, which is the heretic!

Lest some think that Ferré finds annihilationism a less odious option, he understands annihilationism as teaching that "God in this view has children who are so permanently a problem that out of convenience, self-pity or frustrated concern He liquidates them!"[145] He makes the point that "most of the positive drive in view of conditional immortality comes from the desire to escape the Christian contradiction in eternal hell."[146] He dismisses conditional immortality by stating that "at least in the doctrine of eternal hell, life is seriously eternal for each and all."[147]

Fates of the Wicked

Not only does Ferré suffer from an inadequate view of the Scriptures, but he also argues that there are several traditions concerning last things in the Bible. He acknowledges that "we think that it is at least likely that eternal damnation was actually intended by some of the writers of the Bible. We cannot be sure, but we think this to be at least highly probable . . . Whether Jesus taught eternal hell or not is uncertain . . . we must remember that Jesus was far from understood and that his message comes from some distance and with much dilution."[148]

Ferré sees eternal damnation in some of the parables of Jesus, but also believes the Bible teaches annihilation in texts such as Romans 2:12 and 1 Corinthians 1:18. He also believes that final salvation for all is also taught. "We simply have no right to meddle with the New Testament"; Ferré says, "all three teachings are undeniably there." Ferré solves the apparent self-contradictions of the Bible by saying that "only one position is finally consistent with God as *agape*. The other positions are there because preaching is existential."[149]

Jesus: A Deceiver or Merely Uninformed?

Ferré has taken God as *agape* as his governing motif, but he dismisses Matthew 25's teaching regarding the sheep and the goats being sent to eternal destinies (the point is living one's life of Agape). He also minimizes the story of the rich man and Lazarus (mistakenly stating that it is in Luke 17) and the other eschatological parables of Jesus as teaching the doctrine of eternal punishment. He argues that:

> most of the passages mentioning eternal or final damnation are the emphatic scaffolding of parables and not to be taken as specific teachings or literal truth. In other words, Jesus may have preached existential hell, where it is both true and needed, and not hell as an explanatory category. Wooden or leaden thinking on our part on this subject has caused much harm to the spiritually sensitive and the intellectually seeking.[150]

Later he says that the logic of God's sovereign love may have been missed by Jesus. The New Testament is very existential; the implications of God's sovereign love could not be understood by Jesus' disciples and, "it may be, of course, that Jesus himself never saw them."[151] Fortunately, for truth's sake, Ferré claims that the reality of God's sovereign love was captured by twentieth-century theologians who had time to think through the implications of God's all-encompassing love!

Resistance to this rejection of the traditional view of the fate of the wicked is acknowledged by Ferré: "Only those who have tried long and hard to present the glories of God in its full victory can know the astonishing fervor with which people cling to eternal hell as almost the most important part of the Christian message."[152]

Hell and the Problem of Evil

Perhaps Ferré's strongest challenge to conservative theology is his attempt to provide a theodicy concerning the doctrine of hell. In his book *Evil and the Christian Faith*, Ferré says that "without the ultimate salvation of all creatures, men and, we think, animals, God's time and way, it is easy to see that there can be no full solution of the problem of evil."[153] "If one creature is to be eternally tormented, Christ's compassion declares that it were far better that there had been no creation."[154]

Thomas Talbott (1941 –)

One of the best known contemporary universalists, Thomas Talbott, wrote a book entitled *The Inescapable Love of God* [155] in which he attacks the traditional view that those who die without Christ will suffer eternal separation from God. He particularly charges what he calls "Augustinian" Christians with holding a "demonic picture of God" and advocates what he calls "a stunning vision of Omnipotent Love."[156] He argues that God "has but one moral attribute, namely his love . . . ,"[157] a love which will not rest until all His creation is brought back into the fold. This is the time-honored approach of universalists, for if God's final and ultimate nature is love (rather than, say, holiness), He *cannot* eternally reject anyone. "For God is love," says Talbott, "that is the rock-bottom fact about God."[158]

His use of several universalistic-sounding passages (such as Romans 5, 1 Corinthians 15, and Romans 9-11) causes him to conclude that even 2 Thessalonians 1:9's teaching about "eternal destruction" "is itself a redemptive concept"![159]

Because he has written his text to prove that the Apostle Paul was a universalist, he spends relatively little time looking at the teaching of the Lord Jesus Christ on hell. However, in discussing the parable of the sheep and goats in Matthew 25, he writes:

> For even a superficial reading of the Gospels reveals one point very clearly: Jesus steadfastly refused to address in a systematic way abstract theological questions, especially those concerning the age to come. His whole manner of expressing himself, the incessant use of hyperbole and riddle, of parable and colorful stories, was intended to awaken the spiritual imagination of his disciples and to leave room for reinterpretation as they matured in the

> faith; it was not intended to provide final answers to their theological questions."[160]

One could argue that where a person will spend eternity is hardly an "abstract theological question." It must also be asked: "How do we determine Jesus' *intent?*" Rather than intending to "awaken the spiritual imagination of his disciples," I would suggest that Jesus' teaching, especially as we will see in Matthew 25, patently speaks about two (not just one) eternal destinies. Because Talbott is seeking to read the Bible from a universalist perspective, he can declare:

> The more one freely rebels against God, the more miserable and tormented one becomes; and the more miserable and tormented one becomes, the more incentive one has to repent of one's sin and to give up one's rebellious attitudes. But more than that, the consequences of sin are themselves a means of revelation; they reveal the true meaning of separation and enable us to see through the very self-deception that makes evil choices possible in the first place. We may think we can promote our own interest at the expense of others and that our selfish attitudes are compatible with enduring happiness, but we cannot act upon such an illusion, at least not for a long period of time, without shattering it to pieces. So in a sense, all roads have the same destination, the end of reconciliation, but some are longer and windier than others.[161]

We don't have to determine Jesus' "intent"; we can take the text at face-value.

In discussing Jesus' story of the sheep and the goats in Matthew 25, a story which ends by saying that the wicked [the goats] will "go away to eternal punishment, but the righteous [the sheep] to eternal life" (verse 46), Talbott argues that this story does not teach that anyone's eternal fate is sealed at death. Rather, "the purpose of the story is to inform us that our actions, for good or ill, are more far reaching than we might have imagined, and that we shall be judged accordingly; it is not to warn us concerning the ultimate fate of the wicked."[162] But does it not appear patently true that this text is clearly eschatological (pertaining to the end-times), concerns itself with verdicts rendered about the wicked and the righteous, and describes their respective fates as "eternal life" and "eternal punishment"? (v. 46) What part our *imaginations* should play in interpreting the text is unclear to me, unless one is already committed to reading God's Word from, for example, a universalist perspective.

Talbott seems quite interested in the use of human imagination and declares his conviction that " . . . nothing works greater mischief in theology, I am persuaded, than a simple failure of the imagination, the inability to put things together in imaginative ways."[163] I would argue that there is something that works far greater mischief in theology than the failure of imagination and that is *unbelief*. When we refuse to believe God's Word, substituting our own wishful thinking or theological imagination, we should call it what it is: unbelief.[164]

George MacDonald (1824-1905)

In his work *Unspoken Sermons*, MacDonald gives his reasons for rejecting a retributivist theory of punishment (sermon entitled "Justice") and some of the grounds for his hope that God will eventually reconcile all created persons to himself (sermon entitled "The Consuming Fire").[165] In his *Getting to Know Jesus* he ridicules the vicarious penal view of the death of Christ as "the vile assertion,"arguing that "as a theory concerning the Atonement nothing could be worse, either intellectually, morally, or spiritually . . . the idea is monstrous as any dragon. Such a so-called gospel is no gospel . . . It is evil news, dwarfing, enslaving, maddening — news to the child-heart of the dreariest damnation."[166] He refers to the vicarious/penal view of the atonement as "the revolting legal fiction of imputed righteousness"[167] and says that " . . . he who trusts in the atonement instead of in the Father of Jesus Christ, fills his fancy with the chimeras of a vulgar legalism, not his heart with the righteousness of God."[168] He expresses his universalism by saying,

> If your will refuses to work with His you must remain in your misery until — God knows when; God knows what multitudes of terrible sheepdogs He may have to send after you — His wandering sheep — before He can get you to come . . .[169]

Thomas Talbott says that MacDonald was "fond of pointing out that not one word in the New Testament implies that vindictiveness and wrath are ultimate facts about God, or that Christ's sacrifice was required in order to appease a vindictive God."[170]

In describing his understanding of hell, MacDonald says, "I believe that the very fire of hell is the fire of love, but it is a love that will burn the evil out of you."[171] Hell is actually an ally, MacDonald says, "For hell is God's and not the devil's. Hell is on the side of God and man, to free the child of God from the corruption of death. Not one soul will ever be redeemed from hell but by being saved from his sins, from the evil in him. If hell be needful to save him, hell will blaze, and the worm will writhe and bite, until he takes refuge in the will of the Father."[172] God's own person is at stake in this issue, he says: "I believe that God will spare no pain, no trouble, no torture that will be needful to save men from themselves, else it seems true that He could not be God."[173]

Madeleine L'Engle (1918-)

Madeleine L'Engle, a popular novelist among Christians, writes in her *The Irrational Season*:

> I know a number of highly sensitive and intelligent people in my own communion who consider as a heresy my faith that God's loving concern for his creation will outlast all our willfulness and pride. No matter how

> many eons it takes, he will not rest until all of creation, including Satan, is reconciled to him, until there is no creature who cannot return his look of love with a joyful response of love . . . I cannot believe that God wants punishment to go on interminably any more than does a loving parent. The entire purpose of loving punishment is to teach, and it lasts only as long as is needed for the lesson. And the lesson is always love.[174]

D.A. Carson responds to L'Engle's position by commenting, "Regrettably, L'Engle pays little attention to what the Bible actually says, but simply expounds what she can and cannot believe."[175]

It seems that Karl Barth is virtually alone in his abundant use of Scripture to support his theological positions. Talbott uses a few references from the Apostle Paul, forcing other texts which do not agree with his universalism to fit into his "imaginative" way of reading Scripture. Other universalists seem to rely upon "evident reason," or "the nature of God as love dictates that . . . ," or similar arguments. In fact, a number of the theological texts of the men we have discussed have no indices to Scriptures used in their works, obviously because so little Scripture is used.

However, universalists (when they employ Scripture) point to several specific New Testament passages, using them to argue the position that all without exception will be saved. Two of the more prominent texts, Philippians 2:9-11 and Colossians 1:19-20, will now be briefly considered.

Philippians 2:9-11

Paul argues in this text for a Christlike mind to serve fellow believers. Although the doctrinal teaching of Philippians 2 is rich (both His full deity and complete humanity are clearly taught), the imparting of doctrine for doctrine's sake is not Paul's concern. He is emphasizing, rather, the importance of demonstrating one's life in Christ through practical self-giving love.

In His incarnation the second Person of the Trinity assumed the nature of a servant and became a perfect man (Phil. 2:6). His becoming man, Paul says, was for the primary purpose of giving His life in death on the cross (Phil. 2:7-8). The unbeliever Freud ridiculed the idea of Christ's sacrifice: "That the Redeemer sacrificed himself as an innocent man was obviously tendentious distortion, difficult to reconcile with logical thinking." However, reconciliation is exactly the point! Christ's death paid the debt of sin for everyone who believes in Him.

But don't verses 9-11 of Philippians 2 argue that the Father has exalted the Son and "bestowed on Him the name which is above every name," and do not these verses clearly state that at some future point "every knee should bow . . . [at the name of Jesus] in heaven, and on earth, and under the earth, and that every tongue should confess that Jesus Christ is Lord"? (NASB) Barth refers to these verses as recording "the proclamation . . . of the justification of all sinful humanity."[176] The church, says Barth, as "a very small and modest light in this world," began its commission with Jesus' charge to "go therefore and make disciples of all the nations" (Matt. 28:19) and then is brought by God's grace to "its end, that 'at the name of Jesus every knee should bow, of things in heaven, and things in earth, and things under the earth' (Phil. 2:10)!"[177]

Could there be more inclusive expressions than these: "in heaven, and on earth, and under the earth"? This "universal character of the atonement"[178] prompted one evangelical to ask, "Does not 'confessing Jesus Christ as Lord' equal *salvation*?" "After all," he continued, "Romans 10:9 says that 'if you confess with your mouth "Jesus as Lord" and believe in your heart that God raised Him from the dead, you will be *saved*.'"

However, one must point out that the demons in Mark 3:11 were compelled (apparently by the mere presence of Christ) to declare, "You are the Son of God!" That certainly does not equal *saving* faith, but rather a forced acknowledgment of Christ's person. Matthew 8:29 records the demons as expecting not salvation, but *torment*: "What do You want with us, Son of God? . . . Have You come to torture us before the appointed time?" Simply saying the words "Jesus Christ is Lord" does not bring salvation, as any Christian who has dialogued with Jehovah's Witnesses or Mormons knows!

But the eternal state, says one commentator, has no separate room for those "outside" faith:

> Since all things in heaven and on earth, visible and invisible . . . were created by Christ (Col. 1:16) and were to find their consummation in Him, they must come within the sphere of His mediatorial activity: they must ultimately be summed up in Him as their head (Eph. 1:10). Hence in the world of spiritual beings since some have sinned or apostatised, they too must share in the atonement of the cross of Christ and so obtain reconciliation (Col. 1:20) and join in the universal worship of the Son (Phil. 2:10) . . . Since all things must be reconciled and summed up in Christ there can be no room finally in the universe for a wicked being, whether human or angelic. Thus the Pauline eschatology points obviously in its ultimate issue either to the final redemption of all created personal beings or to the destruction of the finally impenitent.[179]

Earlier in Philippians Paul speaks of those who oppose the Gospel and by such opposition set forth "a sure sign . . . that their doom is sealed" (1:28, NEB). One verse later than the text we are considering, Paul admonishes the Philippians to "work out your own salvation with fear and trembling" (2:12). Salvation must be worked *into* one before it can be worked *out* of one.

Paul later reminds the Philippians of those who are "enemies of the cross of Christ: [whose end] is destruction" (3:18-19). Rather than teaching universalism, Philippians 2:9-10 appears to be emphasizing not a confession of personal *faith*, but an acknowledgment by *force* on the part of all unredeemed beings of the supremacy and lordship of Jesus Christ.

Lightfoot understands verse 10 as referring to "all creation, all things whatsoever and wheresoever they be. The whole universe, whether animate or inanimate, bends the knee in homage and raises its voice in praise."[180] Hawthorne, however, suggests that verse 11 refers to the fact that:

> the hope of God is that every intelligent being in his universe might proclaim openly and gladly (Lightfoot) that Jesus Christ alone has the right to reign . . . [However], it is conceivable that beings, who are created with the freedom of choice, may choose never under any circumstances to submit to God or to his Christ. And it is also conceivable that these beings will never be forced to do so against their wills (cf. Rev. 9:20-21; 16:9, 11).[181]

Those particular passages in Revelation cited by Hawthorne emphasize that the impenitence of the wicked will continue (9:20-21), and that even when "seared by the intense heat," men will continue to blaspheme the name of God, refusing to repent and give Him glory (16:9, 11).

Colossians 1:19-20

"But," the universalist might ask, "what if the Bible clearly states that God's desire and action through Christ actually brings back all of creation to Himself? Surely we could not find a clearer biblical statement of such a truth than Paul's words in Colossians 1: 'For it pleased the Father that in Him all the fullness should dwell, and by Him to reconcile *all things* to Himself, by Him, whether things on earth or things in heaven, having made peace through the blood of His cross'" (1:19-20, NKJV, emphasis mine).

At first glance it appears that this text supports the contention that "the goal [of God] is undoubtedly [the] complete conversion of the world to Him"[182] through the reconciliatory work of the Son. Some might even argue that the "all" of verse 19, which emphasizes the full deity of Christ, necessitates that the "all" of verse 20 ("to reconcile all things to Himself") encompasses the full orb of all created beings.

Ferré says that "All men . . . belong within Christ potentially, for God is bound to them with cords of love that can neither break nor wear out. God as eternal Love will not rest satisfied until the children of his love accept his love."[182] However, to understand the truth of the whole Bible, we must look at what all of Scripture teaches. If one holds to the belief that the Bible is not self-contradictory, then one must attempt to reconcile the apparently universalistic force of Colossians 1:19-20 with other passages such as Matthew 25:46 ("these [wicked] will go away into eternal punishment, but the righteous into eternal life," NASB), John 5:29 ("those who have done evil will rise to be condemned"), and Revelation 21:8 ("But the cowardly, the unbelieving, the vile, the murderers, the sexually immoral, those who practice magic arts, the idolaters and all liars — their place will be in the fiery lake of burning sulfur").

Other texts emphasize that Christ's kingdom has an "outside" where there will be "weeping and gnashing of teeth" (Matt. 8:12), that there will be a category of humans who are "cursed" and will be sent "into the eternal fire prepared for the devil and his angels" (Matt. 25:41, NASB), that some will be "guilty of an eternal sin" (Mark 3:29, NASB), that some are "storing up wrath . . . for the day of [God's] wrath" (Rom. 2:5, NASB), and that some of humanity "will be punished with everlasting destruction and shut out from the presence of the Lord and from the majesty of His power" (2 Thes. 1:9).

The contemporary Evangelical Thomas Oden writes that "Hell is the eternal bringing to nothing of corruption and ungodliness. Hell expresses the intent of a holy God to destroy sin completely and forever. Hell says not merely a temporal no but an eternal no to sin. The rejection of evil by the holy God is like a fire that burns on, a worm that dies not."[183]

One writer summarizes the issue by saying that "on the basis simply of numbers, there appear to be considerably more passages teaching that some will be eternally lost than that all will be saved."[184] Another theology text emphasizes that Ephesians 1:10 (" . . . to bring all things in heaven and on earth together under one head, even Christ.") and Colossians 1:20

("by Him to reconcile all things to Himself, by Him, whether things on earth or things in heaven," NKJV) "although not teaching universal salvation . . . suggest that the discord and fragmentation characteristic of the fallen universe ultimately will give way to harmony and unity as Christ sovereignly rules over the created order."[185]

"In context," comments one evangelical text, Colossians 1:20 "cannot mean, unfortunately, that every last individual will be in personal fellowship with God. The cosmic pacification Paul has in mind includes the reconciliation of believers and the disarming of unrepentant enemies of the cross (2:15). Having become impotent, the evil forces must submit to Christ's cosmic victory so that his peaceful purposes will be fully achieved."[186]

Another writer reminds us that "reconciliation" may have more than one meaning. "It is not, however, that universal reconciliation means universal salvation, because we know that, while the work of Christ is sufficient for all, it is efficient only for those who actually accept it. It is indeed God's purpose to save all men, but not all of them will come to Him for life. He impels but never compels."[187] Still another writer expresses his belief that these verses refer "to the cosmic significance of Christ's work, the thought being similar to, but not identical with, that of Romans 8:19-22 . . . . The general sense is that the disorder which has characterized creation shall be done away and divine harmony shall be restored. A reflection of the same thought may be seen in Isaiah 11:6-9. In the present passage perhaps the main idea is that all things eventually are to be decisively subdued to God's will and made to serve His purposes."[188]

It must also be pointed out that Colossians 1 states several verses later that such a reconciliation for human beings is valid only if one continues "in the faith, grounded and steadfast, and . . . [is] not moved away from the hope of the Gospel" (v. 23, NKJV).

Paul clearly speaks of the "sons of disobedience" in Colossians 3:6 (NKJV) and states that "the wrath of God" is coming upon them. Rather than emphasizing that all are saved, or will be saved, Paul appeals to the Colossians to support him in prayer.

He requests that they pray "that God would open to us a door for the word, to speak the mystery of Christ, for which I am also in chains, that I may make it manifest" (4:3-4, NKJV).

Conclusion

Bernard Ramm characterizes Barth's universalism as a "courageous" attempt to bestow meaning on all human beings. Believing that Barth has responded "Nein!" to the question "Are non-Christians the waste products of the plan of salvation?" Ramm concludes, "The compassion of Barth in saving significance for every human life by relating it to God through Jesus Christ is certainly commendable to every person of good Christian sensibilities. He does try to give meaning to billions of persons who under other premises would live completely meaningless lives."[189]

We agree with Ramm that "few things are more un-Christian than a juridical, stony response to the problem of the lostness of billions of human beings."[190] However, is the hope of man to be found in a Gospel which seems compromised from a number of directions?

Barth's doctrine of universalism is open to severe criticism. By its very definition, election to Barth eliminates reprobation for even the most wicked. Because other views of election "have abandoned an original universalism," Barth's doctrine attempts to restore that emphasis. If man's "No" to God is only a *foreword* to God's all-encompassing "Yes," and if God has said "No" to Himself in Christ and "Yes" to humanity ("spoken in the axiomatic certainty of God's judicially binding pronouncement"),[191] *then no one will be lost.* However, the biblical basis for such a doctrine of election is lacking. God's last word to some will *not* be the "Yes" of reconciliation, but the "depart" of kingdom exclusion (Matt. 7:21-23 and Luke 13:24-28).

The necessity of personal faith in the Gospel seems to be weak in Barth's view. Man is not seen as drowning in the sea of his own sin, but is only ankle-deep in his ignorance as to his own election!

If ontologically the old man *cannot* exist in the new heavens and the new earth, and if every man has already been liberated by the atoning work of Christ, then where is the need for repentance?

If faith is seen only as a "silhouette" of God's elective decree, and if the rejector of the Gospel is only a "shadow moving on the wall," then where is the Gospel's urgency? If the eternal verdict of "Not Guilty!" has already been pronounced by God *for every human*, then why should any fear to stand before the Judge of all the earth?

If salvation is only a "gentle and intimate awakening" in the Father's house, then why the need for Calvary? Jesus' teaching in the Gospels seems to paint a picture of a person's worst nightmare if he dies in his sins (John 8:21, 24).

Barth's dream about hell (see page 49) perhaps illustrates the weakness of his universalism. His protests notwithstanding, Barth appears to have forgotten hell, or at least to have so redefined and qualified it that a sinner need not give it a second thought.

Dodd's brand of universalism, as well, leaves a great deal to be desired. He begins with a God who cannot be trusted to act justly (God will finally treat all as *if* they had believed). Of course, to forgive all regardless of their response to Christ is to trample underfoot His atoning work. Why, one might ask, did He even bother?

Basing much of his universalism on his belief that the Bible presents a "developing eschatology," Dodd emphasizes that the last chapter of that eschatology comes through the Apostle Paul who matured out of the concept of eternal judgment. Arguing that the Bible moves from a scheme of exclusion to one of inclusion, Dodd invites all to draw the "inevitable conclusion" of universalism, even though Paul admittedly did not.

Dodd grounds much of his universalism upon the "obvious" truth that "if there is but one God and He wholly good, then all mankind must be His care." Somehow, Dodd argues, God's love will find a way of bringing all people into unity with Him. Dodd's "somehow" is diametrically opposed to Jesus' teaching that "many" are on the broad way that leads to "destruction" (Matt. 7:13).

One is not surprised to hear Dodd say that the traditional doctrine of eternal conscious punishment and the universalist faith are springing from two distinct doctrines of God. Certainly the true God is "not willing that any should perish," but His desire is balanced by His requirement that "all should come to repentance" (2 Peter 3:9, NKJV).

Robinson's brand of universalism equally calls for "a war to the death over two competing doctrines of God." The myths of the Bible (which span Genesis through Revelation and encompass man's creation and his final destiny) are not to be understood literally.

All predictions of man's future fate are valid only if they agree with the nature of God as love and His universal lordship. Also connecting his theological pronouncements to "the nature of God," Robinson makes it clear that "false ideas of the last things are direct reflections of inadequate views of the nature of God."

We completely agree. We will demonstrate in the final chapter of this book that the character of God necessitated the atonement (if man was to be righteously redeemed) and that that same character will require the expulsion of unbelievers from His presence forever.

Ferré easily dismisses the dark clouds of God's wrath by basing his universalism on God's central and foundational attribute, Agape love. Because heaven and hell are mutually exclusive categories, as we noted earlier, "heaven can be heaven only when it has emptied hell."

Again, this universalist agrees with the others that the very character and nature of God is at stake in the discussion of the Other Side. Not to hold to Ferré's view "insults the character of God or sells the power of Christ short."

Ferré forgets that God's omnipotence means that He can do all things that are proper objects of His power, that is, whatever is consistent with His nature. If His nature is allergic to sin, one of the things which God *cannot* do is act contrary to His own holy nature!

"Love never fails," says Ferré. To imply that God's love fails to reach some sinners insults God! But, wait a minute. Parents who love a teenaged son with all their hearts, who practice a godly "tough" love toward him, who would willingly give their very lives for that son, *cannot* be held responsible if that son rebels and insists on drug-induced self-destruction! To say that their love failed (because their son chose to reject that love) is accurate (because their son died), but not an insult to parents who must sometimes submit to wrong decisions by their offspring.

How absurd for Ferré to insist that all sinners will have a part to sing in the final hallelujah chorus! Christ Himself declares that some will only weep, wail, and gnash their teeth due to their righteous judgment imposed by God (Matt. 8:12; 13:42, 50; 22:13; 24:51; 25:30; Luke 13:28).

If the Bible is self-contradictory, as Ferré asserts, and posits several conflicting views of the wicked's fate, then we are free to treat those views much as one making menu selections in a cafeteria. Choose what you like!

To suggest that Jesus did not understand the implications of God's sovereign love, as Ferré does, surely compromises His deity. Mackintosh aptly remarks:

> The suggestion that He [Jesus] may have educated us beyond Himself, enabling us to take wider views, is hardly worth discussion. To call it improbable or unconvincing is a weak expression. Whatever our instinctive wishes, we may well shrink from supposing that we have attained to worthier or more ample conceptions of the divine love, its length and depth and height, than were attained by Jesus.[192]

Furthermore, if the biblical evidences are "inconclusive," then why should we trust Ferré's vision of the finally victorious, all-encompassing love of God? On such a fallible basis, how do we know that *evil* will not ultimately win, that *the gates of hell* will not prevail over those of heaven, and that the universe will not *expire* in a spasm of our most horrible nightmares? Why listen to Ferré if we have no authoritative revelation from above?

Much emphasis is placed by Ferré on his understanding of the nature of God. His primary source is human logic: "if God is like this, then this conclusion follows . . ." This use of human reason is a two-edged sword. If one's conception of God runs counter to the biblical description, then he has the wrong God. If one's conception of the future of humanity without Christ runs counter to the biblical description of the fate of the wicked (as we shall show in chapter 5), then he or she has the wrong Gospel!

Thomas Talbott's "stunning vision of Omnipotent Love" does not take the judgment passages of Scripture seriously. To say that God has but one moral attribute (love) is to go beyond — and against — the total teaching of the Word of God. But Talbott would accuse me of a failure of imagination in not reading Scripture from a universalist perspective. George MacDonald does not hesitate to attack the vicarious penal view of the atonement and sees hell as "a love that will burn the evil out of you." Madeleine L'Engle views God's love as that which will outlast all our willfulness and pride. A famous manufacturer of punching bags is called "Everlast." L'Engle seems to be saying that God will everlastingly pummel the sinner until he or she eventually capitulates. She argues that the entire purpose of loving punishment is to teach, thereby rejecting the clear biblical teaching of retributive (not remedial) punishment.

In speaking of the issue of universalism, J.I. Packer asks the piercing question: "Does not universalism condemn Christ Himself, who warned men to flee hell at all costs, as having been either *incompetent* (ignorant that all were finally going to be saved) or *immoral* (knowing but concealing it, so as to bluff people into the kingdom through fear)?"[193]

Universalism also invalidates man's exercise of freedom. As much as Ferré and others try to argue that man is free to choose against God, they deny that man can ultimately say "no" to the atoning work of Christ. J.H. Bernard acknowledges that man may eternally spurn God's offer of forgiveness: "That the divine intention may be thwarted by man's misuse of his free will is part of the great mystery of evil, unexplained and inexplicable."[194]

Admittedly, God is "not wanting anyone to perish" (2 Peter 3:9). But this passage sets forth *repentance* as the only prerequisite which must be met by sinful man. Some will choose to ignore that prerequisite. Lewis and Demarest emphasize that "[the] general desire or wish of God . . . is constantly assailed by creaturely freedom."[195] Berkouwer asks the question: "Is the human choice — belief or unbelief — really important in universalism, if God in His love actually *cannot* be anything else but merciful to all men?"[196]

C.S. Lewis poses the same question concerning man's freedom. "Is it not a frightening truth that the free will of a bad man can resist the will of God? For He has, after a fashion, restricted His own Omnipotence by the very fact of creating free creatures; and we read that the Lord was not able to do miracles in some place because people's faith was wanting."[197]

Lastly, the Scriptures declare that Christ's kingdom will have an *outside*. As Kuhn so clearly points out, "Protestant orthodoxy . . . [asserts] that the Scriptures are the final court of appeal . . . and that they teach that the final reconstitution of all things in Christ would be accomplished only at the price of the eternal loss of a portion of mankind."[198]

The Word of God is to be our final court of appeal, not a logic which demands that if God is to save any, He must save all. T.F. Torrance asks: "Dare we go behind Calvary to argue our way to a conclusion which we could reach by logic, and which would make the Cross meaningless?"[199] The church's mandate, says Berkouwer, "is not to investigate into the secrets of God, not to soften the Gospel into a communique informing the world that everything is going to come out all right in the end. Its command is to let the voice of the Cross resound through the world with its summons to faith and repentance."[200]

In addressing the issue of universalism over twenty-five years ago, Harold Kuhn said that universalism overlooks at least two biblical concepts. It overlooks the "Eli, Eli lama sabachthani" of the Lord Jesus (His being forsaken by the Father), and also what Kuhn calls:

> the unfathomable horror of the act by which men, in arrogance and proud denial, refuse the ultimate work of love at Calvary . . . [He who understands these two concepts] will see, in the light of the Cross, that hell is no crude medieval invention but hideous reality, prefigured here and now in the wreckage of character evident all about us, and the ultimate and inevitable consequence of the power of men finally to contradict God and to depart from him.[201]

If universalism's view of the Other Side is fatally flawed, what about the concept that the wicked will be consumed by God's wrath? Perhaps the wicked will be excluded from heaven by being excluded from existence. If eternal life is God's gift only to those who believe the Gospel, then maybe those who don't believe will cease to be. A discussion of the alternative known as annihilationism comprises our next chapter.

3

The Other Side: Will It Have Any **Permanent** Occupants?

"The positive teaching of Holy Scripture is that sin and sinners will be blotted out of existence. There will be a clean universe again when the great controversy between Christ and Satan is ended." (W.A. Spicer)

"The fire of hell does not torment, but rather consumes the wicked." (Clark H. Pinnock)

"It is in mercy to the universe that God will finally destroy the rejectors of His grace." (Ellen G. White)

"For our God is a consuming fire." (Heb. 12:29)

A recent Pogo cartoon strip portrayed Pogo and his friends in a baseball game. It was the final game of the regular season, and they were losing 44 to 0 in the first inning. The disappointed catcher made a trip to the pitcher's mound, handed the ball to Pogo and said, "I guess this means we're out of the play-offs, huh?" "Out of the playoffs?" Pogo exclaimed, "we're *metaphysically eliminated*!"

Some evangelicals have embraced the doctrine which teaches that all those who reject Christ will be metaphysically eliminated at God's judgment. That doctrine is known as *annihilationism*, which teaches that, although everyone will survive death and even be resurrected, the impenitent will finally be destroyed. "Conditional immortality," a related term, means that no one survives death except those to whom God gives life; that is, man is immortal by grace, not by nature.

The Church of England Doctrine Commission released its official report, *The Mystery of Salvation*, in 1995. It argued that it is "incompatible with the essential Christian affirmation that God is love to say that God brings millions into the world to damn them . . . Hell is not eternal torment, but it is the final and irrevocable choosing of that which is opposed to God so completely and so absolutely that the only end is total non-being."[1]

In 2000 *The Nature of Hell*, a report of the Evangelical Alliance Commission on Unity and Truth Among Evangelicals (ACUTE), was published. This document affirmed belief in hell, but insisted that "specific details of hell's duration, quality, finality, and purpose which are at issue in the current evangelical debate are comparatively less essential."[2]

One of the driving forces behind the evangelical exodus from the traditional doctrine of hell is that of setting forth a biblical and reasonable theodicy to the world. A "theodicy" is a defense of God's justice in the face of evil's reality. One theologian says that "the idea of everlasting torment (especially if it is linked to soteriological predestination) raises the problem of evil to impossible dimensions. If Christians want to hold that God created some people to be tortured in hell forever, then the apologetic task in relation to theodicy is just hopeless."[3]

This same theologian argues that the problems of Auschwitz and cancer pale in comparison to the problem of God allowing most of His creatures to go ignorantly to hell. The doctrine of annihilation is seen, therefore, as a superior theodicy, for it emphasizes that those who are not saved will not exist forever in a place called hell or the lake of fire, but will either simply pass out of existence or be actively put out of existence by God. A number of prominent contemporary evangelicals advocate annihilationism, perhaps the one who has written the most in its favor being Edward Fudge. His work, *The Fire That Consumes,*[4] provides an almost 500-page challenge to non-annihilationist Evangelicals. Fudge and Robert Peterson co-authored the book, *Two Views of Hell: A Biblical and Theological Dialogue.*[5] Debating the primary issues between annihilationists and non-annihilationists, this text is well worth reading. One of Peterson's more powerful points is made when he challenges Fudge on the issue of the definition of death as cessation of being.

Peterson writes,

> Fudge by implication compromises the doctrine of Christ. To hold that Jesus was annihilated when he died means either that his whole person (deity and humanity) was annihilated or that his human nature alone was annihilated. Either conclusion is disastrous. To hold that the person of Christ ceased to exist in death is to explode the biblical doctrine of the Trinity. It is to assert that the second person of the Godhead went out of existence. It is to assert that the resurrection was a re-creation of the second person of the Trinity so that henceforth one person of the Trinity is a creature, not the Creator.[6]

Other annihilationists include the late Philip Edgcumbe Hughes, John Wenham, and Stephen Travis, as well as John R.W. Stott and Clark H. Pinnock.[7] We will note some of the statements made by the latter two evangelicals and then respond to their reasons for holding to annihilationism.

John R. W. Stott (1921 –)

A highly regarded British Evangelical, John Stott has challenged the Christian community to faithful preaching and steadfast spirituality. Over twenty of his books continue to be published. In one booklet he poignantly argues, "If we come to Scripture with our minds made up, expecting to hear from it only an echo of our own thoughts and never the thunderclap of God's, then indeed he will not speak to us and we shall only be confirmed in our own prejudices."[8]

John Stott engages in a book-length debate with the liberal Anglican David L. Edwards in *Evangelical Essentials*.[9] In that work Stott does a masterful job of faithfully representing evangelical theology, defending the orthodox position on miracles, the deity of Christ, the atonement, and other areas, but departing from the long-held view of the eternal conscious punishment of the wicked.

Stott is put on the spot by Edwards to take a stand either for or against the traditional view of hell. Some have suggested that Stott was baited by Edwards into disclosing his annihilationist view. However, Stott says to Edwards:

> I am grateful to you for challenging me to declare my present mind. I do not dogmatise about the position to which I have come, I hold it tentatively. But I do plead for frank dialogue among Evangelicals on the basis of Scripture. I also believe that the ultimate annihilation of the wicked should at least be accepted as a legitimate, biblically founded alternative to their eternal, conscious torment."[10]

Stott expresses gratitude that he, perhaps after years of holding to annihilationism, could publicly affirm his belief that the wicked will be consumed by the fire of God.

Pleading with evangelicals "to survey afresh the biblical material" on the fate of the wicked, Stott advises that they must open their hearts and minds "to the possibility that Scripture points in the direction of annihilation, and that 'eternal conscious torment' is a tradition which has to yield to the supreme authority of Scripture."[11] He then presents four lines of argument which we will consider shortly.

Clark H. Pinnock (1937 –)

This influential Canadian theologian has challenged the church to defend biblical Christianity and to present the message of the Gospel in a contemporary and relevant manner. Responding to a liberal theologian's review of his *Scripture Principle*, Pinnock writes: "As an evangelical I believe there is a truth deposit in scripture which needs to be guarded (2 Tim. 1:14)."[12]

However, he charges Christians who still hold to the eternal conscious punishment view of the Other Side with failing to come to grips with "the moral horror and exegetical flimsiness of the traditional view of hell,"[13] challenging the evangelical world with the question: "How can one imagine for a moment that the God who gave his Son to die for sinners because of his great love for them would install a torture chamber somewhere in the new creation in order to subject those who reject him to everlasting pain?"[14]

Pinnock sees only three possible options concerning the lost: the traditional doctrine of eternal torment (which he says is "morally and scripturally flawed"), universalism (to which he says "large numbers of sensitive Christians" will turn if the traditional view of hell is not abandoned), and annihilationism (which can be referred to as "fire, then nothing"). The last appears to have the fewest problems to Pinnock. God doesn't raise the wicked in order to torture them eternally and consciously, but "rather to declare his judgment upon the wicked and to condemn them to extinction, which is the second death (Rev. 20:11-15)."[15]

In a dialogue similar to Stott's with David Edwards, Pinnock engages in a *Theological Crossfire*[16] with the liberal Delwin Brown. Beginning with an analysis of theological method, Pinnock then discusses with Brown the doctrines of God, sin, Christ, and salvation. The last chapter concerns the Christian hope and there Pinnock defends his annihilationist view of hell.

Pinnock argues that the New Testament writers "surrendered entirely to Hellenism" in their expectation that God would raise up the whole person in body and soul.[17] He questions the traditional doctrine that Christians go immediately to heaven when they die, stating that "this is not really an accurate way of speaking biblically."[18] He is arguing against what he considers the Greek idea of the existence of man's eternal soul — an issue which we will discuss shortly.

Concerning the question, What will happen to those who finally reject God's love? Pinnock writes:

> [Evangelicals] have taught that there will be a literal fire in which people will be tortured forever and ever. But surely this is both morally intolerable and fortunately biblically unnecessary . . . The belief in hell as everlasting torture is probably based upon the Greek view of the immortality of the soul, which crept into Christian theology and extended the experience of judgment into endless ages.[19]

The traditional doctrine of hell, Pinnock argues, is "a clear example of how moral sense causes us to reopen an exegetical question."[20] He then drops the gloves and issues the challenge: "It's time for evangelicals to come out and say that the biblical and morally appropriate doctrine of hell is annihilation, not everlasting torment."[21]

The liberal Delwin Brown is not convinced that the traditional doctrine of hell as eternal conscious punishment can so easily be abandoned by evangelicals. He asks Pinnock: "Why is belief in hell as eternal punishment not mandatory for evangelicals? Aren't you playing the game you attribute to liberals – 'picking and choosing' what you want to believe?"[22] Although Pinnock believes that Brown has misunderstood him ("I do not in fact deny hellfire"), Brown echoes the position of Ferré (noted in chapter 2) that the Bible sets forth several views of the fate of the wicked. Brown challenges Pinnock:

> Your "reform" of the traditional view of hell is a considerable improvement, in my judgment . . . You

> want in the end to say that what the Bible "really" teaches is the destruction of the wicked, not their everlasting torment. Is it not nearly accurate to say: (a) the Bible contains differing views about what happens to the wicked, (b) there are several more or less plausible ways to construe the biblical message as a whole, and (c) the broad interpretation of the biblical witness that you defend (but not prove) leads you on this particular point to deny conscious everlasting torment and affirm a doctrine of hell as annihilation?[23]

Brown then concludes by saying to Pinnock that "We [liberals] are not picking and choosing anymore than you are. Like you, we find ourselves drawn to the biblical witness and compelled to listen to its manifold voices. Like you, we struggle, amidst the wealth and diversity of these voices, to come to some interpretation of that witness as a whole."[24]

Brown both disagrees and agrees with Pinnock's doctrine of annihilation:

> According to the alternative and more dominant view in the New Testament, hell represents something that has an everlasting reality. This, of course, is the view that became orthodox. You are properly harsh in your criticism of orthodox talk about hell as a literal place, to say nothing of its heinous conception of hell as a place of everlasting torment.[25]

One respects Pinnock for dialoguing with Brown. However, the real issue is simply this: does the Bible present *one* view of the fate of the wicked? If it does, is annihilationism more consistent with the biblical material, or is the traditional view of eternal conscious punishment?

Our position is that the traditional doctrine of eternal conscious punishment makes more sense with the biblical data. To prove our case, we will follow Stott's four lines of argument against the traditional view, interacting with Pinnock's (and others') statements as well.

Scriptural Language

Annihilationists frequently contend that the terms used in the Bible about the wicked's fate are terms more of destruction than of enduring punishment. For example, Stott argues that if "to kill" is to deprive the body of life, "hell" would seem to be the deprivation of both physical and spiritual life, that is, an extinction of being.[26]

An Immortal Soul?

Employing a standard argument of annihilationists, Stott emphasizes that man is not naturally immortal. The concept of man's possessing an immortal soul is a Greek concept, he says, not a biblical one. The Lord "alone is immortal" (1 Tim. 6:16); the gift of immortality is given only to those who respond positively to the Gospel. "Christ . . . has destroyed death and brought life and immortality to light through the Gospel" (2 Tim. 1:10).

Pinnock agrees and argues that it is the "belief in the natural immortality of the soul which is so widely held by Christians, although stemming more from Plato than the Bible, [which] really drives the traditional doctrine of hell more than exegesis does."[27] (One might, of course, remind Pinnock that his rejection of hell is, as he admits, driven more by his "moral revulsion" than by exegetical considerations.)[28] Pinnock says that the traditional view argues that if souls will exist forever, those who reject the Gospel must be put *somewhere*: "I am convinced that the hellenistic belief in the immortality of the soul has done more than anything else (specifically more than the Bible) to give credibility to the doctrine of the everlasting conscious punishment of the wicked."[29]

This argument is hardly new. John Calvin, for example, in his *Psychopannychia* attacked the doctrine of "soul-sleep" (the idea that the believer does not go immediately into the presence of the Lord at death, but that his soul "sleeps" in the grave until the Resurrection. Calvin argues from Jesus' words of comfort to the thief on the cross ("Today, you will be with Me in paradise" Luke 23:43) that the believer is ushered immediately into the presence of Christ at death (cf. Luke 16:22).[30]

Seventy years ago Archbishop William Temple dismissed the traditional doctrine of eternal conscious punishment, making the same point as Pinnock:

> One thing we can say with confidence: Everlasting torment is to be ruled out. If men had not imported the Greek and unbiblical notion of the natural indestructibility of the individual soul, and then read the New Testament with that already in their minds, they would have drawn from it [the New Testament] a belief, not in everlasting torment, but in annihilation. It is the fire that is called *aeonian* [everlasting], not the life cast into it.[31]

Misunderstood Orthodoxy

In a two-part article entitled "Evangelicals and the Annihilation of Hell," Alan W. Gomes responds to the charge that the orthodox have adopted the Platonic concept of an immortal, indestructible soul. Conservatives have *not* come to believe in the immortality of the soul because of extra-biblical Greek thought, Gomes argues. The accusation that hell is an invented abode for the indestructible souls of wicked people is fallacious.

Gomes argues that the conditionalists have not really understood the orthodox teaching on the soul's immortality. Orthodox Christians hold that the soul's immortality is not an absolute but a *contingent immortality*. "The soul, as a created substance, depends on God's continuing providential support just as all other created entities do."[32] Gomes makes the point that the soul is immortal "not because it cannot be reduced to nothing by God, but by God's ordinance in and so far as it is indestructible by second causes. In other words, while the 'immortal' soul is impervious to destruction from both external secondary causes (e.g. people), and internal secondary causes (e.g. diseases, such as can afflict the body), the soul could be annihilated by its primary cause, God."[33] The orthodox do *not* teach the soul's *absolute* indestructibility.

Murray Harris makes much the same point when he writes that, "as for the question of man's original state, we may suggest that he was created neither immortal (see Gen. 3:22-24) nor mortal (see Gen. 2:17) but with the potentiality to become either, depending on his obedience or disobedience to God. While not created *with* immortality, he was certainly created *for* immortality. Potentially immortal by nature, man actually becomes immortal through grace."[34]

Lest annihilationists think they have an ally in Harris, he argues that "conditional immortality" of this variety is quite different from the popular meaning of that expression. That popular meaning is the view that only the righteous will live forever, the unrighteous being consigned to annihilation, either at death or after suffering divine punishment for a period. The Apostle Paul teaches that immortality is conditional in the sense that there is no eternal life apart from Christ.

"This does not imply that existence beyond death is conditional or that unbelievers will be annihilated," Harris says, because "in New Testament usage, immortality has positive content, being more than mere survival beyond death, its opposite is not nonexistence, but the 'second death' (Rev. 20:6, 14) which involves exclusion from God's presence" (2 Thes. 1:9). He emphasizes that "forfeiture of immortality means the deprivation of eternal blessedness but not the destruction of personal existence. All human beings survive beyond death, but not all will become immortal in the Pauline sense."[35] In biblical thought, Harris adds, "life is not equated with mere existence and death with nonexistence, for both life and death are modes of existence."[36]

He concludes that "neither the Old Testament nor the New Testament entertains the possibility of the total extinction of persons. The New Testament contains sufficient warnings of the dire, eternal consequences of rejecting Christ to leave us in no doubt that the early church rejected both universalism and annihilationism."[37]

Louis Berkhof, as well, argues that "God is indeed the only one that has inherent immortality. Man's immortality is derived, but this is not equivalent to saying that he does not possess it in virtue of his creation . . . Eternal life is indeed the gift of God in Jesus Christ, a gift which the wicked do not receive, but this does not mean that they will not continue to exist."[38] Twentieth-century theologian John Murray says, "Man is not naturally mortal; death is not the debt of nature but the wages of sin."[39]

One might grant for argument's sake that man is not naturally endowed with immortality. Although one suspects that the Greeks are getting the credit (blame?) for the doctrine of man's immortality in order to do away with the concept of the everlasting punishment of the wicked, the Bible clearly speaks of the existence of the wicked after death. Hebrews 9:27 emphasizes that "man is destined to die once, and after that to face judgment." As well, the "everlasting contempt" of Daniel 12:2 assumes the continuing existence of the objects of God's hatred (see the discussion of God's "holy hatred" in chapter 6).

Of course, it is quite common for annihilationists to reject the doctrinal validity of the story of the rich man Dives (from the Latin for "rich man") and Lazarus (Luke 16:19-31) (discussed in depth in chapter 5). That is, if that teaching section of Jesus is meant to be understood as authoritative information about the after-death condition of the righteous and the wicked, then annihilationism is *automatically* ruled out as a viable viewpoint for Dives is clearly portrayed, not as destroyed, but as consciously suffering in hell (vv. 23-25, 28). As Reymond argues, "the parable may be describing most immediately the intermediate state, but there is nothing in the parable which suggests that the intermediate state's 'torment' will cease for the lost after their resurrection and judgment."[40]

Terms of Destruction

Stott denies not only man's immortal nature, but makes the basic point that eternal perdition is frequently described in Scripture as "destruction." "It would seem strange," Stott says,

" . . . if people who are said to suffer destruction are in fact not destroyed."[41]

The most common Hebrew term for "destroy" is *abad*, a word with a wide range of meaning. The people of Chemosh were "destroyed," but this refers to their being sold into slavery, not their being annihilated (Num. 21:29). Saul's donkeys were *abad* in 1 Samuel 9:3, 20, but *abad* obviously means "lost," not annihilated, in this text. A "broken" (*abad*) vessel (Ps. 31:12) is one which is rendered unfit for use, not one that has ceased to exist.[42]

In the New Testament the Greek verb *apolumi* is translated "destroy" and its noun form (*apoleia*) as "destruction." Stott cites texts such as Matthew 2:13; 12:14; and 27:[20] (which refer to the plots by Herod and, later, the Jews to kill Jesus) as evidence of destruction. He then employs Matthew 10:28 ("Do not be afraid of those who kill the body but cannot kill the soul. Rather, be afraid of the One who can *destroy* both soul and body in hell," emphasis mine) to prove the soul's total annihilation in hell.[43]

The same term "destroy" (*apolumi*), however, is used in Luke 15 by Jesus of three illustrations of lostness: in verses 1-7 to describe the lost, but existing, sheep; in verses 8-9 to describe the lost, but existing, coin; and in verse 24 to describe the prodigal, but existing, son.[44] Other texts (such as John 11:50; Acts 5:37; 1 Cor. 10:9-10; and Jude 11) also use *apoleia* or *apolusthai* to indicate destruction, but not annihilation. Jesus also refers to Judas Iscariot as "lost" in John 17:12, but annihilation could not have been his point, for Judas had not yet hanged himself.

Although a different term is used, the Apostle Paul says in 1 Corinthians 3:17 that "if anyone *destroys* God's temple, God *will destroy* him" (my emphasis). One lexicon lists this term (and its use in 1 Cor. 3:17) as "*destroy* in the sense [of] 'punish with eternal destruction.'"[45] The term suggests ruination, or perhaps, desecration in the context, but certainly not the idea of annihilation.

In our contemporary language we might say "the Boston Red Sox *destroyed* the New York Yankees last night!" Although George Steinbrenner is capable of accomplishing that task without any outside help, we certainly do not mean annihilation by such hyperbole. We sometimes speak of an automobile as *totaled*, not at all meaning that it has ceased to exist. Charles Hodge points out that "To destroy is to ruin. The nature of that ruin depends on the nature of the subject of which it is predicated. A thing is ruined when it is rendered unfit for use; when it is in such a state that it can no longer answer the end for which it was designed . . . . A soul is utterly and forever destroyed when it is reprobated, alienated from God, rendered a fit companion only for the devil and his angels."[46]

One of the passages which Stott cites to prove annihilation, 1 Corinthians 1:18, tells us that "the message of the cross is foolishness to those who are perishing." This participle is in the present tense, which "describes *existing* people who are *presently* perishing. The verb does not suggest that their *future* state will be non-existence."[47]

The term "death," as well, does not mean cessation of existence. Paul says, for example, that a widow "who lives for pleasure is *dead* even while she lives" (1 Tim. 5:6, emphasis mine). His point is that such an ungodly woman is not just a widow in life — she is a widow in the work of God; she's a "carcass of the church" (Matthew Henry). Paul's emphasis is the waste and *ruination* of her life and ministry, not the cessation of her being.

The wicked are sometimes described in Scripture as those who will be "cut off." Both Fudge and Pinnock cite passages such as Psalm 37:22, 28, 34 and 38 as proving the annihilation of the wicked. The word which is used in those verses is *carath*, the same word which is used of the Messiah being "cut off" in Daniel 9:26! Certainly *carath* in that Messianic prophecy does not indicate that the Messiah would be annihilated.

Other expressions used by annihilationists equally fail to prove their case. Psalm 104:35 records the psalmist praying "Let the sinners be *consumed* out of the earth, and let the wicked *be no more*" (KJV, emphasis mine). However, the same expressions are used prophetically of Christ in Psalm 69:9 ("zeal for your house *consumes* me," emphasis mine) and of Enoch in Genesis 5:24 ("Enoch walked with God; then he *was no more*, because God took him away," emphasis mine). The verbs "burn" or "burn up" used of the wicked in Malachi 4:1-3 and Psalm 97:3 are shown not to mean annihilation by Job 30:30 and Revelation 14:10-11.

Scriptural Imagery

Stott's second line of argument focuses on the picture which Scripture paints of the fate of the wicked. The imagery of hell as "eternal fire" does not primarily emphasize torment, Stott suggests, but destruction. "The main function of fire is not to cause pain," he says, "but to secure destruction, as all the world's incinerators bear witness."[48] Obviously, the main function of fire depends upon the one who sets it. Fire may be used to cook, to provide heat or light, or to be stared at to inspire campfire testimonies!

Although the fire is described as "eternal" (Matt. 18:8; 25:41) and "unquenchable" (Matt. 3:12; cf. Luke 3:17), Stott says it would be very odd if what is thrown into it proves indestructible. "Our expectation would be the opposite: it would be consumed for ever, not tormented for ever. Hence it is the smoke (evidence that the fire has done its work) which rises for ever and ever."[49]

Questions about That Fire

The argument that God's fire will *consume* man, however, seems inconsistent with the "unquenchable fire" of Matthew 3:12. The Greek term "unquenchable" (*asbesto*) lies behind our English word "asbestos," which Webster's defines as "mineral supposed to be inextinguishable when set on fire." Reymond asks, "[W]hy [does] John [the Baptist] characterize the fire as 'unquenchable' if every impenitent sinner at the final judgment is instantly consumed by it?"[50]

The same question might be asked about Jesus' warning about *gehenna* in Mark 9. Referring back to Isaiah's prophecy of judgment of the wicked in Isaiah 66:24 (cf. Isa. 51:8), Jesus declares that it is a place where the wicked's "worm does not die, and the fire is not quenched" (Mark 9:48). As one writer argues, "Worms are able to live as long as there is food for them to consume. Once their food supply has been consumed, the worms eventually die. But the torments of hell are likened to *undying*, not dying worms. This is because their supply of food — the wicked — never ceases."[51]

One might also ask, if the work of destruction is complete, why should there be any smoke at all (Rev. 14:11; 19:3)? A snuffed-out candle continues to exist, even while smoke trickles forth from the "extinguished" wick. Smoke, especially smoke which rises for ever and ever, seems to imply remaining fuel for that fire. As an *unquenchable* (Mark 9:48), *eternal* (Jude 7) fire, the fire of God's judgment is no ordinary one which dies out once its fuel has been consumed. The smoke of the wicked's torment "rises for ever and ever" (Rev. 14:11), evidence not that the fire has done its work (as Stott suggests), but that it is doing its work through an eternal process of endless combustion. As Gomes argues, "Stott replaces the 'unquenchable' fire of Jesus with the 'quenchable' fire of the annihilationists."[52]

Certainly the idea of remedial or temporary suffering does not come to mind when we think of those two expressions: unquenchable fire and undying worms. If God can use a burning bush to communicate to His chosen person in Exodus 3 without consuming *it*, who is to say that His fire of judgment cannot punish those who refuse to believe the Gospel without consuming *them*? (cf. Dan. 3:19-27).

Granted that figurative expressions have limits and that much of the language used to describe the fate of the wicked appears to be symbolic; however, as one writer argues, "the realities [which the New Testament descriptions] seek to represent should surely be understood by us to be *more* — not less — horrible than the word pictures they depict."[53] C.S. Lewis also emphasizes that "the prevalent image of fire is significant because it combines the ideas of torment and destruction. Now it is quite certain that all these expressions are intended to suggest something unspeakably horrible, and any interpretation which does not face that fact is, I am afraid, out of court from the beginning."[54]

Scriptural Justice

Stott and Pinnock argue that the traditional view of eternal punishment seems incompatible with God's justice. That is, sins consciously committed in time do not seem to merit conscious torment throughout eternity. Pinnock minces no words in declaring: "I consider the concept of hell as endless torment in body and mind an outrageous doctrine, a theological and moral enormity."[55] To inflict infinite suffering upon those who have committed finite sins, as Pinnock argues,

> would go far beyond an eye for an eye and a tooth for a tooth. There would be a serious disproportion between sins committed in time and the suffering experienced forever. The fact that sin has been committed against an infinite God does not make the sin infinite. The chief point is that eternal torment serves no purpose and exhibits a vindictiveness out of keeping with the love of God revealed in the gospel.[56]

However, the argument that infinite punishment for finite sin is unjust rules out not only the traditional view of hell, but also the suggested alternative view of annihilation. "On this ground," as one writer argues, "God could not even annihilate the sinner for his sin since annihilation is certainly eternal in its effect."[57]

The argument that finite sins cannot be worthy of eternal suffering is fallacious for two reasons: First, such a position "assumes that the heinousness of a crime is directly related to the time it takes to commit it. But such a connection is nonexistent. Some crimes, such as murder, may take only a moment to commit, whereas it may take a thief hours to load up a moving van with someone's possessions. Yet, murder is a far more serious crime than theft."[58]

Second, one must take into account not only the nature of the sin, but also the *person* against whom the sin is committed. Stealing is a crime, but stealing from one's mother is even more serious because one owes greater respect to one's parents. "Torturing an animal is a crime, but torturing a human being is an even greater crime, worthy of greater punishment."[59] (One might suggest that this distinction is fast disappearing in North America, where it is considered a serious crime to kill a whale, but an even more objectionable offense to prevent the abortion of a human being.)

If one takes into account the nature of sin as well as the person against whom the sin is committed, one might ask:

> How much more serious, then, is even the slightest offense against an absolutely holy God, who is worthy of our complete and perpetual allegiance? Indeed, sin against an absolutely holy God is absolutely serious. For this reason, the unredeemed suffer absolute, unending alienation from God; this alienation is the essence of hell. It is the annihilationist's theory that is morally flawed. Their God is not truly holy, for he does not demand that sin receive its due.[60]

Dr. Daniel Fuller makes the same point from a different perspective in his book *The Unity of the Bible*. Arguing from the doctrine of God's glory, Fuller states that "if God uses his great power to work all things together for the good of those who delight in him, then he must direct the full force of that power against people going in the opposite direction."[61] That is, "God could not be loving to those who seek him if he did not vent the power of his wrath against those who remain impenitent. Far from being irreconcilable opposites, God's love and wrath are simply two ways in which he makes it clear that he himself fully honors his name."[62]

A credible, benevolent government matches the *severity of punishment* to the *enormity of the crime*, Fuller argues. Parking in a "no parking zone" merits a fine, but not a prison term. To give a "slap on the wrist" for rape or murder is a mockery of justice. The point is "if . . . humanity has sinned in the worst possible way against God, then our sense of justice must call for the severest punishment, and the biblical teaching of eternal misery in hell for the impenitent meets that requirement."[63] Rather than compromising God's goodness, this view simply says that "for God to be consistent with his burning desire to be fully benevolent to people, he must punish this *enormity* [of unbelief] with the greatest *severity*. Thus the biblical teaching of eternal torment in hell for rejecting God's mercy should accord fully with our sense of justice."[64] We need the reminder that "God can remain loving *only* by opposing, with the full fervency of his love for his own glory, those who oppose him by scorning the opportunity he gives to enjoy that glory."[65] God finds no pleasure in punishing the wicked, but He "nevertheless does it as something he must do, so that without devaluing his glory he can fully rejoice in being merciful to the penitent."[66]

Carson makes an important point concerning the issue of infinite punishment for finite sins. He writes,

> One might reasonably wonder why, if people pay for their sins in hell before they are annihilated, they cannot be released into heaven, turning hell into purgatory. Alternatively, if the sins have not yet been paid for, why should they be annihilated? The truth of the matter is that annihilation does not account for what Jesus calls "an eternal sin" (Mark 3:29), i.e. for sin that "will not be forgiven, either in this age or in the age to come" (Matt. 12:32).[67]

Shakespeare's Hamlet, toying with the possibility of killing himself with a dagger, gives us that famous soliloquy:

> To be, or not to be – that is the question . . . To die – to sleep – No more . . . 'tis a consummation devoutly to be wish'd.

Wanting to be free from the guilt of his misdeeds, Hamlet considers suicide. His uncertainty, however, is that he could not be guaranteed release from punishment in the hereafter. Shakespeare reflects the sentiment that annihilation would be a welcomed prospect. Fuller comments on this idea in Shakespeare by saying, "In fact, people hardened in wickedness could take real comfort in the thought that they would simply cease to exist at death rather than having to answer to God for their sins."[68] As Peterson argues, "annihilation is relief from punishment; the damned in hell would love to be annihilated, for this would deliver them out of their terrible suffering."[69] Ajith Fernando makes the point that "annihilation is very similar to what orthodox Buddhists view as salvation"![70]

Because there are no small sins against a great God, sin involves infinite demerit. David's confession of his sin against Bathsheba (and her courageous husband Uriah) emphasizes that the eternal God must deal with sin: "Against You, You only, have I sinned and done what is evil in Your sight, so that You are proved right when You speak and justified when You judge." (Ps. 51:4) Jonathan Edwards was right when he said that the reason we find hell so offensive is because of our insensitivity to sin. Fuller criticizes Pinnock's objection to hell as eternal conscious punishment by saying that:

> [Pinnock] does not probe deeply enough into the reason why God sent his Son to die for sinners. He certainly did it because he loved them, but why did this love mean that his Son had to die for them? The scriptural answer is that Christ came to die "as the one who would turn aside [God's] wrath" (Rom. 3:25 margin). Jesus had to appease God's anger so that God would remain just when he forgave sinners and in no wise tarnish his own glory [Rom. 3:26].[71]

To the common question of annihilationists "What purpose does eternal conscious punishment serve in God's justice if it is not remedial?" we would respond, it declares His justice!

Referring to Jonathan Edwards' sermon entitled "The End of the Wicked Contemplated by the Righteous: or the Torments of the Wicked in Hell, No Occasion of Grief to the Saints in Heaven," Fuller points out that it was based on Revelation 18:20 (where God commands the saints to rejoice over Babylon's judgment). Edwards states:

> [I]t will be from exceedingly different principles, and for quite other reasons, that the just damnation of the wicked will be an occasion of rejoicing to the saints in glory . . . It will be no argument of want of a spirit of love in them, that they do not love the damned; for the heavenly inhabitants will know that it is not fit that they should love them, because they will know then, that God has no love to them, nor pity for them . . . [The suffering of the wicked] will be an occasion of their rejoicing, as the glory of God will appear in it . . . God glorifies himself in the eternal damnation of the ungodly men.[72]

Scriptural Universalism

Stott is no universalist, but argues that the Scripture seems to indicate a final reconciliation of all creation to God. Therefore, he says, "the eternal existence of the impenitent in hell would be hard to reconcile with the promises of God's final victory over evil."[73] The apparently universalistic texts are easier to relate to the awful realities of hell if hell means destruction, Stott suggests, rather than if it means eternal conscious punishment.

Any Existing Exceptions?

Although Stott makes it clear that texts such as Colossians 1:20 and Philippians 2:10-11 do not lead him to universalism, they underscore (in his mind) the logic of annihilationism's teaching that the wicked will be put out of existence. Stott asks, "[H]ow [can God] in any meaningful sense be called 'everything to everybody' while an unspecified number of people still continue in rebellion against him and under his judgment?"[74] "It would be easier to hold together the awful reality of hell and the universal reign of God if hell means destruction and the impenitent are no more."[75]

One must respond by pointing out that in Stott's view "the awful reality of hell" is not an *everlasting one* (presumably hell ceases to exist once it has done its job of annihilating the wicked). Yet Scripture indicates that hell (more technically, the lake of fire) is *eternal* (Rev. 14:11; 19:3; 20:10) and its fire is described as *eternal* (Dan. 12:2; Jude 6-7; 2 Thes. 1:9; Matt. 18:8; 25:41, 46).

Further, the term "everybody" need not involve all existing beings to be considered sufficiently inclusive. For example, one might have a birthday party and state after the celebration: "Everybody had a great time!" The context of that remark makes it clear that its reference is only to those who were invited and who came. That statement is obviously not implying that those who did not come to the party ceased to exist.

Unhappy Universalists

The universalist, of course, will not be more enamored with the idea of the annihilation of the wicked than with the traditional view of hell. Barclay, for example, clearly identified himself as a universalist. He wrote, "But in one thing I would go beyond strict orthodoxy — I am a convinced universalist. I believe that in the end all men will be gathered into the love of God."[76] He argues that it is impossible to set limits on God's grace. He suggests that the operation of God's grace is not confined to this world and believes that God's grace will ultimately win every single person. "It is a question of God using an eternity of persuasion and appeal until the hardest heart breaks down and the most stubborn sinner repents."[77]

No person has the power to defeat the love of God. Barclay states:

> There is only one way in which we can think of the triumph of God. If God was no more than a King, or Judge, then it would be possible to speak of his triumph, if his enemies were agonizing in hell or were totally and completely obliterated and wiped out. But God is not only King and Judge, God is *Father* — he is indeed Father more than anything else. No father could be happy while there were members of his family forever in agony. No father would count it a triumph to obliterate the disobedient members of his family. The only triumph a father can know is to have all his family back home.[78]

As we shall see in chapter 4, God has set limits on His grace and the hope of postmortem opportunities for redemption has no scriptural support. As Daniel Fuller states, "Death marks that time when God's patience with evil people ends." The British jurist Fitzjames Stephen aptly remarked that "though Christianity expresses the tender and charitable sentiments with passionate ardour, it has also a terrible side. Christian Love is only for a time and on condition; it stops short at the gates of Hell, and Hell is an essential part of the whole Christian scheme."[79] Barclay also assumes the universal Fatherhood of God, a tenet of universalism which Jesus Himself clearly taught was false (e.g. John 8:44; cf. Eph. 2:3, KJV).

Such apparently universalistic texts as Colossians 1:20 and Philippians 2:10-11 certainly are contradicted in the universalist's mind if even *one* human being is put out of existence. In one sense, annihilationism seems a variation of universalism in that, of all those who continue to exist forever, there will be only *one* class remaining: the redeemed.

The apparently universalistic texts of Colossians 1 and Philippians 2 were treated in chapter 2. The Scriptures clearly indicate the everlasting existence and confinement of the wicked under judgment. To acknowledge the continuing existence of a class of human beings who rejected the atoning work of Christ does not compromise either God's holiness or the new heavens and the new earth.

Victory over an enemy may take a variety of forms, despite Barclay's insistence that "there is only one way in which we can think of the triumph of God." A capital criminal might be sentenced to life at hard labor. To be victorious, God does not need to annihilate His enemies; He need only demonstrate His righteous judgment through and upon them. J.I. Packer rightly argues that "the holy God of the Bible is praised no less for establishing righteousness by retributively punishing wrongdoers (Rev. 19:1-5) than for the triumphs of his grace (Rev. 19:6-10) [and] it cannot be said of God that expressing his holiness in deserved retribution mars his joy."[80]

Stott concludes his defense of annihilationism with the words: "I . . . believe that the ultimate annihilation of the wicked should at least be accepted as a legitimate, biblically founded alternative to their eternal conscious torment."[81] However, one is reminded of the comment written by a university English professor on a student's essay: "Your paper is both good and original. Unfortunately, what was good was not original and what was original was not very good." The annihilationists' arguments for their position are not new, original, or persuasive.

In the final analysis, the issue is not what we finite human beings are able to conceive, imagine, or even tolerate concerning the fate of the wicked. There is only one legitimate question: "What does the Bible teach?" Although we will anticipate some of our later discussion (Chapter 5: "The Other Side According to Jesus"), we want to pose two questions to those who are annihilationists.

How Long Is "Eternal"?

Evangelical annihilationists are up against the ropes when it comes to the biblical language describing the fate of the wicked. They will affirm (as does Stott) that "forever and ever" means "everlasting" in Revelation 14:11, but that it applies only to the smoke of God's fire which has consumed the wicked (not to their eternal conscious punishment). Apparently in that text "forever and ever" means "forever and ever." Rene Pache says that the word "eternal" is used sixty-four times to refer to "the divine and blessed realities of the other world . . . In all these cases, it is beyond all doubt a question of duration without end."[82]

However, when Matthew 25 is discussed, a different approach is taken by annihilationists.

Two Flocks

Jesus speaks there of the judgment of the sheep and goats, pointing out that those who had demonstrated their salvation through their works will be commended by Christ and invited into the "kingdom prepared for you since the creation of the world" (v. 34). Those whose faith produced no corresponding works Jesus will describe as "cursed" and He will tell them "depart from Me . . . into the *eternal* fire prepared for the devil and his angels" (v. 41, emphasis mine). Jesus' own words conclude this parable, somber words which declare that "[the goats] will go away to *eternal* punishment, but the righteous to eternal life" (v. 46, emphasis mine).

Pinnock honestly admits that "the interpretation of everlasting, conscious torment can be read out of [verse 46] if one wishes to do so." He acknowledges that scholars such as Murray Harris and Robert Gundry read verse 46 in that way, and quotes the latter's comment that "the parallel between eternal punishment and eternal life forestalls any weakening of the former."[83]

Pinnock goes on to argue, however, that Jesus does not define the nature of the eternal life or the eternal punishment in Matthew 25: "He just says there will be two destinies and leaves it there. One is free to interpret it to mean either everlasting conscious torment or irreversible destruction."[84]

Jesus Our Interpreter

But we must respond that Jesus does not just leave it there. Within this same context of Matthew 25, Jesus declares that the righteous will enter the blessedness of the kingdom prepared for them since the creation of the world (v. 34). The wicked's fate Jesus describes as "eternal punishment" (v. 46) in the place "prepared for the devil and his angels" (v. 41). As we shall see later, that place is not left undefined in the Bible. Jesus clearly describes the nature of the wicked's fate throughout the Gospel of Matthew. Jesus does *not* allow for *either* the annihilationist *or* the eternal conscious punishment view in Matthew 25. The place to which the "goats" will be sent will be the "eternal fire prepared for the devil and his angels" (v. 41). Granted, Jesus does not detail what that eternal fire will involve in Matthew 25, but He has spoken a number of times about the nature of hell up to this point in Matthew's Gospel, and His teaching supplies the basis for the traditional view of eternal conscious punishment. If the Bible, however, clearly declared that the fate of the devil and his angels would be annihilation, then that would, of course, be His meaning in Matthew 25:41. However, such is *not* the case.

How can one deny that the "place" which has been prepared for the "devil and his angels" (Matt. 25:41) is not the same "place" — ("the lake of burning sulfur") — into which he will be thrown at the judgment (Rev. 20:10)? Those human beings whose names are not found in the Book of Life (Rev. 20:15) will be, as far as we can discern, the same ones (described as "goats") that Jesus will reject and send "into the eternal fire" (Matt. 25:41). That "place" will be a place of unceasing torment (Rev. 20:10). If it is just for God to eternally torment the devil and his angels, why would it not be just for the wicked who merit His wrath to experience the same fate?

After dismissing the story of the rich man's "torments" in Luke 16:19–31 as "Jewish imagery," and arguing that that text is referring only to the intermediate state, Pinnock expresses a basic agnosticism about the fate of the wicked: "I would not say that either side wins the argument hands down largely because the Bible does not seem concerned to deal with this question as precisely as we want it to."[85] If Pinnock is correct, then his own attacks on the traditionalist view should be greatly tempered (such as when he describes the traditional view as "morally and exegetically flawed").

If the argument is "up for grabs," then how can Pinnock declare that the traditionalist "position is in fact very weakly established biblically"?[86] Although he writes that "whether the wicked perish or suffer endlessly, hell is a very grim prospect, and I and the others are not trying to lessen it,"[87] we believe that is indeed what is happening with the evangelical "annihilation" of hell.

A few words must be said about the charge that traditionalists "smuggle" the term *conscious* into the doctrine of the wicked's punishment. Adjectives begin to multiply when those who seem not to accept biblical teaching use the same terminology to deny that teaching. We agree with Gomes who states that "once we have said the word 'punishment' we have also said, at least by implication, the word 'conscious.' Punishment, per se, is conscious or it is not punishment. A punishment that is not felt is not a punishment."[88] He continues, "Someone cannot be punished eternally unless that someone is there to receive the punishment. One can exist and not be punished, but one cannot be punished and not exist. Nonentities cannot receive punishment."[89]

The expression "eternal punishment" in Matthew 25:46 rules out the possibility that the wicked are annihilated. William Shedd rightly argues that:

> the extinction of consciousness is not of the nature of punishment. The essence of punishment is suffering, and suffering is consciousness. In order to be punished, the person must be conscious of a certain pain, must feel that he deserves it, and know that it is inflicted because he does. All three of these elements are required in a case of punishment. To reduce a man to unconsciousness would make his punishment an impossibility. If God by a positive act extinguishes, at death, the remorse of a hardened villain, by extinguishing his self-consciousness, it is a strange use of language to denominate this a punishment.[90]

Eternal Opposites

Stott actually hurts the annihilationist cause by his declaration that "the more unlike . . . [heaven and hell] are, the better."[91] Does it not make sense that if heaven represents inexpressible joy, then hell should be indescribable (not nonexistent) sorrow? "Yet," as one critic points out, "the whole point of the annihilationist's argument is to mitigate the horror of eternal suffering for the lost, not to increase it."[92]

As much as annihilationists would like Matthew 25:46 to say that it is the punish*ment* that is eternal, not the punish*ing*, "the Bible uses the adjective 'eternal' to describe the *punishment itself*, not merely the result of the punishment."[93] The adjective *aionion*, although it can at times refer to an "age" or period of time, seems most likely to mean "unending" or "everlasting" here in Matthew 25:46 for a simple reason: *aionion* is used to describe both the length of punishment of the wicked and the length of eternal life for the redeemed. "One cannot limit the duration of punishment for the wicked without at the same time limiting the duration of eternal life for the redeemed."[94] John Broadus' commentary on Matthew clearly declares: "It will at once be granted, by any unprejudiced and docile mind, that the punishment of the wicked will last as long as the life of the righteous; it is to the last degree improbable that the Great Teacher would have used an expression so inevitably suggesting a great doctrine he did not mean to teach."[95]

Who Cares About the Devil?

A Scottish proverb states that "the devil is a busy bishop in his own diocese." Some who deny his diocese begin to doubt the reality of the bishop. One is not surprised that some who distance themselves from the biblical doctrine of hell eventually question the personality and reality of Satan. But the Bible sets forth with equal clarity both Satan's reality *and* his destiny. Unless one is prepared to deny Satan's real, personal existence, it is clear that those who reject Christ will share Satan's fate.

Revelation's Wrath

The Book of Revelation teaches much concerning God's judgment of the wicked. Referring to human beings who "worship the beast and . . . receive his mark", God tells us in Revelation 14 that such a person will "drink of the wine of God's fury [and] . . . he will be tormented with burning sulfur in the presence of the holy angels and of the Lamb. And the smoke of their torment rises for ever and ever. There is no rest day or night for those who worship the beast and his image, or for anyone who receives the mark of his name" (vv. 9-11).

We then read of the seven bowls of God's wrath being poured out on human beings in Revelation 16. Verses 8-9 of that chapter describe the fourth bowl which, when poured out, gives the sun power to scorch people (*anthropoi*) with fire. Those people are then described as "seared by the intense heat and they cursed the name of God, who had control over these plagues, but they refused to repent and glorify him"(v.9). Contrary to the common idea that the wicked will experience remorse when they feel God's judgment, these individuals intensify their blasphemous unbelief and impenitence.

Revelation 20 declares that the devil, who deceived the nations, "was thrown into the lake of burning sulfur, where the beast and the false prophet had been thrown. They will be tormented day and night for ever and ever." (v. 10) There is no exegetical basis whatsoever in this text for suggesting that the devil, if he is indeed a personal being, will be put out of existence at the end of time.

God's Books

This passage goes on to declare that at the Great White Throne of judgment two sets of books will be opened. One set contains the record of all the works which the dead have done (20:12). Apparently, God will take the time to show those who rejected Christ that they neither measured up to His holiness, nor to their own moral standards.

The second set of books is described as "the book of life," referred to again in verse 15 of this chapter, as well as in

Revelation 3:5 and 21:27 (cf. Luke 10:20; Dan. 12:1-2). Revelation 20:14 defines the "second death" as the being cast into the lake of fire (not annihilation, as some suggest),[96] which is the fate of the devil, the beast, and the false prophet described four verses earlier (v. 10).

Would one not at this point have to concede, that if this passage (Rev. 20) goes on to state that wicked human beings will be cast into the same place as that unholy trinity, then the fate of those wicked human beings *cannot* be annihilation? This is in fact what Scripture teaches. Revelation 20:15 declares that "If anyone's name was not found written in the book of life, he was thrown into the lake of fire." Can there be any doubt that the fate of the wicked, predicted by the Lamb of God Himself in Matthew 25:41, is not reiterated here in Revelation 20:10-15?

Pinnock is in error when he interprets Revelation 20:10 as saying that "John's point seems to be that everything which has rebelled against God will come to an absolute end."[97] That, as Gomes says, may be Pinnock's point, but "John's point is that the Devil, the beast, and false prophet will be tormented day and night, forever and ever. To read the text is to refute Pinnock."[98] Incidentally, Revelation 20:10's expression "for ever and ever" (also used of the wicked in Revelation 14:11) is designed to emphasize the concept of eternity. R.C.H. Lenski points out that:

> the strongest expression for our "forever" is *eis tous aiônan tôn aiônôn*, "for the eons of eons"; many aeons, each of vast duration, are multiplied by many more, which we imitate by "forever and ever." Human language is able to use only temporal terms to express what is altogether beyond time and timeless. The Greek takes its greatest term for time, the eon, pluralizes this, and then multiplies it by its own plural, even using articles which make these eons the definite ones.[99]

This same phrase is the strongest form in which the idea of eternity is conveyed in the Bible, and is used several times to refer to the duration of God's own existence (Rev. 1:18; 4:9-10; 10:6; 15:7).

Identical Fates

Pinnock is correct when he declares that "the Devil, the beast, and the false prophet . . . cannot be equated with ordinary human beings, however we should understand their nature."[100] Gomes responds: "Of course an angel's nature is different than a human being's nature. But the point of 'equivalence' is not the *nature* of the beings (i.e. angels as disembodied spirits vs. human beings as psycho-physical unities), but their ultimate *fate*."[101] Texts such as Matthew 25:41; Revelation 14:11; 19:20; and here (Rev. 20:15) declare that their fates will be identical. Isaac Watts was not biblically incorrect when he penned these words:

> There is a dreadful Hell,
> And everlasting pains;
> There sinners must with devils dwell
> In darkness, fire, and chains.[102]

One must also point out that the eternal conscious punishment of the devil and his angels disproves Pinnock's point concerning the unjustness of infinite judgment for finite sin. That is, the devil and the demons are not eternal beings, yet their eternal fate is eternal punishment (Rev. 20:10) for finite rebellion.

Unless annihilationists like Stott and Pinnock are prepared to declare that the devil, the beast, and the false prophet are abstract symbols, or insist that one cannot derive doctrine from the symbolic Book of Revelation or from Jesus' Parable of the Sheep and the Goats in Matthew 25, we hope they will reconsider their rejection of the traditional view.

Demonic Expectation

There are several other deficiencies in the annihilationist position. For example, even though Satan is a "liar and the father of lies" (John 8:44), he and his minions sometimes (perhaps by force) speak the truth. One such occasion concerns the healing of two demon-possessed men in Matthew 8. When Jesus approached them, the demons cried out, "What do you want with us, Son of God? Have you come here to *torture* us before the appointed time?" (v. 29, emphasis mine) The same Greek verb *basanitzô* is used here as is used in Revelation 14:10 and 18:7-8 (see discussion in chapter 6). The parallel account in Luke 8 records the demon speaking through one of the men saying, "I beg you, don't *torture* me!" (v. 28, emphasis mine) Mark's version of the same incident describes the man as shouting at the top of his voice and crying out "Swear to God that you won't *torture* me!" (5:7, emphasis mine)

Of course, annihilationists might suggest that the demons want to deceive us into believing that God is a tormenting fiend, but these accounts seem patently genuine, reflecting terror on the part of these satanic spirits. Perhaps they know their certain fate and thought Jesus was jumping the eschatological timetable. At any rate, their expectation was punishment, not annihilation.

Degrees of Punishment

A few years ago I learned first-hand the meaning of the expression "Achilles heel." My Achilles tendon ruptured when I was playing basketball, requiring surgery and an extended period on crutches. The "Achilles heel" of a position is that point at which it seems especially vulnerable. Annihilationism's Achilles heel appears to be the issue of *degrees of punishment.*

Jesus rebukes the cities of Korazin and Bethsaida for their unbelief in Matthew 11:20-24 (parallel: Luke 10:13-16), indicating that more severe judgment will be given to those who have received greater opportunity for belief. Jesus declares that "it will be more bearable for Sodom and Gomorrah on the day of judgment than for that town" (Matt. 10:15) which does not receive the disciples' witness.

Luke 12:47-48 teaches the same truth of degrees of punishment at the judgment. However, the doctrine of annihilation posits a final, undifferentiated nonexistence for all the wicked. Those who hold this view might grant that a temporary punishment of hellfire, its duration commensurate with the wicked person's just desserts, will occur, yet the final result is the same for every member of that class: they are all, equally, no more. Grounds points out that "instead of absolute equality, Scripture indicates an infinite *inequality* in punishment. There will be the 'few stripes' and the 'many stripes.'"[103]

We are not surprised to hear Fudge's response to Matthew 11:22-24 that "Jesus here indicates that there will be degrees of punishment at the end, based on degrees of culpability . . . [But] Jesus here personifies cities, however, and we do not wish to make too much of these words in our study of the final punishment of individual sinners."[104]

An Invitation to Return

Finally, Pinnock acknowledged earlier his commitment to guard the "truth deposit in Scripture" (cf. 2 Tim. 1:14). If the biblical data supports the traditional view of hell, is it too harsh to suggest that he has made a "withdrawal" from that truth deposit by denying the doctrine of eternal conscious punishment? His "thought experiment,"[105] the advocating of annihilationism, and his attack on evangelicals who proclaim a "pseudo-gospel"[106] (including the eternal conscious punishment view) are cause for concern. Although he considers the annihilation of the wicked "a grim prospect," we would suggest that he reconsider his doctrinal change.

The "pilgrimage" of Clark Pinnock, chronicled by Barry L. Callen in his *Clark H. Pinnock: Journey Toward Renewal: An Intellectual Biography*,[107] causes some to rejoice and others to weep. Callen says that "his [Pinnock's] current faith hypotheses are well-tested and worthy." What are some of his "current faith hypotheses"? Apart from calling into question the truthfulness of Scripture (*The Scripture Principle*), Pinnock postulates a variety of on-the-edge (if not outside the pale of Evangelicalism) theories which cause many to question his theological orthodoxy.

With his pivotal work, *Unbounded Love: A Good News Theology for the 21st Century*,[108] Pinnock reiterates his orientation to see God as love, rather than as an authoritarian and austere judge. Along with his *Most Moved Mover: A Theology of God's Openness*,[109] it appears that Pinnock's theological momentum might move him into some form of universalism. One wonders what factors have kept him from becoming a "wishful universalist," for he has seriously submitted a wide variety of options to avoid the tragic truth of an everlasting hell (annihilationism, postmortem conversionism, salvific general revelation, a wider hope view, and open theism).

In endorsing Callen's work on Pinnock, Stan Grenz says that " . . . no story of evangelical theology in the twentieth century is complete without the inclusion of his fascinating intellectual journey from quintessential evangelical apologist to anti-Augustinian theological reformist." I recall back in the 1970's one Evangelical debater being so sharp with his unbelieving antagonists that the audience of Christians was reported as rooting *against him* in the debate! Along came Pinnock and in his public debates with people like Madeline Murray O'Hare he was marked by a gentle and persuasive and winsome approach. In the last few years the gloves have come off and Pinnock has caustically attacked fellow Evangelicals on a number of fundamental issues. I believe a strong case could be made that Pinnock's hypotheses have, indeed, been well-tested (throughout church history) and have been found wanting.

John Stott's sensitive recommendation of annihilationism as a viable biblical alternative certainly merits our respect, even if we believe his position is a wrong one. We are reminded of a statement in his pamphlet *Our Guilty Silence*. There he tells about the seventeenth century Jesuits in China who, in order not to upset the social sensitivities of the Chinese, excluded the crucifixion and certain other details from the Gospel. Professor Hugh Trevor-Roper, Stott says, responded by writing: "We do not learn that they made many lasting converts by the unobjectionable residue of the story."[110] The redefining of hell along annihilationist lines, we believe, should be reconsidered by Stott.

For those who move in this theological direction of denying the biblical doctrine of hell (and perhaps even further), we believe Walter Brueggemann's warning is not too harsh and should be carefully heeded: "The gospel is too readily heard and taken for granted, as though it contained no unsettling news and no unwelcome threat . . . It is a truth that has been flattened, trivialized, and rendered inane."[111]

4

The Other Side: Will It Have Any **Redeemable** Occupants?

"Those who assert the possibility of a future chance do not make death the decisive barrier of time for people to make a decision of faith." (John E. Sanders)

"Some interpreters [hold] that death is the occasion when the unevangelized have an opportunity to make a decision about Jesus Christ." (Clark H. Pinnock)

"We do not wish to build fences around God's grace . . . and we do not preclude the possibility that some in hell might finally be translated into heaven." (Donald Bloesch)

"For Christ . . . also . . . went and preached to the spirits in prison." (1 Peter 3:18-19)

In the film *Flatliners*, a group of young medical students experiment with death. Through medical technology they take turns rendering each other clinically dead, the others bringing back to life each student who had volunteered for the "journey." A rather tense competition soon develops to determine who can stay dead longer than the rest and still be successfully resuscitated.

Although those who experience that induced "death" state differ in their religious beliefs about the afterlife, a common theme characterizes their journeys: the consequences of one's earthly actions follow one into the next world. After returning to life, some of the students make amends with those they had wronged in this world.

Strong theological and medical objections might be raised about this movie's plot, but *Flatliners* sets forth death as an opportunity to realize some of one's mistakes in life and to repent. Could it be that Hollywood is, for once, right? That is, some theologians argue today that perhaps God will use death to offer the Gospel to the billions who have never heard in order that they may repent. This view (sometimes referred to as *postmortem* conversion) appears to be a possible answer to the thorny problem of the countless numbers of men and women made in the image of God, who through no fault of their own, never receive the Good News about Christ.

If one affirms the truth of Romans 10:14 ("How then shall they call on Him in whom they have not believed? And how shall they believe in Him of whom they have not heard?" NKJV), is it not logical that those who have never heard in this life must receive an opportunity to hear in the next life?

Does not the New Testament itself indicate that Jesus descended into hell and "preached to the spirits in prison" (1 Peter 3:18-20)? Certainly a God of love, One who "takes no pleasure in the death of the wicked" (Ezek. 33:11), and One who is "not willing that any should perish, but that all should come to repentance" (2 Peter 3:9, NKJV), would provide an opportunity to those who have never heard, would He not? If

God is loving and God is just, would it not be unfair to condemn those who have not *believed* simply because they have not *heard*?

Although there are some theologians who suggest that God will present the Gospel as often as needed to finally convince *all* unbelievers to repent (see chapter 2), we are not here considering a second chance offer of the Gospel. Our question concerns those who have not heard even once. The view that all will have the Gospel presented to them at least once has sometimes been called "universal explicit opportunity" and says that every person will hear the Gospel in an overt fashion, even (if necessary) after his or her earthly demise.

One evangelical roundly criticizes Christians who "seriously maintain and defend the notion that God will be sending to hell millions upon millions of people who lacked the opportunity to call on the name of Jesus."[1] "What drives people more than anything else into the camp of theological relativism," suggests this same writer, "is the impression they have that the God of orthodox theology is harshly exclusive by nature." To correct this impression we must make it as clear as possible "that classical Christology does not entail a restrictive soteriological scenario."[2]

But life itself appears to entail a "restrictive soteriological scenario," does it not? That is, a very small percentage of the total world population hears and responds to the Gospel of Christ. Therefore the suggestions are made that either God might save the unevangelized through general revelation, supernaturally reveal Christ to the one seeking, or even use death as the avenue of proclaiming the Good News of Christ to those who have never heard.

But before we discuss the possibility of after-death opportunities to hear the Gospel, we must ask some questions about general revelation. Every human being, according to Romans 1 and Psalm 19, is daily exposed to information about the God of creation. Perhaps the truth received through general revelation, if properly responded to, can save those who never explicitly hear the Gospel of Christ.

Can General Revelation Save?

In the children's classic *Rebecca of Sunnybrook Farm*, Rebecca struggled with whether or not she should become a missionary. She says to herself: "It isn't as if the heathen really needed me; I'm sure they'll come out all right in the end . . . they'll find God somehow, sometime." "What if they die first?" asked Emma Jane. "Oh, well, they can't be blamed for that; they don't die on purpose."[3]

What about those who die before they hear the Gospel? William Cowper, the eighteenth-century English poet, once asked, are thousands "lost in endless woe, for ignorance of what they could not know?" Biblical statements such as John 14:6 ("I am the way and the truth and the life. No one comes to the Father except through me"), Acts 4:12 ("Salvation is found in no one else, for there is no other name under heaven given to men by which we must be saved"), and Romans 10:14 ("How can they hear without someone preaching to them?") appear to exclude the possibility of salvation apart from an explicit presentation of the Gospel.

According to *Operation World 21st Century Edition*, of the world's 12,000 ethnolinguistic peoples, "about 3,000-3,600 are 'World A' peoples in which less than 50% are likely to have heard the gospel."[4] With a population of over 6 billion, there are many who have not heard a clear gospel witness.

Twenty years ago demographers predicted that by the year 2,000 the world's population would number close to ten billion — "the world's projected ultimate population size."[5] Although that prediction did not come to pass, it was also said back in 1981 that there were between 25,000 and 30,000 "people groups" in the world of which about 3,000 "unreached people groups" are identified and cataloged. "Some 10,000 languages and dialects are said to exist in the world of which only 1,500 have even a part of the Word of God," this researcher wrote. The need for cross-cultural missionaries is great for "ninety-five percent of all missionaries work among peoples who have already been evangelized. Unless present missionaries are redeployed and new missionaries are directed to the unreached, the dark side of the globe will not only continue in darkness but will continue to multiply in that darkness."[6]

There is some encouraging news, however, according to *Operation World.* The "Jesus" film project "has had 4.1 billion individual viewings — maybe representing 3 billion people and has yielded over 128 million enquirers."[7]

If it is true that "most human beings who have ever lived have never heard about the redeeming work of our Lord Jesus,"[8] then the crucial question is quite simply: "[D]oes a person have to hear about and believe in Christ before death in order to receive salvation?"[9] Theologians are divided on the issue of whether the unevangelized billions are really lost without an explicit presentation of the Gospel of Christ.

Salvation Apart from an Explicit Gospel Presentation

One writer, representing the viewpoint which says that if the unevangelized respond to the light they have they can be saved, comments on the apparently exclusive biblical texts (John 14:6; Acts 4:12; and Rom. 10:14) by saying that "it is not certain from these passages that one must hear of Christ in this life to obtain salvation. They simply say there is no other way to heaven except through the work of Christ; they do not say one has to know about that work in order to benefit from the work."[10]

However, Jesus clearly said to the Jews of His day: "If you do not believe that I am who I claim to be, you will die in your sins" (John 8:24). His statement specifically implies that a certain amount of knowledge of and positive response to His person is a necessary requirement for *not* dying in one's sins. Those who hold that the unevangelized can be saved apart from an explicit presentation of the Gospel might respond to this text by saying, "The Jews had Jesus right in front of them! They were responsible for the incredible light they received. This argument cannot be applied to those who have never even heard of Jesus!"

Some theologians attempt to solve the problem of the untold billions by suggesting that God's revelation of Himself through man's nature, the world's history, and the created universe might bring salvation. If someone who has not heard the Gospel were to respond to what is revealed of the Creator God through those three avenues, he might be redeemed on the basis of the work of Christ (although unknown to him). It seems reasonable, it is argued, that a person will be judged by the knowledge that he possesses, not condemned for information he does not have. As one writer put it, "there is a possibility of salvation for the hidden peoples who, by the way of grace through faith, recognize their need and repent before God, seeking his forgiveness."[11]

Frequently an appeal is made to those under the Old Testament economy who were saved without any explicit knowledge of Christ. Osburn says, "If the eternal God . . . has applied Christ's blood to people of faith in the Old Testament who [had] no knowledge of Jesus, why can he not do likewise for the unreached person today who has no explicit knowledge of Christ but may believe in the One who raised Jesus from the dead (cf. Rom. 4:23-24)?"[12]

Salvation apart from an explicit Gospel presentation is also supported, it is said, by Revelation 5:9 which states that Christ's blood "purchased men for God from every tribe and language and people and nation." Osburn continues his argument emphasizing:

> This is not only a great source of comfort for those missionaries who feel that their work is bearing no fruit but also a fulfillment of Genesis 12:3 (that all the peoples of the earth would be blessed through Abram). Yet if there will be Christians in heaven from among every people group and language, what can be done with those civilizations and small tribes who have disappeared without ever having a missionary witness because of war, or disease, or natural calamity? These verses seem to indicate that there may be members of even these peoples who will be in heaven, so God must have dealt with them in a special way.[13]

"Perhaps conservative Christianity should at least allow for the possibility of the salvation of those very few unreached people who apparently do seek God, grope for him, and find him (cf. Acts 17:27)," concludes the above critic. We must avoid a "too-confident and sweeping dogmatism against the feasibility of salvation for some of those who have never heard," warns this writer, or we will be "adding unnecessarily to 'the offense of the cross.'"[14]

Sir Norman Anderson grappled with the issue of those who have never heard and asked the pointed question: "Might it not be true of the follower of some other religion that the God of all mercy had worked in his heart by his Spirit, bringing him in some measure to realize his sin and need for forgiveness, and enabling him, in his twilight as it were, to throw himself on God's mercy?"[15]

God is certainly capable of saving those who have never received an explicit presentation of the Gospel on the basis of their response to the witness of general revelation, say certain scholars. However, others suggest that because general revelation cannot save, but only condemn, special revelation about Christ is needed for conversion.

Salvation Comes Only by an Explicit Gospel Presentation

One argument used by these theologians is that the unevangelized *have* heard the witness of creation (as expressed in Rom. 10:18) and that creation's witness brings enough information about God to convince the seeker that he or she is lost. According to Romans 1:18-21, man's own conscience condemns him, revealing his inadequacy to live up to his own moral standards. "Scripture gives no clear statement on the salvation of those who have never heard the name," emphasizes Bruce Nicholls. He further states, "We have little evidence of those who without knowing the name of Jesus fulfill the condition of salvation. We can only affirm that salvation from beginning to end is the work of God in Christ. None are saved by their good works or because they have lived according to the light they have received. In practice general revelation becomes a vehicle for divine judgment and not for salvation."[16]

Responding to S.D.F. Salmond's contention that, "We need nothing beyond Paul's broad statement that those who have the law shall be judged by the law, and that those who are without law shall be judged without law," J. Ronald Blue argues that this reference to Romans 2:12 misses Paul's point entirely. Paul is not arguing that some will not be judged because they did not have the law. Rather he is arguing that all will be judged according to the information they have. The term "judged" is better translated "perish," that is, "those who have sinned without the Law will perish just as surely as those who have sinned with the Law . . . The argument of the passage is not to excuse men but to show that they have no excuse."[17]

Harold Lindsell also emphasizes the fact that "general revelation, to be a vehicle of salvation, must insist that God is revealed sufficiently so as to restore the broken relationship with man . . . But the essence of special revelation is the truth that God is not revealed unto salvation in general revelation . . . This much is perfectly evident: general revelation is totally insufficient as a vehicle for salvation."[18]

Blue makes it clear that "the judgment of God in relation to the untold billions of the world is not based on their response to unrevealed truth but to revelation they *have* received."[19] God's truth is made clear to all men through conscience and creation, according to Romans 1:19-20. Humans are without excuse. Blue expresses this thrust of Romans: "There is sufficient knowledge for each person after the fall to be criminally liable for sin."[20] "The issue therefore," he says, "is not that the unevangelized have not put their trust in a Person of whom they have never heard, but that they have suppressed the truth they have both received and understood."[21]

The purpose of Romans 1:18-32 is "to show that the wrath of God is being revealed against all godlessness and wickedness of men who suppress the truth by their wickedness."[22] "Clearly in Paul's mind," asserts Nicholls, "there is no salvation in God's universal revelation in nature or in conscience, not because they are not valid paths to a true knowledge of God, but because of the enormity of human sin and rebellion so that all men are blinded to their truths."[23] The Bible makes it clear that "though all men have the possibility of a true knowledge of God, all are under the wrath of God, for there is no salvation for those who reject or pervert God's universal revelation of love and justice."[24]

Clark Pinnock, on the other hand, argues that a lack of knowledge of Christ is not sufficient to send one to hell. "Of one thing we can be certain: God will not abandon in hell those who have not known and therefore have not declined His offer of grace. Though He has not told us the nature of His arrangements, we cannot doubt the existence and goodness of them."[25]

Blue takes great exception to Pinnock's position. God *has* told us of His arrangements, says Blue. He then summarizes the main argument of Romans 1 and 2 by stating that the apparently innocent "heathen" are far from innocent. Their consciences and creation itself clearly reveal God's existence and attributes. However, the unevangelized have repressed God's truth through general revelation, giving expression to that rejection through degraded thoughts, emotions, and actions. "No matter how isolated a man may be from the revelation of God's righteousness in the Gospel of Jesus Christ," Blue argues, "that man is entirely without excuse. The wrath of God is on him because of his ungodliness and unrighteousness, not because of his lack of faith in Christ."[26]

Blue also points out that those who hold to the possibility of salvation apart from an explicit presentation of the Gospel sometimes even suggest that the idolatrous actions of the unevangelized reveal their search for the real God. "Idolatry is viewed as piety and reverence yet to be perfected. Nothing could be further from the truth. These are not gropings for God. They are evidence of rebellion against God. 'The idolatrous systems of the world,' says Watts, 'are actually states of man's departure from God and expression of his desire for other gods rather than the true, living God.'" [27]

"The world's untold billions are *lost*!" Blue proclaims, and they *need* to hear the Gospel. Only Jesus Christ can bridge the gap between a holy God and sinful men and women. How will the unevangelized hear? "Human agents must be mobilized by the Lord to cross the frontiers that stand as barriers to Gospel presentation. God has so willed it . . . There is not a single line in the Book of Acts to suggest that God can save a human being without employing a human agent. On the contrary there are several examples of God's going to great lengths to secure the active cooperation of one or another of His servants."[28]

Those who grapple with the truth of the untold billions might be sincere in suggesting that they can be saved through general revelation, but they are sincerely (and scripturally) mistaken. Special revelation is needed for salvation.

Supernaturally-given Special Revelation

The New Testament reveals God as one who not only can supernaturally whisk away Philip from an Ethiopian convoy (Acts 8), but who can also convert an accessory to murder by the name of Saul of Tarsus through a miraculous vision on the road to Damascus (Acts 9). This God of the New Covenant is also free to rather unexpectantly (and supernaturally) provide the very orthodox Peter with a smorgasbord of unclean entrées to teach him to share the Gospel with the Gentile Cornelius (Acts 10).

One observer suggests concerning the one who has not heard the Gospel:

> If he sincerely accepts the verdict of guilty handed down by his conscience, thereby recognizing that he is a sinner in desperate need of the Lawgiver's grace, then the stage is set for that person's encounter with God's special revelation. This may consist of the Gospel or the Scriptures, but it may also be in the form of dreams or visions (Daniel 2; Acts 9:3ff.), an angel (Rev. 14), or through oral tradition.[29]

In some situations that supernaturally-given special revelation may be the provision of a missionary who has seen that "the fields . . . are ripe for harvest" (John 4:35). Many converts from other religions to Christianity "recognize the continuity between their new experience of God in Christ and their former search for God."[30] Don Richardson, the late veteran missionary who held that special revelation is needed for salvation, points out in *Eternity in Their Hearts* that many tribal communities immediately respond to the Christian Gospel when they first hear it because they understand it as the fulfillment of their search for atonement or appeasement in sacrifice.[31]

God is certainly free to supernaturally reveal Himself to those who never receive a Gospel witness, but such a hope should not weaken our missionary efforts or concern for the unevangelized. Although Paul's conversion came through his miraculous vision, he pursued his calling to be a witness to the Gentile and Jewish worlds through the time-honored practice of wearing out shoe leather – personally going to those who needed to hear the Gospel.

J.I. Packer aptly warns us that "we have no warrant from Scripture to expect that God will act [to bring salvation through general revelation] in any single case where the Gospel is not yet known. To cherish this hope, therefore, is not to diminish in the slightest our urgent and never-ending missionary obligation . . . Living by the Bible means assuming that no one will be saved apart from faith in Christ, and acting accordingly."[32] "Our job, after all," Packer reminds us, "is to spread the Gospel, not to guess what might happen to those to whom it never comes."[33]

We agree with those evangelical scholars who "see lostness as the most agonizing question concerning the Christian church especially in those contexts where Christianity is a minority faith."[34] Although God may (if He so chooses) save those (who never hear an explicit gospel presentation) on the basis of their positive response to the witness of general revelation or might supernaturally provide special revelation about Christ to such people, we cannot build our mission strategies on such speculations.

But what about those who die before a missionary or a vision ever gets to them? Is it possible that evangelical Christians have been far too pessimistic about death? Are the billions who have died without ever hearing of Christ eternally lost? Perhaps Bible-believing Christians have made too much of death.

Death and Fences

The story is told of a lawyer who was on his deathbed, busily thumbing through his Bible. "Bill," a friend said to him, "I didn't know you were religious." "I'm not," the lawyer replied, "I'm looking for a loophole!" Might death itself provide such a "loophole" for those who have never heard the Gospel?

The evangelical theologian Donald Bloesch states: "We do not wish to build fences around God's grace . . . and we do not preclude the possibility that some in hell might finally be translated into heaven."[35] This writer is certainly correct that Christians have not been given the task of fence building. It sounds very spiritual to say that God's grace has no fences, or to imply that such fences are not as imposing as once thought.

However, are there *no* fences around God's grace? The failure to recognize God-revealed limits to His grace, as explained in the Scriptures, is a serious error. Jesus declared that one day the "door" will be shut (Luke 13:25), and He Himself is described in Revelation as the One who "holds the key of David. What He opens no one can shut, and what He shuts no one can open" (Rev. 3:7). There will come a time when it will be "too late" for salvation (cf. Luke 12:35-48).

Bloesch has expressed an agnosticism concerning the fate of the wicked by saying that "we cannot know on the basis of what is revealed in Scripture . . . whether God will . . . transform into his likeness even the most rebellious of his enemies, or . . . destroy those forms of life that are out of harmony with his new creation."[36]

Such universalistic or annihilationist speculations sound merciful, but does Jesus not clearly state that "broad is the road that leads to destruction" and "small is the gate and narrow the road that leads to life, and only a few find it" (Matt. 7:13-14, NIV)? Does the Lord not also emphasize that between those in hell and those in heaven there is a "great gulf fixed, so that those who want to pass from here to you cannot, nor can those from there pass to us"? (Luke 16:26, NKJV) A *chasm*, rather than merely a fence, is the biblical image here.

We observed in chapter two that some hold the view that hell will be a kind of school which will drive men and women to accept the Gospel. What purgatory does for the Roman Catholics, hell (in the minds of some theologians) does for those who have not received Christ. However, Dorothy Sayers seems much more in line with the teaching of Scripture when she says in her introduction to Dante's *Inferno* that

> hell itself is not remedial; the dead who have chosen the "eternal exile" from God, and who thus experience the reality of their choice, cannot profit by that experience. In that sense, no living soul can enter Hell, since, however great the sin, repentance is always possible while there is life, even to the very moment of dying. But the vision of Hell, which is remedial, is the soul's self-knowledge in all its evil potentialities — the revelation of the nature of impenitent sin.[37]

To suggest that there will be potential transfer from the realm of the wicked dead to the fellowship of Christ in heaven is to reason contrary to Christ's teaching in Luke 16. Apparently (according to such scholars), there will be no "chasm" as Jesus taught (v. 26). Presumably He was either perpetuating Jewish myths about the fate of the wicked, or He was wrong about hell's permanence.

C.S. Lewis' story of a bus trip from hell to heaven (*The Great Divorce*), as Lewis himself tells us, is not meant to "arouse factual curiosity about the details of the afterworld."[38] It is written to show the many reasons why some, even if given an opportunity to take a day excursion from hell to heaven, would not be happy there; it would simply not suit them.

Jesus is clearly teaching in Luke 16 that no missionary efforts from the heavenly realms will be allowed to reach into hell. Furthermore, none in hell will be able to change locations. Presumably, in their blasphemous rebellion they will not want to.

It is interesting in the Luke 16 passage that the rich man is not concerned about escaping hell himself; he only requests, first, water to alleviate his tormented tongue, and, second, a warning for his five brothers that they would not follow him to that "place of torment" (v. 28). Evidently he knew that no eternal change of residence was possible. As C.S. Lewis has expressed it, sin is man saying to God throughout his life, "Leave me alone, God!" And hell is God's way of finally saying to man, "You may have your wish."

The Finality of Death

"If I sold my house and my car, had a big garage sale and gave all my money to the church, would that get me into Heaven?" I asked the children in my Sunday School class. "NO!" the children all answered. "If I cleaned the church every day, mowed the yard, and kept everything neat and tidy,would that get me into Heaven?" Again, the answer was, "NO!" "Well, then, if I was kind to animals and gave candy to all the children, and loved my wife, would that get me into Heaven?" I asked them again. Again, they all answered, "NO!" "Well", I continued, "then how can I get into Heaven?" A five-year-old boy shouted out, "YOU GOTTA BE DEAD!"

Richard Leakey, the Kenyan anthropologist and author, was once asked the question: "What happens after death?" To which he replied, "I don't think anything need happen." Comedian Woody Allen once remarked: "It's not that I'm afraid to die; I just don't want to be there when it happens!" *Newsday* magazine once asked a number of celebrities to write their own epitaphs. The comedienne Joan Rivers wanted hers to read: "Wait! Can we talk?" The late Erma Bombeck once said: "I have learned to take labels seriously. I have devoted my life to making sure my yeast doesn't expire, my film doesn't run out of time, or my batteries pass away." But was *she* ready to die?

In an article entitled "Whistling Past the Graveyard,"[39] author Marvin Olasky discusses the range of books which need to be published regarding death. "Someone needs to answer the question, 'How then shall we die?'"[40] Olasky gives quotes of several famous people about death: For example, American liberal minister Henry Ward Beecher's last words were: "Now comes the mystery." Mark Twain, who became a bitter man as he approached old age, wrote in his private notebooks, "O Death where is thy sting? It has none. But life has." George Santayana, a popular philosopher, said, "There is no cure for birth and death but to enjoy the interval." Woody Allen said, "I don't want to achieve immortality through my work. I want to achieve it through not dying." Science-fiction novelist Isaac Asimov declared his dislike for both heaven and hell: "I don't believe in an afterlife, so I don't have to spend my whole life fearing hell, or fearing heaven even more. For whatever the tortures of hell, I think the boredom of heaven would be even worse."[41]

But is death as innocent and insignificant as some imply? Those who suggest that death should not be seen as the "decisive barrier of time for people to make a decision of faith"[42] must come to grips with the teaching of the New Testament on the issue.

The Teaching of Paul

Paul, for example, in a passage teaching the resurrection of believers, writes that if Jesus did not rise from the dead, then "those who have fallen asleep in Christ are lost" (1 Cor. 15:18). The expression "fallen asleep in Christ" obviously refers to physical death (sleep is frequently used as a metaphor of a believer's death, see John 11:11 and Acts 7:60). Paul's point is that "the foundational assumption of . . . all of Scripture . . . is that one's spiritual condition at death determines whether or not he will inherit eternal life."[43]

In a passage which argues against the doctrine of "soul-sleep," Paul claims that to be "at home in the body" is to be "away from the Lord" and to be "away from the body" is to be "at home with the Lord" (2 Cor. 5:6-9). The apostle certainly appears to be teaching that the one who has trusted Christ goes immediately into His presence at death. Likewise, the one who is not redeemed goes immediately to a place of torment and separation from God's presence (Luke 16).

Paul did not consider death as an opportunity to receive the Gospel. Rather, he describes death as "the last enemy to be destroyed" by the reigning Christ (1 Cor. 15:26).

The Teaching of Jesus

Jesus had much to say about the morbid subject of death and its finality. His poignant question, "What good is it for a man to gain the whole world, yet forfeit his soul?" (Mark 8:36) implies that one may so conduct his affairs in life that he not only misses *this* life, but the *next* as well. "Or what," Jesus asks in the passage, "can a man give in exchange for his soul?" (Mark 8:37) The forfeiture of one's essential being (one's "soul") is the issue here.

In John's Gospel Jesus deliberately discusses death. For example, Jesus teaches that "whoever hears My word and believes in Him who sent Me has eternal life and will not be condemned; he has crossed over from death to life" (John 5:24). "Death" in this verse seems to refer to a condition of spiritual separation from God. That decision to move out of the realm of spiritual death into the realm of eternal life is made in this life, not after one has died!

As the One who has the power to raise the dead (John 5:21), Jesus declares that a day is coming when "all who are in their graves will hear his voice and come out — those who have done good will rise to live, and those who have done evil will rise to be condemned" (John 5:28-29). No hint is given by Jesus that one can add to one's record of deeds *after* death, nor does Jesus give any support to the idea that one's spiritual status may be altered in any way after physical death.

With words that should have sent shivers down their spines, Jesus warns the Jews of the danger of unbelief, "I am going away, and you will look for me, and you will die in your sin. Where I go, you cannot come" (John 8:21). Jesus uses this same expression of "dying in one's sins" three verses later where He says: "I told you that you would die in your sins; if you do not believe that I am the one I claim to be, you will indeed die in your sins" (v. 24). The finality of one's earthly response to Christ in all the horror of "dying in one's sins" is clear.

"My sheep," Jesus says, "listen to my voice; I know them, and they follow me. I give them eternal life, and they shall never perish; no one can snatch them out of my hand" (John 10:27-28). The giving of eternal life occurs prior to one's physical death. Jesus' promise that such shall "never perish" must refer to spiritual separation, because *He* perished, as did all of His disciples (most by martyrdom). Physical death His followers will experience; spiritual death will not, however, be their portion.

An undertaker in Washington, D.C. drives a hearse with a license plate on the back which reads "U-2-1-DAY" and closes his business letters with the expression "Eventually yours"! The denial of death's finality is understandable when one is grappling with the issue of the "untold billions who are still untold." However, we dare not go beyond Scripture's clear teaching that one's eternal destiny is settled at death. 2 Kings 20:1 makes it clear that the putting of one's house in order occurs in *this* life.

Hebrews 10:31 declares that "It is a dreadful thing to fall into the hands of the living God." The context of Hebrews 10 is that of ignoring the truth, rejecting the law of Moses, and dying without mercy on the testimony of two or three witnesses (v. 28). If one rejects God's truth in this life, "no sacrifice for sins is left, but only a fearful expectation of judgment and of raging fire that will consume the enemies of God" (vv. 26-27). God is a God who will repay; "It is mine to avenge"; "the Lord will judge His people" (v. 30). Then verse 31 says that "It is a dreadful thing to fall into the hands of the living God."

The late Canadian novelist Robertson Davies once prayed, "Oh God, don't let me die *stupid*!" Those who die without trusting Him, Jesus says, are like an astute farmer who built bigger barns but forgot the unpredictable inevitability of death and ignored the fate of his soul (Luke 12:13-21).

Hebrews 10:31's declaration that "it is a dreadful thing to fall into the hands of the living God" is in the context of Jews who had the law of Moses. What about the billions who have not even heard of Moses? Is there any scriptural evidence that they, after death, might receive an opportunity to hear the Gospel?

Christ's "Descent into Hades"

In C.S. Lewis' *The Great Divorce*, one of the ghosts who took the bus trip from hell to heaven asks one of heaven's "solid people," "Since you people are so full of love, why did you not go down to Hell to rescue the Ghosts? One would have expected a more militant charity!"[44]

Is there evidence, perhaps, of Jesus Himself going down to the realm of the wicked dead and, by an act of "militant charity," proclaiming the Gospel to those who have never heard? Some argue that "if people will be condemned only for their rejection of the Savior, then they will have to be given an opportunity, sometime, to accept or reject him."[45] Perhaps that opportunity will be after death. Although those who hold to a postmortem opportunity for conversion acknowledge that the biblical support for this position is lacking, 1 Peter 3:18-20 is sometimes brought forth. Those three verses simply state:

> For Christ died for sins once for all, the righteous for the unrighteous, to bring you to God. He was put to death in the body but made alive by the Spirit, through whom also he went and preached to the spirits in prison who disobeyed long ago when God waited patiently in the days of Noah while the ark was being built. In it only a few people, eight in all, were saved through water.

History of the Doctrine

The Apostles' Creed uses the expression "He descended into hell (Hades)," the Latin phrase being *descendit in inferna.* The idea that Jesus descended into Hades between His death and His resurrection was espoused by Clement of Alexandria (ca. 155-ca. 220), who included the heathen with the saints, martyrs, and Old Testament prophets as those to whom the Gospel was preached. Eusebius of Caesarea (ca. 265-ca. 339) also held to the descent into Hades doctrine.

One of the strongest advocates of the doctrine was Origen (ca. 185-ca. 254), the scholar who was the church's first universalist. He argued that "[Christ's] soul, stripped of the body, did there (in Hades) hold converse with other souls that were in like manner stripped, that He might there convert those who were capable of instruction, or were otherwise in ways known to Him fit for it."[46]

Other church fathers who held to the descent into Hades view were Cyril of Jerusalem (ca. 310-ca. 386), Athanasius (ca. 296-ca. 373), Ambrose (ca. 339-ca. 397), and Jerome (ca. 345-ca. 419). Augustine rejects the view, listing it as a heresy.

Although the descent into Hades view was tenaciously held during the Middle Ages (between the fall of Rome in 476 and the Protestant Reformation, beginning about 1500), the Reformers rejected it for three reasons. The first reason was that it was simply a traditional, rather than a scriptural, doctrine. The second reason was that it appeared to give some support to the Roman Catholic dogma of purgatory. The third reason was that it appeared late in the creeds of the church. The phrase "He descended into hell" does not appear in the AD150 or the AD350 versions of the Apostles' Creed; it is not until AD700 that the phrase occurs.

Suggested Interpretations

Many Christians are probably not aware of the significance of the expression "He descended into hell" when they recite the Apostles' Creed. The idea of Christ's "descent" is usually connected with 1 Peter 3:18-20, which we shall examine presently.

Roman Catholic writers suggest that between His death and resurrection Christ descended to a place designated as *limbus patrum* (a chamber for Old Testament saints who were waiting to be admitted to the presence of God). The teaching is that Christ in His spirit went to the *limbus patrum* while His body lay in the grave and in His resurrection brought forth the spirits of the Old Testament saints and conducted them to heaven.

Lutheran writers understand the descent as Christ proclaiming His victory over the powers of darkness, pronouncing their sentence of condemnation. John Calvin takes a metaphorical view of the expression ("He descended into Hades"), concluding that it refers to the penal sufferings of Christ on the cross, where He really endured the pangs of hell.

Some theologians put great hope in the descent into Hades doctrine, assuming that it is solidly based on the 1 Peter passage. Theologian Donald Bloesch confidently declares, "We can affirm salvation on the other side of the grave, since this has scriptural warrant (cf. Isa. 26:19; John 5:25-29; Eph. 4:8-9; 1 Peter 3:19-20; 4:6); yet we cannot preach that any of those who are banished to hell will finally be saved."[47]

This same theologian also argues that Hades "is not yet hell" and that the intermediate state of the lost ("Hades") is a "state of inner torment or lostness." "It should nonetheless be pointed out," he says, "that God is present in this so-called realm of the dead, and is in absolute control . . . . This realm is not outside the compass of the Gospel, since our Lord preached to the spirits who were in prison (1 Peter 3:19-20)."[48]

Another writer, commenting on the passage in 1 Peter, is in agreement with this position and states that "Jesus, as a spirit, appeared to fallen spirits, to some as Conqueror and Judge, to others, who still stretched out to Him the hand of faith, as a Savior . . . the preaching of Christ begun in the realms of departed spirits is continued there . . . so that those who (here) on earth did not hear at all, or not in the right way, the good news of salvation through Jesus Christ, shall hear it there."[49]

Clark Pinnock is optimistic in his application of 1 Peter 3 to the fate of those who have never heard. He states that "Peter in his first epistle adds an important clue when he speaks of the Gospel being preached to the dead. Though far from exegetically certain, it is held by some interpreters (as reputable as Cranfield and Pannenberg) that death is the occasion when the unevangelized have an opportunity to make a decision about Jesus Christ."[50]

John Sanders is honest in his treatment when he acknowledges that "on biblical grounds it is quite uncertain whether 1 Peter or the doctrine of Christ's descent have anything to do with a future opportunity to hear the Gospel."[51] He does argue, however, that "the concept of God giving the unevangelized a future opportunity to accept or reject Christ is on solid ground theologically . . . It seems correct to say that people will be condemned only for rejecting Jesus Christ. This would make it essential that they be given an opportunity to do so either in this life or the next."[52]

Five views of this "descent into Hades" have been commonly held:[53]

> (1) One popular view is that Christ preached through the Holy Spirit through Noah as he was building the ark. He was preaching to those who were unbelievers on the earth but now are people in hell ("spirits in prison"). Augustine and Aquinas held this view.
>
> (2) Another view is that Christ personally went and preached to people in hell between His death and resurrection, offering them a second chance of salvation. Several commentators hold this position.
>
> (3) The third view is similar to the second in that Christ preached between His death and His resurrection to people in hell, but rather than offering them a second chance of salvation, He was declaring His triumph and their condemnation. The seventeenth century seemed to favor this third view, sometimes referred to as the "orthodox Lutheran theory."

(4) Another view holds that after Christ died, He declared release to the people who had repented just before they died in the flood. He then led them out of their imprisonment in purgatory into heaven. This has been a common Roman Catholic position.

(5) The final view appears to be the dominant view today. It holds that after Christ's death He traveled to hell and announced His triumph over the fallen angels who had sinned by intermarrying with human women before the flood. However, with the evangelical drift away from the finality of death and the doctrine of hell, one would not be surprised to see the second view (a second-chance salvation position) become the most popular of these interpretations.

Wayne Grudem suggests that the three pivotal questions to be asked of this text in 1 Peter are: (1) Who are the "spirits in prison"? (2) What did Christ preach? and, (3) When did He preach?[54] We will briefly discuss each in turn.

Who Are the "Spirits in Prison"?

Grudem's answer to this question is that the "spirits in prison" must be understood to be human spirits, not angelic spirits.[55] He observes, "When Peter defined the 'spirits in prison' as those 'who disobeyed in the days of Noah when God's patience waited during the building of the ark,' it is very unlikely that he would have expected his readers to identify them as disobedient angels . . . Our conclusion is that the 'spirits in prison' are the human beings who disobeyed at the time Noah was building the ark and who were destroyed in the flood."[56]

What Did Christ Proclaim?

The focus in the text is that of Noah's preaching, or more accurately, Christ's preaching by means of the Spirit through Noah. The Greek verb for "preach" (*kerysso*) in the text suggests a preaching of repentance, rather than a preaching of condemnation (the latter sitting better with views three or five above).

View four, which says that Christ proclaimed to Old Testament believers His finished work of redemption, is also not supported by the context. As Grudem argues, "The mention of 'prison' and disobedience, as well as the waiting of the patience of God, and the comment that only eight were saved, all point to preaching directed to sinners who needed repentance, not to righteous saints waiting to hear a glad cry of victory."[57]

The proclamation to sinners of their need to repent and trust in God fits the overall context of 1 Peter, that is, of being a good witness in the circumstance of hostile unbelievers. The immediate context, that of "always being ready . . . to give an account for the hope . . . in you" (3:15-16, NASB), seems to support this view that Christ was proclaiming the need to repent through Noah.

When Did Christ Preach?

If, indeed, the "spirits in prison" are people who disobeyed God during Noah's lifetime and the message preached to them was that of the need for repentance, then views three, four, and five are eliminated. Grudem argues that a decision between view one (Christ preached through Noah at the time the ark was built) and view two (Christ preached between His death and resurrection, giving those who disobeyed before the flood a second chance for salvation) can be decided if one can establish the time at which the preaching took place.[58]

This preaching of Christ could have occurred chronologically after His death and resurrection, for verse 18 of the text refers to Christ's being "put to death" and then being "made alive by the Spirit." We are then given the statement that "by whom also He went and preached to the spirits in prison" (v. 19). Grudem argues that Peter's use of the phrase "by whom" does not necessarily imply that the preaching must follow chronologically the death and resurrection of Christ. Sometimes Peter uses this stylistic phrase as a literary device when changing to a different subject.[59]

From a logical point of view, the interpretation that Christ proclaims the message of salvation sometime after His death to the spirits in prison appears to violate Peter's message to his readers to persevere as faithful witnesses. What sense would this view make of the context in which Peter urges his readers to be faithful witnesses even if they should have to suffer, if "he then proceeds to tell them that even the worst sinners in all history . . . can be given another chance to repent after they have died?"[60] Such a view seems to be contradictory to his purpose in writing.

If view two (the second-chance view) is the correct one, "why [are] only sinners who disobeyed during the building of the ark . . . given another opportunity to repent?" "Why not others as well, especially those who had no chance to hear the warnings to repent?"[61] Grudem rightly points out that "the idea of a chance of salvation after death is difficult to reconcile with other parts of the New Testament (cf. Luke 16:26; Heb. 9:27)."[62]

In support of view one (that Christ was preaching through Noah during the building of the ark), Peter himself refers to the "spirit of Christ" moving the prophets to predict the "sufferings of Christ and the glories to follow" (1 Peter 1:11, NASB). Therefore, it is not inconceivable that Peter understood that the spirit of Christ was active in Noah as he preached to the generation prior to the flood.

Grudem shows several parallels between view one and the larger context of 1 and 2 Peter.[63] He summarizes by saying, "[View one] sits well with Peter's purpose of encouraging suffering believers that they need not fear to be righteous and to bear faithful witness to the hostile unbelievers surrounding them, for Christ is at work in them as he was in Noah, and they, like Noah, will certainly be saved from the judgment to come."[64]

"In fact," he continues, "it is the remarkable similarity between the situations of Noah and of Peter's readers which best explains why Peter, in reaching back to the Old Testament for an encouraging example, selects the incident of Noah preparing the ark. Far from being surprising or unusual, this example is contextually quite appropriate."[65]

Grudem argues that the phrase "who formerly were disobedient" (1 Peter 3:20) should really be translated as an adverbial use of the participle: "when they formerly disobeyed." He concludes that Christ preached to the spirits who are now in prison but He did so "when they formerly disobeyed," that is, during the preaching ministry of Noah.

To the question "why did Peter not say that Christ preached 'through Noah?'" Grudem responds that it is very difficult to answer why a writer did not write something in a particular way. Furthermore, Peter's readers would have understood verse 20 ("when they formerly disobeyed") "much more readily than we do, especially since our minds are cluttered by English translations which say 'who formerly disobeyed.'"[66] That is, Peter's readers would have understood that Christ's preaching was during the time of and through Noah, rather than between His death and resurrection.

Grudem concludes this discussion by paraphrasing verses 19 and 20 as follows: "In the spiritual realm of existence Christ went and preached through Noah to those who are now spirits in the prison of hell. This happened when they formerly disobeyed, when the patience of God was waiting in the days of Noah while the ark was being built."[67]

Grudem's view agrees with that of Louis Berkhof who argued that "Scripture certainly does not teach a literal descent of Christ into hell."[68] He could not have bodily descended into hell, for His body was in the grave. If He did descend into hell, then He did so only by means of His soul, and, Berkhof argues, "this would mean that only half of His human nature shared in this stage of His humiliation (or exaltation)."[69] Furthermore, this descent could not have been a triumphal march, for Christ had not yet risen from the dead. As well, at the time of His death Christ commended His spirit to His father, which "seems to indicate that He would be passive rather than active from the time of His death until He arose from the grave."[70]

The debate concerning whether or not general revelation can save those who never heard the Gospel will continue. Our responsibility [illegible] the Gospel wherever we can, for the [illegible]

[illegible]

5

The Other Side According to **Jesus**

"Who is responsible for this God-defaming doctrine of a hell of torment? The promulgator is Satan. His purpose in introducing it has been to frighten the people away from studying the Bible and to make them hate God." (Jehovah's Witnesses)

"There is no way of avoiding the conclusion that Jesus firmly accepted the fact that there was a counterpart to heaven for those who were condemned before God." (Donald Guthrie)

"I believe that Jesus Christ taught eternal punishment — I do not accept it on his authority!" (Theodore Parker)

"Be afraid of the One who can destroy both soul and body in hell." (Jesus, Matt. 10:28)

"Hell as professionally believed and taught is the doctrine of the devil and not of God," observed one writer in a 1982 issue of *Eternity* magazine. Ellen G. White, revered by the Seventh-Day Adventists as a prophetess of God, minces no words when she declares that the originator of the doctrine of hell is the devil himself. She writes in *The Great Controversy*, "[T]he prince of darkness, working through his agents, represents God as a revengeful tyrant, declaring that He plunges into hell all those who do not please Him, and causes them ever to feel His wrath; and that while they suffer unutterable anguish and writhe in the eternal flames, their Creator looks down upon them with satisfaction."[1] She emphasizes that Satan is in fact clothing God with Satan's own attributes. "How utterly revolting," she exclaims, "is the belief that as soon as the breath leaves the body the soul of the impenitent is consigned to the flames of hell!"[2]

Leon Morris asks the question, "Why does anyone believe in hell in these enlightened days? Because Jesus plainly taught its existence. He spoke more often about hell than he did about heaven. We cannot get around this fact . . . He said plainly that some people will spend eternity in hell . . . He spoke plainly about hell as well as about heaven, about damnation as well as about salvation" (emphasis mine).[3]

As Ligon Duncan says in an article entitled "Speaking Soberly and Sensitively about Hell," "One of the most important reasons to talk about hell is that it was a regular theme of Jesus' sermons. Those who argue against the existence of hell directly contradict Jesus Himself."[4]

It is important to point out that we do not need more than the biblical revelation to learn what God wants us to know about hell. Mary K. Baxter's book *A Divine Revelation of Hell*[5] purportedly records her trip to hell and Jesus' direct revelations to her. In conjunction with her *A Divine Revelation of Heaven*[6] in which she claims she toured heaven and had personal conversations with Jesus, works such as these are poor substitutes for the authoritative – and sufficient – teaching of God Incarnate, the Lord Jesus Christ.[7]

But what exactly *did* Jesus teach? This chapter will examine the claim that Jesus taught more about hell than He did about heaven. We will then survey the Gospel of Matthew for our Lord's specific teaching. Then we will focus upon one particular passage (Luke 16) which is often disputed. Finally, we will summarize Jesus' teaching about this difficult subject.

A Quantitative Question

Evangelists and other Bible-believing Christians have often claimed that Jesus taught more about hell than He did about heaven. Is this claim, however, supported by the biblical evidence?

One way to test this claim is to count the times Jesus used the terms "hell" and "heaven" in the four Gospels. Two words are translated "hell." The term *hades* (the region of the departed spirits of the lost) occurs eleven times in the New Testament and is translated ten times as "hell" and once as "grave" in the King James Version. Jesus is the source of three uses of the term *hades*.

The term *gehenna* (the place of the wicked dead) is used twelve times in the New Testament. It is a form of the word *Hinnom*, a valley outside Jerusalem. The wicked king Ahaz instituted fire worship and child sacrifice in that valley (2 Chron. 28:3). That heathen practice was followed by Mannaseh, as 2 Chronicles 33:6 tells us. "The valley of Hinnom, Gehenna, therefore," Barclay states, "was the scene of one of Israel's most terrible lapses into heathen customs."[8] That valley was declared unclean by Josiah in his reformation (2 Kings 23:10) and was subsequently set apart as a place where refuse was discarded and burnt. Gehenna became a "type or symbol of Hell, of the place where the souls of the wicked will be tortured and destroyed . . . the word roused in the mind [of] every Israelite the grimmest and most terrible pictures."[9] Jesus is the source of eleven of those twelve uses of the term.

However, the term most often used for heaven (*ouranos*) is used in the New Testament 268 times, quite frequently by the Lord Himself. A simple counting of the terms used for "hell" (*gehenna* and *hades*) and the one used for "heaven" (*ouranos*) shows that Jesus used the term "heaven" far more than He did the terms relating to the fate of the wicked.

Therefore, to prove or disprove the claim that Jesus spoke more about hell than He did about heaven we must move beyond a mere counting of individual terms. The real question is did Jesus *teach* more about avoiding hell than He did about going to heaven.

Matthew's Gospel and Hell

To answer this question one should survey all four Gospels and ask the same question of each section of Jesus' teaching concerning eternity. Does the Lord seem to be primarily speaking about missing hell or about gaining heaven? We will look only at the Gospel of Matthew because it records Jesus' fullest teaching on the issue.

We will follow two guidelines in this study: (1) the didactic or teaching sections under consideration need not necessarily use the terms "heaven" or "hell" in order to be teaching about one's eternal destiny, and (2) the application or conclusion of the Lord's teaching should appear to emphasize either or both of the two destinies.

If one looks carefully at the Lord's teaching in Matthew, it seems obvious that He spoke more of avoiding hell than of gaining heaven. The following division of the teaching sections of Christ bear this out.

No reference to heaven or hell is made by Christ until He begins His public ministry in Matthew 4. Although He emphasizes the need for repentance in Matthew 4:17, the point He seems to be making is that "the kingdom of heaven is near" in the Person of the Son. Therefore, the issue of where one will spend eternity does not appear to be the force of this passage.

In His Sermon on the Mount (Matt. 5-7), the Lord emphasizes the blessedness of those who live for the kingdom of heaven. Christ does stress in Matthew 5:12 the fact of a "reward in heaven" for those who live on the basis of kingdom principles.

He challenges His followers to let their lights shine so that men will glorify their "Father in heaven" (5:16). The "least in the kingdom of heaven," Jesus says, will be those who set aside even the least of the law's demands (5:19), while those who keep the law and teach others to do the same will "be called great in the kingdom of heaven" (5:19).

He warns that the righteousness of the Pharisees and the doctors of the law will not gain entrance to the kingdom of heaven (5:20). A severe warning is then given to all who nurse anger against their brothers. Matthew 5:22 states that the one who calls his brother "fool" (Gr., *moron*) shall be in danger of hell (*gehenna*) fire.

In a passage marked by severe language, Jesus warns that it is better for one to pluck out his eye or cut off his hand (and to be saved) than "for your whole body to go into hell" (*gehenna*, 5:27-30). Matthew 18:9 is a similar statement and emphasizes that it is better for the sinner to gouge out and throw away his right eye than to retain both eyes and be thrown into the fire of hell (*gehenna*). Mark 9:43-47, a parallel passage, is also talking about the sinner apparently doing himself bodily harm that he might not be prevented from going to heaven. However, Mark's account of Jesus' words includes the triple idea of cutting off one's hand, cutting off one's foot, or plucking out one's eye. Mark's account uses *gehenna* three times (vv. 43, 45, and 47).

Jesus is obviously using exaggeration for effect, but let us not water down His point. Jesus is teaching that hell is the horrible reality behind the hyperbole; spiritual amputation may be necessary to save one's soul. Nothing in life, including the precious and well-protected parts of one's body, is of more value than gaining heaven. As C.S. Lewis reminds us: "You cannot take all luggage with you on all journeys; on one journey even your right hand and your right eye may be among the things you have to leave behind."[10]

Rewards, Fear, and Judgment

The Lord emphasizes in Matthew 6 (vv. 1-4) the importance of doing good deeds anonymously. "Your Father, who sees what is done in secret," Jesus says, and "will reward you." However, the reward promised seems to relate to earthly life.

Much of the emphasis in chapter 6 concerns the love and care of our "Heavenly Father." Although Jesus challenges us to "store up for yourselves treasures in heaven" (v. 20), the primary teaching is that we should not doubt our value to God (v. 26), nor should we panic about our physical needs (v. 32), but we should "seek first His kingdom" throughout our earthly lives (v. 33).

In Matthew 10:28 Jesus teaches that we are not to fear those who kill the body, but cannot kill the soul. We are, however, to fear Him who can "destroy both soul and body in hell" (*gehenna*). Jesus is not referring to an idea popular in the Middle Ages that the devil will be the king of hell (for he too will be its prisoner), but to the truth that God alone is to be revered by man.

Luke 12:4-5 is a parallel statement to Matthew 10:28, except that Matthew's statement "fear Him who is able to destroy both soul and body in hell" is reported by Luke as "fear Him who, after He has killed, has power to cast into hell" (NKJV). The NIV renders verse 5 as "Fear him who, after the killing of the body," which does not necessarily imply that it is God who does the killing.

If the NKJV translation is the correct understanding, however, it draws our attention to the fact that, although recognizing God as the One who has the power of death, we seldom draw the conclusion that on occasion it is He who kills (and not simply that He allows death to occur)! We will discuss the malevolence of God in our last chapter, but it should be said here that people are to fear God, not because He puts the wicked out of existence, but because He has the power to cast the wicked into a place called hell.

In Matthew 11:21-24 Jesus uses the expression *hades* to refer to Capernaum's fate:

> Woe to you, Korazin! Woe to you, Bethsaida! If the miracles that were performed in you had been performed

> in Tyre and Sidon, they would have repented long ago in sackcloth and ashes. But I tell you, it will be more bearable for Tyre and Sidon on the day of judgment than for you. And you, Capernaum, will you be lifted up to the skies? No, you will go down to the depths [*hades*]. If the miracles that were performed in you had been performed in Sodom, it would have remained to this day. But I tell you that it will be more bearable for Sodom on the day of judgment than for you.

Jesus is possibly using hyperbole again, but His purpose is not to say that Tyre, Sidon, and Sodom had insufficient evidence of God (that particular challenge is thrown in Abraham's face by Dives, as we shall see later in our study of Luke 16). Rather the emphasis of Jesus in this passage appears to be on the biblical principle that when greater light is given and ignored there will come greater judgment. After all, Capernaum was Jesus' headquarters on the north shore of Galilee. Its townspeople could see and hear Jesus almost any time they wished. But they didn't bother.

More on Hades and Gehenna

Hades is used for a second time in Matthew 16:18. In Jesus' declaration to Simon, He changes Simon's name to Peter (*petros*, a "stone") and states "on this rock [*petra*, a "rock"] I will build my church, and the gates of *Hades* [hell] will not overcome it." The picture Jesus is using is not that of the church on the defense and hell on the offense (as is commonly thought), but rather the church on the offense and hell (*hades*) on the defense. The church, composed of all those who make the same confession about Christ as Peter made, are storming the gates of hell, rescuing those who are, in a sense, already its captives!

The contemporary Christian portrayal of Jesus as meek and mild is shattered by Jesus' next usage of the term *gehenna* in Matthew's Gospel. Jesus had obviously not read the latest edition of "How to Win Friends and Influence Jewish Leaders" when He declared in Matthew 23:15:

> Woe to you, teachers of the law and Pharisees, you hypocrites! You travel over land and sea to win a single convert, and when he becomes one, you make him twice as much a son of hell [*gehenna*] as you are.

Evangelism Pharisee-style takes quite a beating from Jesus in this text. But strong deviation from the truth requires strong correction; a severe cancer necessitates the radiation of Jesus' rebuke.

Assuring that He had made His point, Jesus employs the term *gehenna* one last time in Matthew's Gospel in this same chapter. Although most of us would never think of Jesus as being a name caller, He utilizes what to the Jews of His day is rather offensive language: "You snakes! You brood of vipers! How will you escape being condemned to hell [*gehenna*]?" (Matt. 23:33)

Ready for His Return

Matthew 24:36-51 records Jesus' teaching about being ready for His second coming. Jesus uses three images to describe the conditions of His return. First, He portrays His return as a parallel to the destructive and devastating flood of Noah's day (vv. 36-41). Second, He compares His coming to the rude breaking and entering of a cat burglar (vv. 42-44). Third, Jesus states that His coming will be like a master who returns from a trip, greatly surprising one of his wicked, unoccupied servants. The servant had actually engaged in drunken brutality against his fellow servants during the master's absence. Jesus then states that:

> The master of that servant will come on a day when he does not expect him and at an hour he is not aware of. He will cut him to pieces and assign him a place with the hypocrites, where there will be weeping and gnashing of teeth (vv. 50-51).

The Parable of the Ten Virgins (Matt. 25:1-13) is used by Jesus to emphasize the cruciality of being prepared for His coming. Those who were ready "went in with him to the wedding" (v. 10); those who were not ready were shut out from the banquet (vv. 10-13). Jesus certainly is teaching that the wedding banquet is by invitation only and that some will be too late for the bridegroom's recognition and welcome.

The Parable of the Talents follows immediately (Matt. 25:14–30) and teaches the importance of faithful service for the master. The wicked, lazy servant who buried his talent is severely judged and the parable concludes with the strong words: "Throw that worthless servant outside, into the darkness, where there will be weeping and gnashing of teeth" (v. 30). The motivation for faithful service is, of course, the anticipated approval of the master (note the term "happiness" in vv. 21 and 23). However, an equal emphasis in this passage seems to be on the penalty for unfaithfulness, which is the misery of being cast into the painful, outer darkness.

Two Prepared Places

One of the most crucial texts pertaining to the doctrine of the wicked's fate occurs next in Matthew 25. Verses 31-46 record Jesus' sheep and goats' analogy. One is reminded of the late Keith Green's powerful rendition of Jesus' teaching in this passage concerning service done (or not done) in the name of Jesus.

The "sheep" (those who unknowingly served Christ as they ministered to the needy) are commended by the Lord: "Come, you who are blessed by my Father; take your inheritance, the kingdom prepared for you since the creation of the world" (v. 34). The "goats" (those who failed to serve Christ by failing to serve the needy), however, are sent to another prepared place: "Depart from me," Jesus will say, "you who are cursed, into the eternal fire prepared for the devil and his angels" (v. 41).

This sheep and goats' judgment passage is concluded with Jesus' very clear summary: "These [the goats] will go away to everlasting punishment, but the righteous [the sheep] into eternal life" (v. 46, NKJV). One should hardly be surprised that those who hold to the eternal conscious punishment view put a great deal of emphasis upon the fact that the everlastingness of the destiny of the wicked ("the goats") seems to be equivalent to the everlastingness of the destiny of the righteous ("the sheep"). To imply that the destiny of the righteous is quantitative and that of the wicked is not, or that "eternal life" indicates possession whereas "eternal punishment" indicates an eternal effect, seems to strain the text.

Summary of Hell in Matthew's Gospel

Although Jesus uses the term *hades* on only two occasions in Matthew, He emphasizes that the judgment of the wicked will be based on their opportunity to respond (Matt. 11:21-24) and that the defensive gates of *hades* will not be able to withstand the Gospel's assault (Matt. 16:18).

Jesus' uses of the term *gehenna* warn of the danger of hell fire (Matt. 5:22) and the relative insignificance of losing a bodily part (and going to heaven) in comparison to remaining whole but being wholly lost (Matt. 5:29-30). Similar hyperbolic language of self-mutilation is used by Jesus on a second occasion in Matthew 18:9.

Perhaps anticipating the persecution of His disciples, Jesus reminds them whom to fear. God is the One to be feared, for He alone has the power to "destroy both soul and body in hell," (or *gehenna*, Matt. 10:28).

Jesus' teaching in Matthew indicates that He knew of hell's reality. One might ask, "If we are on our way to hell, wouldn't it make sense for Jesus to first tell us how to avoid that destination? If we were in a spiritually neutral condition, then perhaps instruction about heaven might be more appropriate." However, no one is spiritually neutral. Every human being is either in the category of the "sheep" who are doing God's will or the "goats" who are outside His will. Eternal destinies await both –"eternal life" or "eternal punishment" (Matt. 25:46).

The other uses of the term *hades* in the New Testament (Luke 10:15; 16:22-23; Acts 2:26-32; 1 Cor. 15:55; Rev. 1:18; 6:8; 20:13-

14) appear to relate to the intermediate state (the time between one's death and physical resurrection) into which wicked persons have passed at their death.

Gehenna is used only once outside the Gospels (James 3:6). However, a study of its twelve occurrences in the New Testament leads to the conclusion that *gehenna* is a place of condemnation and terrible punishment. The wicked, after their resurrection, will be cast into *gehenna* to remain forever. Revelation 20:13-14 indicates that *gehenna* and "the lake of fire" are synonymous terms, referring to the everlasting destiny of the wicked after the reunion of their bodies and their disembodied personalities.

An Oft-Disputed Parable?

The story of the rich man and Lazarus (Luke 16:19-31) would seem to be tailor-made to answer a number of questions about the Other Side of the Good News. However, many who reject the traditional concept of eternal conscious punishment dismiss this passage as only a parable, not intended to be pressed in its details about the after-death condition of the righteous and the wicked. The Jewish scholar Alfred Edersheim emphasizes that "its parabolic details must not be exploited, nor doctrines of any kind derived from them, either as to the character of the other world, the question of the duration of future punishments, or the possible moral improvement of those in *Gehinnom*."[11]

Edersheim's major reason for his position is that this parable is addressed to the Pharisees, "to whom Christ would scarcely have communicated details about the other world, on which He was so reticent in His teaching to the disciples."[12]

Another commentator agrees that "it would be rash to attempt a description of the afterlife from the details" given in this story.[13] It has been argued that "the aim of the parable is not to acquaint us with details of the life to come, but to confront us with our duty in this life."[14]

One evangelical theology textbook states that "it is probably better to see the story not as revealing details of life after death, but rather as giving a different twist to commonly held views about afterlife. [Jesus'] story is intended to reveal truths about the kingdom."[15]

Such restrictions on Luke 16 certainly are well-intentioned. However, 2 Timothy 3:16 reminds us that "All Scripture is God-breathed and is useful for teaching, rebuking, correcting, and training in righteousness." Unless one is prepared to suggest that Jesus is passing on inaccurate information about the afterlife, why should Luke 16 not be understood to reflect a general picture of what happens to the righteous and the wicked at death?

Murray Harris, for example, agrees that Luke 16's purpose is "not to satisfy our natural curiosity about man's anthropological condition after death." But, he adds, "it is not illegitimate to deduce from the setting of the story the basic characteristics of the postmortem state of believers and unbelievers." Among those characteristics set forth are man's consciousness, memory, and rationality in the intermediate state.[16] Millard Erickson's popular textbook *Christian Theology* comes to the same conclusions, but also understands Luke 16 as a refutation of universalism as well as the Roman Catholic idea of a second chance to accept the Gospel after death.[17] Charles Ryrie, in his *Basic Theology*, also agrees with these general conclusions.[18]

James Oliver Buswell argues that Luke 16:19-31 "is the most important New Testament passage bearing on the meaning of Hades . . . . These thirteen verses, in the words of Christ Himself, give us the fullest account we have of the meaning of the word."[19] They teach that it is a place of disembodied, conscious spirits who are capable of communication. The one who is wicked is "in torments;" the one who is righteous is in Abraham's loving fellowship."[20]

The respected theologian Louis Berkhof, as well, uses Luke 16:19-31 to support several doctrinal conclusions:

(1) the fact of the conscious existence of the soul after death. He states that "the rich man and Lazarus converse together."[21] This is not exactly accurate, for no conversation

between Lazarus and Dives actually takes place in our text. Abraham, one might say, does Lazarus' talking for him;

(2) the fact that the future state of believers is a state in which they are truly alive and fully conscious;[22]

(3) the fact that believers enjoy a conscious life in communion with God and with Jesus Christ *immediately after death*;[23]

(4) the belief that the state of unbelievers after death is a fixed state. He argues that "the most important passage" to prove the fixity of one's eternal fate is this text, Luke 16:19-31.

(5) the fact that the wicked experience subjective punishments. That is, Luke 16 portrays *hades* as "a place of torment";[24] and

(6) the assertion that the annihilation of the wicked is ruled out by Luke 16:19-31. This text clearly teaches "the continued existence of the wicked."[25]

Another writer agrees that three "truths concerning the life to come are . . . inescapably insisted on in the parable."[26] The *first* of these truths is the finality of death as far as human destiny is concerned. That is, "the state of the individual soul after death is irrevocably settled during his lifetime." The *second* truth which Luke 16 clearly teaches is that the lot of the righteous is infinite happiness and of the ungodly indescribable distress. Both destinies are not only conscious realities, but the memory of this life with its lost opportunities subsists in the Beyond. The *third* truth recorded in Luke 16 with an equal insistence is that there is for all humankind a sufficient guide to heaven in the Scriptures.[27]

The annihilationist Edward Fudge states that there is "no clear exegetical basis in Luke 16 for any conclusions concerning the end of the wicked,"[28] which one would expect him to assert. If there were any section of the teaching of Christ which could be dismissed as parabolic and not be taken as an accurate description of the fate of the wicked, Luke 16 would be first on the hit list of universalists, annihilationists, and postmortem conversionists.

However, is Luke 16 so easily dismissed? The use of parables, one of the characteristic forms of the teaching of Jesus, is a fascinating study. Matthew's Gospel uses the term "parable" seventeen times, Mark's Gospel thirteen times, and Luke's Gospel eighteen times.

Although one commentator understands Lazarus to be "an allegorical representation . . . of the ideal disciple,"[29] the use of the proper name "Lazarus" (which means "God help!") indicates that this may not be a parable. The respected biblical scholar G. Campbell Morgan writes, "Jesus did not call it a parable. Luke does not call it a parable. Moreover, the fact that, while the rich man is not named, the beggar is named, makes it probable that He was naming an actual case. It may be a parable. If so, at least it is striking that it is the only parable of Jesus in which a name is given to a person."[30]

Lest one too hastily decide that Luke 16:19-31 is *not* a parable, it must be pointed out that the familiar stories of the Good Samaritan (Luke 10:30-36), the mustard seed and the leaven (Luke 13:18-21), as well as the great banquet (Luke 14:16-24) are also not specifically called parables by Jesus or Luke in this third Gospel. Although the story of the rich man and Lazarus follows the parables of the Lost Sheep, the Lost Coin, the Prodigal Son, and the Shrewd Manager in Luke 15-16, the debate will continue concerning whether Luke 16:19-31 is parabolic.

Erickson states that "while it was not Jesus' primary intent here to teach us about the nature of the intermediate state, it is unlikely that He would mislead us on this subject."[31] If we may assume that the story of the rich man and Lazarus should not be dismissed merely as parabolic, and that Jesus is not seeking to mislead us, this raises a question: What does this passage teach in general concerning the other side of eternity?

The passage is easily divided into two sections: (1) The earthly scene (vv. 19-22) and (2) The eternal (or after-death) scene (vv. 22-31). Let's examine each more closely.

The Earthly Scene (Luke 16:19-22)

We discover in the first section that the rich man (Dives) is anonymous from God's perspective. Although unnamed, we are told that he lived the "good life." If there had been a "Lifestyles of the Rich and Famous" in the first century, Dives would have headlined Robin Leach's first broadcast!

This man wore the finest clothes; perhaps the linen which he wore was the Egyptian material described as "woven air."[32] The Greek term used indicates that what he wore was the next best material to silk, which was worth its weight in gold. Dives "fared sumptuously every day" (v. 19, KJV). The term "sumptuously" is from the Greek word *lampo* which means "to radiate." Dives dined "flamboyantly" every day, one commentator writes.

In great contrast is "a beggar named Lazarus" who is "covered with sores" — perhaps from malnutrition (v. 20). To illustrate his plight, Lazarus is described by Jesus as having his sores licked by the dogs (v. 21, KJV), not as an alleviation of his suffering, but as an aggravation of his condition (dogs are always represented in Scripture as unclean animals). We are also told that he "was laid" at Dives' gate (a term meaning a gate of beauty). The verb "was laid" might be better translated "was flung," probably indicating that his bearers were glad to throw down their unwelcome burden.

Lazarus literally waited for the crumbs which fell from the rich man's table. Barclay points out that Dives, "a figure of indolent self-indulgence," ate with his hands (which was customary in a time when there were neither knives nor forks nor napkins). In very wealthy houses, "the hands were cleansed by wiping them on hunks of bread, and then the bread was thrown away. It was that bread which Lazarus was waiting for."[33]

The word "desiring" (v. 21, KJV) may suggest that his longing for crumbs remained unsatisfied. Certainly not a very happy life, according to worldly standards.

The earthly scene closes rather abruptly with the deaths of both the beggar Lazarus (perhaps on Dives' very doorstep) and the rich man. Verse 22, however, says that the beggar had an angelic escort to "Abraham's bosom" (KJV), a Jewish metaphor for the presence of God. The rich man, we are informed, "also died and was buried." G. Campbell Morgan points out that "the man with all his wealth could not bribe the grim rider upon the pale horse."[34] It is reasonable to assume that Dives' funeral was first-class and as flamboyant as his life.

Morgan makes an interesting point in discussing the death of Lazarus:

> The probability is that [Lazarus] never was buried, for at that time in Jerusalem, unknown and unclaimed beggars who died by the highway were carried to Tophet, Gehenna, and flung out where the fires were burning to destroy offal [the waste parts of butchered animals].The possibility is that the man whose business it was to clean things up, the scavenger, got the sore-infested body, and pitched it out to Tophet, the actual Gehenna, burning outside the city.[35]

Unknown to men, Lazarus is known by God. And although his body was unclaimed by men, the angels of God claim his spirit and escort him to "Abraham's bosom."

As much as those who hold to soul-sleep might prefer the story to end at this point (with the rich man in the grave), the story continues in doctrine-overhauling fashion with the rich man described as being "in hell" (Hades, v.23). Jesus is already hinting at a reversal of destinies, for the beggar's body, tossed into "Gehenna" (which many scholars understand to have been a garbage pit outside Jerusalem) would have probably been evidence to the Jews of the beggar's lost condition. Dives' elaborate burial would have been understood as proof of his favor with God and his heavenly reward. Edersheim points out that although Jesus' story is consistent with Jewish stories, "there is this very marked and characteristic contrast, that in the Jewish legend the beatified is a Pharisee, while the sinner tormented with thirst is a Publican!"[36]

The Eternal (or After-Death) Scene (Luke 16:22-31)

This section records what the rich man experienced, what he saw, and an incredible conversation he had with Abraham.

What Dives Experienced

In no uncertain terms Dives experienced torment. Four times we are told of that torment. Jesus, the One telling the story, portrays him as "in torment"(v.23). In unyieldingly overwhelming thirst, the rich man describes himself as "in agony in this fire" (v. 24). In his conversation with Abraham, the rich man is told by Abraham that he is getting what he deserved. Lazarus "now . . . is comforted," Abraham says, "and you are in agony" (v. 25). Later, the rich man expresses his concern that his (still living) brothers not "come to this place of torment" (v. 28).

Medieval theologians made a distinction between *poena damni* (the pain of loss, i.e. the loss of the vision of God) and *poena sensus* (the pain of sense) of the wicked in hell. We will touch on the issue of *poena damni* later; at this point, however, it must be asked how anyone could suggest that the rich man's pain and punishment (*poena sensus*) is not portrayed in Luke 16 as *real?*

What Dives Saw

Verse 23 says that Dives "lifted up his eyes and saw Abraham afar off, and Lazarus in his bosom" (NKJV). One is reminded of John the disciple who leaned on Jesus' breast (John 13:25; 21:20). Different Greek words are used in the two passages (the term *stethos* is used in John 13:25 and 21:20 and means "that which stands out"; the term *kolpos* is used of Lazarus' position in both verses 22 and 23 and means "the front of the body between the arms." This term *kolpos* is used figuratively of "a place of blessedness with another, as with Abraham in Paradise."[37] This same word *kolpos* is also used of Jesus Christ's eternal and essential relation with the Father in John 1:18 which speaks of Christ as "the only-begotten Son, who is in the bosom of the Father" (NKJV). The term used here to describe Lazarus' location certainly seems to indicate heaven.

At least on this one occasion, the wicked dead person is allowed to catch a glimpse of some of the blessed condition of the righteous person! Conversely, we are not told that Lazarus sees the suffering of the rich man.

Not only did the rich man see the blessedness of Lazarus, he also acknowledged the reality of the "great gulf fixed" (NKJV) between the two destinies (v. 26). Edersheim states that "above all, and as marking the vast difference between Jewish ideas and Christ's teaching, we notice that there is no analogy in Rabbinic writings to the statement in the parable, that there is a wide and impassable gulf between Paradise and Gehenna."[38]

We get our word *chasm* from this Greek word "gulf," which is used only here in the New Testament. A yawning or unbridgeable abyss is the emphasis.

The term "fixed" comes from a Greek verb *sterizo* which means "to set forth, make fast, fix." This word denotes "firmness of purpose" or "that which has been established."[39] Romans 16:25 records Paul praying on behalf of the Roman believers "to him who is able to *establish* you by my Gospel" (NIV, emphasis mine). More importantly, the same term is used in Luke 9:51 to refer to Jesus as He "stedfastly *set* His face" (KJV, emphasis mine) to go to Jerusalem. Might not one say that the same resoluteness which caused the Son of God to go to Calvary marks the fixed bounds of hell for those who ignore His work? Perhaps the English word *sterilize* comes from this Greek term. This verb "fixed" in Luke 16:26 is in the perfect tense, indicating action completed with abiding results. Robertson suggests that its thrust is to show a "permanent chasm."[40] It is interesting that the story records no request of the rich man that he might escape his own condition. Perhaps he knew that his circumstances were unalterable.

A Conversation across a Chasm

The rich man makes two requests in this passage. His first request concerns his own thirst, and he pleadingly asks Abraham to send Lazarus "to dip the tip of his finger in water and cool my tongue" (v. 24). How ironic! In the earthly sphere, the rich man's response to Lazarus' suffering was to permit him to have the crumbs which fell by the sheer force of gravity (not compassion) to the floor. Now he asks that Lazarus serve as his waterboy, presumably to enter the flames himself to bring Dives relief!

The rich man's second request seems to be other-directed (vv. 27-28). Again he pleads that Lazarus be sent on an errand (one should not overlook the fact that he does not ask to go himself), this time to warn his five living brothers about "this place of torment" (v. 28). Many commentators falsely conclude that Dives shows repentance or at least a concern for others in this second request. This suggestion will be examined momentarily.

Principles in This Passage

Some commentators insist that Luke 16:19-31 is primarily about stewardship, others that it is about one's treatment of the poor. The noted scholar R.C. Trench sees the primary point of this passage to be unbelief:

> It is not the primary purpose of the parable to teach the fearful consequences which will follow the abuse of wealth and contempt of the poor, but the fearful consequences of unbelief, of having the heart set on this world, and refusing to believe in that invisible world, here known only to faith, until by a miserable and too late experience the existence of such an unseen world has been discovered. The sin of Dives in its roots is unbelief: the squandering of self, and contempt of the poor, are only the forms which it takes . . . . It is most important to keep in mind that this, the rebuke of unbelief, is the central thought and aim of the parable.[41]

We disagree with the commentator who said that "whatever elements of man's ultimate destiny are present in this story are of secondary application."[42] The eternal fate of the righteous and the wicked are clearly spoken of by Jesus in this text, and several general principles may be discerned. Those principles find support in other passages of the Word of God, as we shall see.

A Righteous Reckoning

The *first* principle is that after death one receives perfect judgment based on an infallible evaluation of one's earthly life (v. 25). It would be inappropriate to draw the conclusion that all poor people go to heaven simply because they are poor or that all rich people go to hell simply because they are wealthy, for the overall point of the passage is to challenge the Pharisees "who loved money" (v. 14). One's use of wealth discloses whether one is rightly related to the God who gives wealth.

Abraham emphasizes to the rich man that he is not being unfairly treated, nor is Lazarus receiving what is out of harmony with what is right. "In your lifetime," Abraham says, "you received *your* good things" (v. 25, emphasis mine). Perhaps Abraham means that the rich man, by neglecting God, enjoyed only the good things which his own human hands could provide. The "evil things" (v. 25, NKJV) which Lazarus experienced are not described by Abraham as *his* "evil things." That is, Lazarus was not being punished for sins which he had committed. The first lesson which the rich man (and we) should learn is that God is just; "a man reaps what he sows" (Gal. 6:7).

A Final Destiny

The *second* principle of this passage is that one's eternal destiny is fixed (established) at death. Although Dives is not alone in *hades* (the "you" of v. 26 is plural), he appears unaware of anyone else's presence. There is a "great gulf" which is "fixed" (v. 26). James Moffatt renders this expression "a great gulf yawns," while J.B. Phillips translates it as "a great chasm has been set."[43]

This chasm, Abraham emphasizes, has a twofold purpose. It rules out any short-term, heavenly missionary outreach (by those enjoying God's blessedness) *to* hell, as well as any holiday excursions (by those separated from the joy of God's presence) *from* hell. Moffatt's translation of verse 26 states that a "great gulf yawns . . . to keep back those who want to cross from us to you." In light of recent attempts to overhaul hell, or at least to question God's justice in sending the wicked there, one is reminded of Oswald Chambers' statement, "It is possible to have such sympathy for our fellow man as to be guilty of red-handed rebellion against God."

Although two different words are used to mean "pass" in this verse (*diabaino* and *diaperao*), the thrust is certainly on the impossibility of bridging that chasm. C.S. Lewis' provocative book *The Great Divorce* notwithstanding, opportunities to move from hell to heaven are ruled out by that yawning chasm.

A Reasonable Warning

The *third* principle is that sufficient evidence has already been given in the Scriptures for faith. Dives requests that Lazarus be told by Abraham to leave the blessedness of God's presence and return to earth as a messenger to his five living brothers, "so that they will not also come to this place of torment" (v. 28). What a presumptuous, non-repentant request on Dives' part! He expresses no remorse for how he treated Lazarus during his earthly life; now he simply expects Lazarus to be his messenger boy.

Sometimes the enemies of God's grace most eloquently proclaim His truth. The rich man obviously believes that it is only in one's earthly life that a decision can be made which keeps one out of hell. Dives harbored no hope that his brothers could decide for God in any *postmortem* condition. He wants his brothers to receive the testimony of Lazarus (v. 28). Dives, we must not forget, had never taken the time to hear Lazarus' testimony in his comfort-crowded and gusto-filled life. Recognizing and believing that no one from heaven could rescue his soul because of that "great gulf fixed," he nevertheless hopes that one could leave paradise and persuade those on earth not of the seriousness of living for God, but of the reality of the place of punishment.

Abraham's response to this second request (v. 29) from the rich man might be paraphrased: "Your five brothers have the five books of Moses; let them hear them!" Presumably those five brothers would have to invest some time and energy to go to the synagogue to hear the Old Testament read to them or to request a private audience with the priest (the brothers not having their own copy of the Scriptures). One commentator suggests that Dives' unbelief is most shown "in supposing that his brethren, while refusing to give heed to the sure word of God, would heed a ghost."[44] How simple it is to suggest that the reason people don't believe is that the evidence is insufficient. Perhaps the problem was simply that they couldn't be bothered (as the rich man himself probably felt while he was alive). It is far easier to sit back and expect God to take the extra measures to thoroughly convince the wicked to repent!

Barclay suggests that the sin of Dives was not that he was deliberately cruel to Lazarus. "The sin of Dives was that he never noticed Lazarus, that he accepted Lazarus as part of the landscape . . . [Dives'] was the punishment of the man who never noticed."[45] Blaise Pascal, the seventeenth-century mathematician and theologian, once stated that:

> There are two kinds of people who can be called reasonable: those who serve God with all their hearts because they know Him, and those who seek Him with all their hearts because they do not know him . . . But as for those who live without knowing Him and without seeking Him, they adjudge themselves so little worthy of their own concern that they are unworthy of the concern of others.[46]

The rich man rejects Abraham's evaluation, a rather disrespectful attitude toward the father of Israel. Trench says that "the man's contempt of God's word, which he showed on earth, follows him beyond the grave."[47] Dives protests that a visit from the dead will bring repentance to his brothers (v. 30). How could he be so certain? Edersheim says that "the request seems to imply an attempt at self-justification, as if, during his life, he had not had sufficient warning."[48]

This term *testify* which Dives uses (v. 28, NKJV) concerning his hoped-for errand is an old Greek word which has the connotation of a "solemn and thorough witness,"[49] as if the witness of the five books of Moses had not been thorough. Rather than expressing a concern for souls, it may be that Dives uses his five lost brothers as evidence of God's lack of clarity about the afterlife. Perhaps one element of the atmosphere of hell will be a self-justifying blaming of God for insufficient evidence. Not the clarity of the truth, but the callousness of man's heart is the issue here.

Appropriate Pain

A word should be said at this point about the concept of *poena damni*. As was mentioned earlier, medieval theologians suggested that the wicked will suffer both *poena sensus* (a pain of sense) as well as *poena damni* (a sense of loss at not seeing God). However, the idea of *poena damni* seems to imply a remorse or repentance or mental anguish which many think will characterize the wicked in hell.

One writer said that "hell is truth seen too late." We believe that the Scriptures provide stronger support for the position that hell is truth twisted and thrown in the face of God! That is, impenitence and blasphemy will mark the wicked in hell, not remorse. Revelation 16:9 teaches that those who had martyred God's witnesses "were seared by the intense heat and they cursed the name of God, who had control over these plagues, but they refused to repent and glorify Him." It appears in Luke 16 that Dives twists God's truth, or at least questions God's fairness and the Old Testament gospel's clarity.

Abraham abruptly concludes the conversation across the chasm by emphasizing that if one does not respond to revelation already given, he will not be open to new and additional truth

(v. 31). (Christ makes the same point in His challenge to the Jewish leaders in John 5:45-47.) Overtly miraculous evidence (someone rising from the dead) will not bring persuasion to those who have rejected previous installments of God's message. If one returned from the dead, he would communicate the same truth which "Moses and the prophets" proclaimed so long ago (v. 31, cf. Luke 24:25-26). Perhaps this is why the resurrected Christ appeared only to His disciples; the enemies would simply explain away the appearances. The continuity of God's truth through Moses and the prophets is evident; if one ignores that truth from written witnesses, he will ignore that same truth from risen witnesses!

King Saul, one commentator observes, "was not led to repentance when he saw Samuel at Endor nor were the Pharisees when they saw Lazarus come forth from the tomb. The Pharisees tried to put Lazarus to death and to explain away the resurrection of Jesus."[50] Alford comments on the curious fact that Lazarus was the name of one who *did* rise from the dead but whose return "was the immediate exciting cause of their crowning act of unbelief."[51]Rather than believing this latter Lazarus' testimony, the Jews began conspiring to do him in (John 12:10).

The episode of "Doubting Thomas" (John 20), some might suggest, seems to be an exception to this rule of sufficient evidence. However, one must point out that Thomas is better decribed as "Adamantly Unbelieving Thomas" (as the Greek of John 20:25 shows), rather than as "Doubting Thomas." He already had sufficient evidence of Christ's resurrection (John 20:1-25). Furthermore, he is not commended by Jesus for demanding a personal resurrection appearance; he is rather soundly *rebuked* by the Savior for his postponed faith (John 20:29).

In summary, Luke 16 teaches much about the two destinies awaiting humans. We agree with Trench who cautions concerning parables that "doctrines otherwise grounded may be illustrated, or even further confirmed by them; but it is not allowable to constitute doctrines first by their aid."[52] The general principles about the afterlife contained in Jesus' story find support in other Scriptures. The idea of the wicked's conscious torment is taught in passages such as 2 Thessalonians 1:8-9, Revelation 14:10-11 and 20:10-15. Paul writes of God's justice and reminds those who were experiencing persecution that "He will punish those who do not know God and do not obey the Gospel of our Lord Jesus. They will be punished with everlasting destruction and shut out from the presence of the Lord and from the majesty of His power" (2 Thes. 1:8-9).

The Apostle John emphasizes that every human being who worships the beast and receives his mark

> will drink of the wine of God's fury, which has been poured full strength into the cup of his wrath. He will be tormented with burning sulfur in the presence of the holy angels and of the Lamb. And the smoke of their torment rises for ever and ever. There is no rest day or night for those who worship the beast and his image, or for anyone who receives the mark of his name (Rev. 14:10-11).

Revelation 20:10, although referring to the fate of the unholy three (the devil, the beast, and the false prophet), uses similar language and speaks of "the lake of burning sulfur where . . . they will be tormented day and night for ever and ever." Although many would prefer to think of this fate as awaiting only those three, we are told in this same chapter of Revelation that all human beings whose names are not found in the Book of Life will be thrown into that same lake of fire (Rev. 20:15).

The idea of the fixity of one's fate at death, taught in Luke 16, has already been discussed in our previous chapter. Hebrews 9:27 certainly seems to indicate that judgment follows one at death (allowing no possibility for a change of spiritual status). Jesus twice teaches that those who are not rightly related to Him by faith will die in their sins (John 8:21, 24).

The concept of the sufficiency of God's testimony concerning His Son is also supported elsewhere in Scripture. Jesus Himself confronted the Jewish leaders with their refusal to believe the writings of Moses: "If you believed Moses," Jesus said, "you would believe Me, for he wrote about Me. But since you do not believe what he wrote, how are you going to believe what I say?" (John 5:46-47) The Scriptures are able to make one "wise unto salvation" (2 Tim. 3:15, KJV) if one will only listen. Although the Ethiopian eunuch needed Philip to explain the meaning of Isaiah 53, there was sufficient Gospel content in the Old Testament for the eunuch to come to faith.

The conscious blessedness and immediate presence of the believer after death with the Lord is taught by Paul in 2 Corinthians 5:6-9. As Murray Harris writes, "[A] temporal distinction can hardly be drawn between the destruction of the earthly house (2 Cor. 5:1) and departure from the mortal body (2 Cor. 5:8). As soon as residence in physical embodiment ceases, so too does absence from the Lord (cf. 2 Cor. 5:6)."[53] Likewise, when Paul expresses his desire "to depart and be with Christ" (Phil. 1:23), the word "and" (*kai*) is explicative and means that to depart this life is to be immediately with Christ. Harris emphasizes that the "*postmortem* state of the believer is qualitatively superior to his spiritual life on earth."[54]

Apart from the conversation between Abraham and Dives in Luke 16, the major points of the story of the rich man and Lazarus find support in other biblical passages. If one wishes to dismiss the afterdeath teaching of Luke 16:19-31, he or she is also likely to explain away other Scriptures (such as Rev. 14:10–11; 20:10–15) as hyperbole or figurative language not meant to be literally understood. We shall show in our final chapter that such a position is exegetically weak, to say the least.

Jesus was no accommodator to Jewish views about the afterlife, nor was He simply trying to put the fear of God in the Pharisees so they would use their riches for better purposes than self-entertainment. Rather than seeing Luke 16:19-31 as an elaborate story told *only* to warn about the wise use of wealth, isn't it more reasonable to see the issue of riches as a springboard to Jesus' discussion of two destinies, one of anguish and isolation from God, the other of joy and fellowship in His presence? Truly it is difficult for a rich man to enter the kingdom of God. For those who ignore Moses and the prophets, there is only one other destiny.

A Summary of Jesus' Teaching

"Whether Jesus taught eternal hell or not is uncertain," declared the universalist Nels Ferré.[55] Our study has shown that the primary source for the doctrine of the Other Side of the Good News is, indeed, Christ Himself. Jesus not only firmly accepted the fact that there was a counterpart to heaven for those who were condemned before God, but warned of hell on numerous occasions. As Carl Henry writes, "Jesus' teaching makes it patently obvious that no correct view of final judgment can be elaborated that empties hell of its terrors and depicts God's last judgment as benevolent toward the impenitent and ungodly."[56] For those self-righteous, spiritual-looking Jewish leaders, Jesus used appropriately strong language to speak of judgment. The Good Shepherd (John 10) will be the wrathful Lamb (Rev. 6:16) on Judgment Day.

In his book *Heaven and Hell* Peter Toon writes that "it can never be said that heaven and hell were given an equivalent emphasis and value in [Christ's] preaching and teaching . . . Hell is . . . a secondary feature of his teaching, not a primary one."[57] We would disagree and argue that, quantitatively, it appears that Jesus spoke more about hell than about heaven because He knew that God's wrath presently abides on all who are not rightly related to Him. As He teaches in John, "Whoever rejects the Son will not see life, for God's wrath remains on him" (John 3:36). He knew that "the wages of sin is death" (Rom. 6:23) and one day will be payday.

Judgment has already been declared: "Whoever does not believe stands condemned already because he has not believed in the name of God's one and only son" (John 3:18). "Whoever hears My word and believes Him who sent Me has eternal life and will not be condemned; he has crossed over from death to life" (John 5:24). Several verses later Jesus states that "a time is coming when all who are in their graves will hear His voice and come out — those who have done good will rise to live, and those who have done evil will rise to be condemned" (John 5:29). In a world sold on self-creative faith, we need to say to the unsaved: "You will stand before God's judgment even if you don't think you will!"

C.S. Lewis emphasizes that "there is no neutral ground in the universe: every square inch, every split second, is claimed by God and counterclaimed by Satan."[58] Man is not spiritually neutral; he is on his way to a most horrific place and needs to be rescued. One who is rapidly approaching a deadly waterfall does not need instruction on the joys of outdoor camping; he needs to be warned of imminent danger and rescued from certain death!

Jesus taught that hell is a place (Matt. 24:51; Luke 16:28; cf. Rev. 21:8; Acts 1:25b) to be avoided at all costs (Matt. 5:22, 29, 30). He taught that it will be a place of enforced separation from His presence (Matt. 7:23; cf. 2 Thes. 1:8-9). As a place of darkness, its only sounds will be weeping and the gnashing of teeth (Matt. 8:12). Hell is a fate far worse than one's physical death (Matt. 10:28) and will contain punishments varying in severity (Matt. 11:22-24).

Jesus used several images to convey truth about the fate of the wicked. They are like *weeds* which the angels will weed out and "will throw . . . into the fiery furnace, where there will be weeping and gnashing of teeth" (Matt. 13:42). Second, as *bad fish*, the wicked will be separated from the righteous and the angels will "throw them into the fiery furnace, where there will be weeping and gnashing of teeth" (Matt. 13:49-50). The wicked, third, are like a *wedding guest* who came to the wedding banquet improperly dressed. Commentators tell us that the king routinely provided the required wedding clothes. This man had simply not bothered to ask for them. The king then tells his attendants: "Tie him hand and foot, and throw him outside, into the darkness, where there will be weeping and gnashing of teeth" (Matt. 22:13).

As the One who came to baptize with the Holy Spirit and fire, Jesus will one day "clear His threshing floor, gathering His wheat into the barn and burning up the chaff with unquenchable fire" (Matt. 3:11–12). Lest one think that the wicked will be consumed, that fire is described as *unquenchable*, a Greek word from which we get our English word "asbestos," indicating "mineral supposed to be inextinguishable when set on fire"[59] (as we pointed out in chapter 3). Jesus utilizes the "fire" imagery on a number of occasions to describe the place to which the wicked will be cast (Matt. 18:8-9).

One writer makes the following point concerning such language used to describe the fate of the wicked: "Doubtless much of the language of Scripture describing the unseen world must be understood figuratively. But figurative language, if it has any meaning at all, intends something literal, and it is my conviction that the figure of 'unquenchable fire,' in the light of other Scripture references, intends unending conscious *misery*."[60]

God's original intention was not to send men and women to a place called hell. Jesus is presently preparing "a place" (John 14:1-3) for all those who love Him. However, that other place originally "prepared for the devil and his angels" (Matt. 25:41) will finally be occupied by the devil, his angels, and all "whose names are not found in the Book of Life" (Rev. 20:15). No exegetical evidence exists to show that the final destiny of the *human* wicked is different than the final destiny of the *angelic* wicked.

Lastly, although God is "not willing that any should perish" (2 Peter 3:9, NKJV), some will indeed perish by their own choosing. They will ignore all of the signposts erected by God to miss hell. For them there will indeed be a destiny, not a "non-destiny" (as annihilationism would have us believe). That destiny is described as "eternal punishment" (Matt. 25:46).

John Wenham, although himself an annihilationist, points out that "Christ taught the existence of hell with a wealth of terrifying images."[61] But we must add that Jesus' teaching on the fate of the wicked must not be viewed as morbid speculation, but as sorrowful (yet authoritative) declaration. As He looked over the city of Jerusalem, Jesus cried, a cry recorded in both Matthew and Luke: "O Jerusalem, Jerusalem, you who kill the prophets and stone those sent to you, how often I have longed to gather your children together, as a hen gathers her chicks under her wings, but you were not willing" (Matt. 23:37; cf. Luke 13:34).

Jesus is our primary source for the doctrine of hell. As John Gerstner points out, "The irony is that while we attempt to use Christ to assure ourselves that there is no hell, it is Christ Himself who tells us most about hell."[62] His authority is to be trusted. As the late Kenneth Kantzer stated so well:

> I give serious consideration; indeed, I must confess, I am deeply impressed by the arguments of brilliant thinkers like Tillich, and Ferré and Bultmann and Brunner and Barth, not to mention John of Damascus and Thomas Aquinas, the Pope, Nietzsche, Feuerbach, Bertrand Russell, and many more. But what do these men *know*? What are the *data* on which they base their judgments? When it comes to the important question, "What is man's destiny after this life?" I prefer Jesus Christ, the God-man as my authority, to Paul Tillich. I prefer Jesus Christ to Rudolf Bultmann. And above all, lest you misunderstand me, I prefer Jesus Christ to my own blind human guesses based on woefully inadequate data.[63]

6

Must We **Decide** about the Other Side?

"The safest road to Hell is the gradual one — the gentle slope, soft underfoot, without sudden turnings, without milestones, without signposts." (C.S. Lewis)

"The hottest places in hell are reserved for those who, in a time of great moral crisis, maintain their neutrality." (Dante)

"It often seems to me that we face not just a few minor changes on the outskirts of historic Christian conviction but a virtual revolution in fundamental beliefs." (Clark H. Pinnock)

"Before every man there lies a wide and pleasant road he thinks is right, but it ends in death." (Prov. 16:25, TLB)

A student loaned me a recording of a sermon preached by his black pastor. The sermon was entitled "What in Hell Do You Want?" As he announced his sermon title, he got some laughter from his congregation. "I wanna' know, brothers and sisters," he shouted in a Southern drawl, "what is it that you *want* there in hell?" He vigorously described hell, using several images in Scripture, and concluded his sermon by saying that "every letter in the word hell represents somethin'! The letter h stands for *hot*! Listen to me, children! and e — hell is *e-vil*! and l — are ya' listenin'? Hell is a *low* place and l agin' — it's *lonely* down there! Which leads me to ask one mo' time — what in hell do you want?"

If we are honest with ourselves, we would have to say to this preacher, "There's *nothing* in hell that we want. In fact, we wish we didn't have to talk about it at all."

But we need to talk about hell, says one missionary writer:

> In our witnessing attempts today we tend to focus strictly on the good news of the Good News. Rarely is the bad news part of the gospel message mentioned: that eternal damnation is in line for those who do not acknowledge Jesus Christ as the Son of God . . . . Without question, hell is real (Mark 9:43, 45), terrible (Isa. 66:24), and eternal (Dan. 12:2). Whatever wishful-thinking trap we fall into, the fact won't change: lostness is forever.[1]

Some might suggest that the Christian's time would be better spent on issues other than the doctrine of hell. Admittedly, one would almost prefer to agree with Thomas Browne when he said: "I thank God, and with joy I mention it, I was never afraid of Hell, not ever grew pale at the description of that place. I have so fixed my contemplations on Heaven that I have almost forgot the idea of Hell."[2]

The Fight Is On

The evangelical Christian, who can't forget hell, often seems, in boxing terms, to be up against the ropes. In the matter of the destiny of the wicked, he is taking body blows from the cults who insist that a God who allows a hell of eternal conscious punishment is unworthy of one's faith. He then returns to his corner for some encouragement and promptly receives several left hooks from his own manager (some evangelical leaders who argue that "everlasting torment is intolerable from a moral point of view because it makes God into a bloodthirsty monster who maintains an everlasting Auschwitz for victims whom He does not even allow to die").[3] One is hardly surprised that some young fighters for the faith seem ready to throw in the towel.

Obviously, no follower of Christ wants to be guilty of presenting God as one more heinous than Hitler. However, if the Bible is clear on this issue, the Christian must *not* throw in the towel.

One commentator, suggesting that there may be "remedial discipline and growth in the unseen world," understands the story of the rich man and Lazarus (Luke 16) to provide some "hope of salvation" after this life. His reasoning? "Christ . . . significantly places the torment of Dives in *Hades*, the abode of the departed awaiting the resurrection, and not in *Gehenna*, the place of the finally lost (v. 23)."[4]

Although this same writer continues by saying that there is no scriptural evidence of a second chance to receive the Gospel for those who have clearly heard and turned away, he suggests that this parable may teach that:

> the destiny of most ordinary folks after death . . . is neither that highest bliss which will be the rewards of those who on earth have made it their joy to love and serve Christ, nor the pains of everlasting damnation, but a state of growth . . . Therefore discipline and growth beyond the grave are to be taken seriously.[5]

Apparently there are three, not simply two, possible destinies for humans.

If unbelief might be called a sin of the intellect, (it is, of course, more than that), then could not one say that hope not firmly based on Scripture is a sin of the heart? We have no right to declare anything that deviates from the biblical teaching about the fate of the wicked. Barth's universalistic hope of none being lost, for example, runs counter to the teaching of Scripture (see chapter 2). Annihilationism's exegetical basis seems rather thin, its being "a more humane view" of the fate of the wicked notwithstanding (as noted in chapter 3). The postmortem conversionists' hopes are also without solid scriptural support (as was noticed in chapter 4). Any suggestion of a change in one's eternal status after death is certainly ruled out by Scriptures such as Luke 16:19-31 (as we showed in our previous chapter).

If it is a crime to shout "fire" in a crowded theater when there is no fire, how much more criminal is it not to shout at all when the fire is raging all around and people are asleep in their seats? The biblical Christian does not want to be alarmist, but he ought to be sounding the alarm!

Lessening the severity of hell or redefining its biblically declared nature is, in our opinion, more dangerous than outright denial. To promote the hope that hell will be a place of growth (rather than a place of groaning) is to twist the tenor and content of Christ's teaching. Redefinition is more serious than total rejection, not only because the one doing the redefining appears to still be a member of the camp. Redefinition does nothing to change that which is being redefined; it only causes less caution to be taken in the face of a dangerous reality. A cup of poison relabeled Kool-Aid is not less lethal, only more enticing.

A liberal theologian who says, "I can't accept what the Bible teaches on this issue" appears to be fairly easy to refute. The really dangerous theologians are those who profess to be part of the family and want to call the church back to "moral sanity" by redefining hell.

How should the Bible-believing Christian respond when a respected evangelical theologian declares, "I consider the concept of hell as endless torment in body and mind an outrageous doctrine, a theological and moral enormity, a bad doctrine . . . which needs to be changed"?[6] We do not want to cling to "outrageous" doctrines nor do we want to be characterized as holding to "a theological and moral enormity." However, pejorative language aside, we are required to respond to those who question our theological and moral sensitivities. More importantly, our responsibility is to submit to what the Bible teaches as did the Berean believers who "searched the Scriptures daily to find out" about the doctrines which were being recommended (Acts 17:11, NKJV).

The Inadequacy of Alternative Positions
One of the foundational tenets of evangelical Christianity is the complete reliability of the Bible as our guidebook for life and doctrine. Those alternative positions that do not take the Bible seriously or that twist the teachings of the Bible to fit an already-decided-upon viewpoint often receive the lion's share of publicity and must be responded to.

The Unitarian minister Theodore Parker, for example, once remarked: "I believe that Jesus Christ taught eternal punishment — I do not accept it on his authority!" One wonders if any evangelical Christians ever said to him, "Parker, if Jesus Christ taught it, and if He indeed is God manifest in the flesh, *you'd better believe what He said!*" Perhaps some did; presumably he was not persuaded, and now it is too late.

The Authority of the Bible

We saw in chapter 2 that a universalist such as Ferré held a low view of the Bible (it is a "first century museum," an "umbrella" which "cloaks the spirit and implications of the gospel," etc.) One is hardly surprised that he rests his view of the Other Side solely on his understanding of God's "love." Jonathan Edwards clearly declared that "A true love of God must begin with a delight in his holiness, and not with a delight in any other attribute; for no other attribute is truly lovely without this."[7] But what about evangelicals who deny or redefine the doctrine of hell?

We are reminded again of Stott's comment that "If we come to Scripture with our mind made up, expecting to hear from it only an echo of our own thoughts and never the thunderclap of God's, then indeed he will not speak to us and we shall only be confirmed in our own prejudices."[8] One suspects that some evangelicals are muting the thunderclap of God's voice when they deny the biblical teaching about hell. Thunderclaps, as most Boy Scouts know, help to calculate how far away the lightning is. Lightning, a suitable image for God's judgment, strikes lethally with tremendous destructive power.

A Doctrinal Modification

A modification of one's doctrine of the Bible does not appear to be a necessary part of rejecting the traditional doctrine of eternal conscious punishment (note the high doctrine of Scripture held by annihilationists such as John Wenham, Philip Edgcumbe Hughes, John Stott, etc.) However, when men like Donald Bloesch speculate about the possible transference of a sinner from hell to heaven, or declare that "redemptive love is present in hell,"[9] one wonders how authoritative the biblical material is to his theology.

If one is going to consistently deny the biblical teaching on hell, a revision of one's doctrine of the Bible may be likely to occur. Pinnock, for example, makes a number of statements which reflect a different view of the Bible than he embraced in previous years. Although his doctrine of the Bible appears to have changed before his doctrine of hell, a cause/effect connection may be possible, but cannot be proven. This same scholar, who said in one of his earlier books that "To cast doubt on the complete veracity and authority of Scripture is a criminal act creating a crisis of immense proportions for theology and faith,"[10] made the following declarations in *Tracking the Maze*:

> (1) Jesus cannot be shown to have taught exactly what conservative Protestants believe about the Bible if only because their beliefs are very complex when properly explained.[11]

(2) One's insistence on the core historicity of the central Christian claim does not imply that every single episode in the Bible's extensive narrative is historical to the same extent . . . I would want to admit that there are things in the Bible that are historylike but not likely to be historical.[12]

(3) I do not think we should consider the historical value of the Sampson [*sic*] or Elisha stories on the same level with the Exodus and the Resurrection of Jesus. We are not bound to deny the Bible the possibility of playful legend just because the central claim is historical . . . . Unquestionably, Jesus' Resurrection had to happen for the gospel story to be true; but the same does not hold for Elisha's axehead or the fate of Lot's wife . . . Why is this such a delicate point for some people? Because some Christians put a great deal of stock in a version of rational certainty and fear it being weakened in any way. If Lot's wife did not actually turn to salt, all the certainty of their faith is lost. This is because their hope rests not on the story of salvation but on the Bible being a book free of legendary elements.[13]

(4) [Concerning John Stott's dialogue with the liberal Anglican David Edwards (*Evangelical Essentials*), Pinnock says] Stott does not really reply to Edwards' question about the need to believe all the miracles of the Bible (Did Moses' rod actually become a snake and his hand leprous? etc.) *Surely the honest answer is no.*[14]

(5) We have consistently inflated the importance of inspiration up to a level where it actually rivals Jesus Christ. As soon as the answer people give to the question, "On what foundation do you rest your hope of salvation?" is the Bible and not Jesus Christ, we are in deep trouble.[15]

(6) I think we have exaggerated the supernaturalness of inspiration. The text plainly bears the mark of humanness . . . . Together the books reveal a variety of viewpoints. They

do not stand above the relativity that affects all things human . . . Whatever was the case with the original manuscripts, the present Bible we have in our hands is not divinely perfect, and we must stop pretending otherwise.[16]

(7) We will need to be sensitive to the fact that Scripture does not speak in a uniformly rigid manner. We will need to acknowledge that elements in Scripture derive from the culture of the writer, not from revelation, and that a dialogue going on between the Spirit and the believer when Scripture is read creates the distinctive way each believer has of encountering the Bible.[17]

Alarming Implications

A few questions need to be asked concerning the above statements. How does one decide what is "historylike" and what is "history"? Pinnock refers to the book of Jonah in another place as possibly "a didactic fiction, serving a prophetic function." He then asks: "Could it not be a storylike narrative pointing forward to Jesus Christ?"[18] Is Jesus' Resurrection more "history" because of its centrality to the Gospel message, but Jonah's existence and experience not so historical? Rather than merely being fiction with a function, was Jonah not considered by Jesus as historical as His own predicted burial and resurrection (Luke 11:29-32; Matt. 12:38-42)?

When Pinnock expresses surprise that some Christians' faith would be lost if Lot's wife did not literally turn into a pillar of salt, he may be only raising a rhetorical question. One might nonetheless point out that the biblical material specifies that an actual event of judgment took place (Gen. 19:23-26). With an economy of words, Jesus challenged His disciples with the truth of His Second Coming: "Remember Lot's wife" (Luke 17:32).

When Pinnock asserts that Moses' rod did not actually become a snake, nor did Moses' hand literally become leprous, one should not be apologetic in responding that that is what the Scripture declares occurred (Ex. 4:3-9 and 7:9-12).

When Pinnock declares that the books of the Bible "reveal a variety of viewpoints" and that "they do not stand above the relativity that affects all things human," it is not wrong for evangelicals to be concerned. From such a viewpoint, one should not be surprised that Pinnock does not understand the Bible as being "a book free of legendary elements."

We believe that Pinnock sets forth a false antithesis in suggesting that one's assurance of salvation is not primarily what God has declared in His Word, the Bible, but in "Jesus Christ." But Christ's revelation to mankind *is* the Bible; the *written* Word does not stand in competition with the *Living* Word. Pinnock is right when he warns us not to treat the Bible as a magic book (which seems to be how the Jewish leaders treated the Old Testament Scriptures, John 5:39-40), but we have no authoritative revelation of Jesus Christ apart from the Bible.

Caution lights ought to flash in the evangelical's mind upon hearing Pinnock say that "a dialogue going on between the Spirit and the believer when Scripture is read creates the distinctive way each believer has of encountering the Bible." Such language appears to put the emphasis upon one's subjective experience of the Word, rather than upon the objective revelation of God through the Bible.

"There is something terribly wrong when we argue about the Bible more and enjoy it less," said Pinnock on one occasion.[19] One is reminded of the comment by the late American evangelical Dr. Harold J. Ockenga when he said, "It is apparent that those who give up an authoritative, dependable, authentic, trustworthy, and infallible Scripture must ultimately yield the right to the use of the name 'evangelical.'"[20] Pinnock's own position appears to be that he doubts some of the statements of biblical revelation while at the same time holding that revelation has not ceased!

It is, therefore, hardly surprising that Pinnock states in his dialogue with the liberal theologian Delwin Brown:

> I was led to question the traditional belief in everlasting conscious torment because of *moral revulsion* and broader theological considerations, not first of all on scriptural grounds. *It just does not make sense* to say that a God of love will torture people forever for sins done in the context of a finite life . . . *It makes no sense* to suppose that, alongside the new creation, tucked away in some corner of it, there exists a lake of fire with souls burning ceaselessly in it. It's time for evangelicals to come out and say that the biblical and morally appropriate doctrine of hell is annihilation, not everlasting torment.[21]

I was led to doubt the traditional doctrine initially because I found the notion of endless torture even for the most wicked *morally intolerable* and not because first of all I doubted its biblical status.[22]

Other factors than exegesis entered into the decision [to abandon the traditional view of hell] . . . I have already mentioned the role played by *simple moral revulsion.* Then I had to consider the biblical understanding of resurrection and immortality, where it became obvious that the traditional view of hell rested on the Hellenistic and unscriptural belief in the immortality of the soul. I also had to look at the issue of justice as it bore upon the concept of hell and consider the metaphysical implications in terms of an everlasting dualism implicit in the traditional doctrine. Finally, I was forced to look at the few difficult passages that seem to teach everlasting conscious punishment but which, I found, do not necessarily do so.[23]

A Challenge to Re-evaluate

A few observations must be made on Pinnock's forthright explanation of why he has rejected the eternal conscious punishment view. Several times he uses the expression "moral revulsion." Similarly, he twice says that the eternal conscious punishment view "just does not make sense." Without wanting to sound simplistic, might not those two points be challenged by insisting that one's sense of morality as well as the certainty of one's logical conclusions ought to *flow from*, and not be *brought to*, the Word of God? Let's assume for the moment that Pinnock's annihilationism is clearly a wrong position and that the biblical doctrine is clearly the doctrine of eternal conscious punishment. Would he (and perhaps we) not still respond that, to our moral way of reasoning, hell is morally revolting and "just does not make sense"? But it would still be the truth of God. Surely in our sin-twisted, fallen humanity we do not think that we will agree with all of God's actions (nor did the patriarchs, see 2 Sam. 6:8-10).

And what if the Bible has specifically declared that God will eternally *torment* those who reject Christ? Granted, it may be more comfortable for us to believe that God only allows the wicked to be tormented, but what do the Scriptures say about the terrible subject of torment?

We read, for example, in Revelation 14:10 that those receiving the mark of the beast will be "tormented . . . in the presence of the holy angels . . . and of the Lamb." Revelation 18:7-8 speaks of the harlot being punished: "give her as much *torture* and grief as the glory and luxury she gave herself . . . . She will be consumed by fire, for mighty is the Lord God who judges her" (emphasis mine). In Matthew 8:29 Jesus is asked by the demons: "Have you come here to *torture* us before the appointed time?" (emphasis mine) The evil spirit in the demon-possessed man pleads with Jesus in Mark 5:7, "Swear to God that you won't *torture* me!" (emphasis mine) Later, Jesus uses a story to emphasize judgment in Matthew 18. The man who was unmerciful to his fellow servant is severely judged: "his master turned him over to his jailers to be *tortured*" (v. 34, emphasis mine). "This is how my Heavenly Father will treat each of you unless you forgive your brother from your heart," Jesus says in the next verse (v. 35). In each of these passages the same Greek verb (*basanitzo*) is used to indicate torture.

Superior Sensitivity

The implication from Pinnock seems to be that all evangelicals prior to our day who held to the eternal conscious punishment view were moral misfits not facing up to the horror of the wicked's fate. Such is obviously not the case. On a related issue, Dr. George Murray, an evangelist, tells the story of his trip to L'Abri, the Swiss chalet run by Francis and Edith Schaeffer years ago for spiritual seekers: "The conversation after dinner was typically deep and theological. Then someone asked Dr. Schaeffer: 'What will happen to all those who have never heard of Christ?' Dr. Schaeffer didn't give an intellectual, deep, profound answer. He simply bowed his head and wept." We evangelicals ought to be bowing our heads and weeping far more than we are, yet we must be faithful to what Scripture truly teaches.

J.I. Packer understandably reacts to the annihilationists' tone of moral superiority. He asks, "Who can take pleasure in the thought of people being eternally lost? If you want to see folks damned, there is something wrong with you!"[24] He continues:

> What troubles me most here, I confess, is the assumption of superior sensitivity by the conditionalists. The feelings that make people want conditionalism to be true seem to me to reflect, not superior spiritual sensitivity, but secular sentimentalism which assumes that in heaven our feelings about others will be as at present, and our joy in the manifesting of God's justice will be no greater than it is now. It is certainly agonizing now to live with the thought of people going to an eternal hell, but it is not right to reduce the agony by evading the facts; and in heaven, we may be sure, the agony will be a thing of the past.[25]

The conditionalist or annihilationist could equally ask if those of us who hold to the eternal conscious punishment position do not do so out of a desire to see people other than ourselves tormented. However, if our morality and our theology flow from what the Bible teaches, then we must correct our moral sensitivities (as well as our insensitivities) by the biblical data. If God is as holy and man is as sinful as the Bible declares, then the doctrine of eternal conscious punishment makes more sense than the concept that all sinners (regardless of their degree of sinful activity) receive the same fate: extinction of being, as in annihilationism.

An Unfair Fate

Pinnock's rejection of eternal punishment for "sins done in the context of a finite life" is a standard objection to the eternal conscious punishment view. Of course, annihilationism is susceptible to the same challenge: annihilation is eternal in its effects, is it not?

The question, however, seems to be, "Does the traditional doctrine of hell set forth an inequity, i.e. infinite judgment for finite sinfulness?" We would respond by pointing out that the believer in Christ is infinitely rewarded for a finite acceptance of the atoning work of Christ. (Granted, it is not the believer's finite faith, but rather the infinite work of Christ received which is the basis of salvation.) Many acts in this finite life have consequences which extend far beyond the mere moment of their being committed. A momentary lapse of concentration by a driver can lead to lifelong paralysis; a brief departure from one's moral standards can lead to pregnancy; a finite (although lifelong) rejection of Christ will lead to eternal separation from Him.

An Eternal Plague Spot?

Finally, Pinnock argues that "it makes no sense" to suppose that "alongside the new creation, tucked away in some corner of it, there exists a lake of fire with souls burning ceaselessly in it." He seems to be attacking either the idea of an eternal dualism between good and evil or the problem of an eternal plague spot in the new heavens and the new earth.

Concerning the dualism objection, we agree with Pinnock that if the continued existence of sin and sinners implies two equal and opposing principles in the new heavens and the new earth, such does not appear to be taught in the Scriptures. However, the continued existence of sinners, confined as prisoners in a place called the lake of fire, is clearly taught (Rev. 20:11-15).

We must also argue that if God can be completely holy and good and yet allow evil (although restrained) to be present *now* in His creation, why not *forever* (but confined to a place called the lake of fire)? The Bible speaks of God being vindicated at the end of time, but there is more than one way for the Victor to display His triumph over His enemies than by putting them out of existence. He can give them life at hard labor; or, in connection with the holy God of the Bible, He can consign them to eternal (second) death, separating them forever from His presence and kingdom.

Concerning the "plague spot" objection, we must say that it makes better sense of the language used of the fate of the wicked (e.g., that they will be thrown "outside" the kingdom, that their "place" will be with the devil and his angels) to hold that they will continue to exist forever, cut off from God's grace. If God's kingdom has an *outside*, then it is not a compromise of that kingdom to faithfully proclaim that some will suffer eternally outside its gates.

The Myth of a Safe God

In the classic children's story *The Lion, the Witch, and the Wardrobe*, Lucy was soon to meet Aslan the lion (a Christ figure). Greatly apprehensive about meeting him, she says to Mrs. Beaver: "Is he – quite safe? I shall feel rather nervous about meeting a lion." "Safe?" said her husband Mr. Beaver. "Don't you hear what Mrs. Beaver tells you? Who said anything about safe? "Course he isn't safe. But he's good. He's the king, I tell you."[26]

Not safe – but good. Some of today's evangelicals have made a megashift to a "kinder and gentler" God who appears to be both safe and good – or maybe only safe. They find it difficult to hold to the biblical images of Christ as the Lamb of God as well as the Lion of Judah. They seem to prefer that Christ remain a lamb, perhaps not remembering that the Book of

Revelation depicts Him as a wrathful Lamb at the judgment (6:16; cf. 19:15).

The Malevolence of God

William Temple once commented that "It is much worse to have a false idea of God than no idea at all." Frankly, we're more comfortable with the idea of God *allowing* suffering and death than that of His actively *causing* them. Perhaps the reason why we're so repulsed by the idea of hell is that we've conditioned ourselves to think of God as solely pure, passive, and pacifistic.

One of the major objections to the eternal conscious punishment view is that it appears to compromise God's love and portrays Him as One who "out-Auschwitzs Hitler." Our insensitivity to the gravity of sin combined with an ignorance of God's malevolence render the traditional view of hell simply "unthinkable."

What a foreign idea it is to many that God is one who *hurts* as well as One who *heals*. Jeremiah records the Lord's declaration against His own people: "I myself will fight against you with an outstretched hand and a mighty arm in anger and fury and great wrath. I will strike down those who live in this city – both men and animals – and they will die of a terrible plague" (21:5-6). (One can almost hear today's vivisectionists protesting, "Why the destruction of innocent animals?") The Lord continues through Jeremiah by stating: "'I have determined to do this city harm and not good,' declares the Lord." (21:10) One cannot support the concept of a harmless God from Jeremiah's prophecy!

Lest one respond with the liberal "that's the-wrathful-God-of-the-Old-Testament" approach, Jesus Himself pictures the Heavenly Father as one who will one day torment all those who do not forgive their brothers from their hearts (Matt. 18:21-35). Rather than thinking of God as the One whose primary agenda is the sustaining of our physical lives, we must realize that on occasion (thankfully not always) He executes those who have incurred His wrath.

In his instruction about the Lord's Supper, Paul reminds the Corinthians that their abuse of that solemn ceremony led to God's judgment. By failing to properly partake of that meaning-packed remembrance feast, this group of believers was severely judged by God: "That is why many among you are weak and sick, and a number of you have fallen asleep", Paul declares (1 Cor. 11:30). If God takes away the physical lives of those who have abused the ceremony commemorating Christ's death, what will He do to those who ignore the One who died? Jesus did not teach that all will be well in the end, particularly with those who die in their sins.

How disappointed we are when a young person is allowed by God to die in his or her prime; how much more disappointed some might be with God when He will actively cause many to be permanently cast out of His presence into eternal death! John Wenham comments about the god of liberal theology by saying, "It is in fact easier to accept the God of the Bible than it is to accept a liberalized God whose character has ceased to be terrible."[27]

Are the wicked going to be punished? God's Word says that they will. Will that punishment be only self-inflicted mental grief? No! The God of the Bible will inflict just punishment as proof that He is both love and holy wrath. Rather than understanding Hebrews 10:31 correctly ("It is a dreadful thing to fall into the hands of the living God."), some seem to have paraphrased it to say: "It is a (yawn) boring thing to fall into the hands of a harmless God!" We want God to be both holy and harmless, an impossible combination of attributes. The existentialist philosopher Jean-Paul Sartre understandably admitted: "The last thing I want is to be subject to the unremitting gaze of a holy God."

Meek and Mild Jesus?

The King James translation of Hebrews 7:26 speaks of our high priest Jesus as "holy, harmless, undefiled." A better rendering is that He is "holy, blameless, pure." The term *blameless* is a Greek term used only here and in Romans 16:18 and means "without evil or guile."[28] He is the guileless, blameless high priest for all who are covered by His atoning sacrifice. However, God's holy wrath borne by Christ did not exhaust or empty His anger against those who reject His Son. The idea of Jesus being meek and mild, holy and harmless is a myth! God hates sin! It cost His Son His life. We must warn the world with strong language: "If you hug your sin and reject His Son, He'll do more than rap your knuckles. You will receive only His wrath."

It is hard for us to picture the Good Shepherd as the Great Avenger. But if a good shepherd breaks the leg of a wayward sheep to keep it from straying, what will He do to a sheep who smites the Shepherd? Are we implying here that the Good Shepherd will kill His *own* sheep? No! That's precisely the point: some are wolves in sheep's clothing and a loving Shepherd won't tolerate a wolf running free among His chosen sheep! How could anyone think that the One "who did not spare His own Son," (Rom. 8:32) will spare a wolf, who seeks to destroy the flock of God which Christ purchased with His own blood? Such action will be taken, not because the Shepherd isn't good, but because there is a world of difference between a sheep and a wolf. A wolf, of course, will gobble up the sheep, for that's what wolves do (Acts 20:28-31).

Existence in Hell

As harsh as it might sound, could we not twist Ferré's phrase and say that Heaven can only be heaven when it has *filled* hell? We are not suggesting that God delights in the death of the wicked (Ezek. 18:23, 32; 33:11) nor that He looks forward to eternally judging them (John 3:17) nor that He has any desire to fill hell (2 Peter 3:9). However, the Bible does describe heaven as God's kingdom separated from all wickedness (Rev. 21:1-8).

C.S. Lewis imagines that the wicked, if allowed to visit heaven from hell, would be marked by a desire to extend hell, "to bring it bodily, if they could, into Heaven."[29] In *Mere Christianity*, Lewis states:

> Christianity asserts that every individual human being is going to live forever, and this must be either true or false. Now there are a good many things which would not be worth bothering about if I were going to live only seventy years, but which I had better bother about very seriously if I am going to live for ever. Perhaps my bad temper or my jealousy are gradually getting worse — so gradually that the increase in seventy years will not be very noticeable. But it might be absolute hell in a million years: in fact, if Christianity is true, Hell is the precisely correct technical term for what it would be.[30]

In the popular movie *Ghost* of a few years ago, Patrick Swayze stars as the spirit of a character who is murdered. He communicates to his earthly lover (played by Demi Moore) about his new existence: "It's amazing, Molly – the love inside – you take it with you." Might not the Christian suggest that hell is the sinner eternally taking all his sins with him?

The commonly held view that the wicked experience repentance in hell is *incorrect*; the Bible teaches that their impenitence will continue forever (Rev. 16:9). Edersheim, referring to the expression "weeping and gnashing of teeth" (Matt. 8:12; 22:13; 24:51; 25:30; Luke 13:28), points out that "weeping" is associated in Rabbinic thought with sorrow, but "gnashing of teeth" almost always with anger (not, as generally supposed, with anguish).[31] Is it not, therefore, reasonable to assume that those who reject the work of Christ, if they were offered the opportunity to leave hell, would rush to spread their sin and unbelief among the blood-bought children of heaven? We are speculating a bit here, no doubt, but some Christians have argued that hell is a protection of the redeemed from the wicked. Although universalists object that hell, if not remedial, is wasted punishment, we would respond and say that it is sometimes appropriate to separate a criminal from society and to give him life at hard labor. Such is not a denial of human value, but its affirmation in the sense that the righteous are being protected. In Matthew 21:33-41 Jesus tells the parable of a landowner who rented out his vineyard to some farmers. When the landowner sent servants to collect his fruit, the farmers mistreated the servants, killing several of them. Finally the landowner sent his own son, assuming that they would respect him. Jesus then explains that they threw the landowner's son out of the vineyard and killed him (v. 39).

Jesus concludes the parable by asking His audience what the landowner should do to the farmers. Matthew's account records the chief priests and elders responding "He will bring those wretches to a wretched end" (v.41). The parallel accounts in Mark 12:1-12 and Luke 20:9-19 record Jesus stating that the owner would come and kill the tenants and give the vineyard to others. Certainly the parable is given by the Lord as a prediction of His coming rejection and execution by Israel's leaders. The parable describes the harsh judgment that will befall those who mistreat the landowner's son! Rather than the heavenly landowner being meek and mild, He will exercise severe (yet just and appropriate) judgment on the wicked.

The idea of the harmlessness of God is foreign to the biblical picture that He executes those who presumptuously touch the ark (2 Sam. 6:6–7), who offer unauthorized fire on His altar (Lev. 10:1-2), or who lie to the Holy Spirit (Acts 5:1-11). In his excellent book *Disappointment with God* Philip Yancey relates the story of lightning striking the church of a liberal English bishop, David Jenkins, who had denied the Virgin Birth and the deity of Christ. Some conservative Christians rejoiced in what appeared at the time to be an act of God's judgment against unbelief, but Yancey responds to such a perspective by asking: "Why should David Jenkins provoke divine wrath when the outright blasphemer Bertrand Russell lived unpunished into cranky old age? If God consistently sent lightning bolts in response to bad doctrine, our planet would sparkle nightly like a Christmas tree."[32]

The fact is that God does not consistently send lightning bolts to judge bad doctrine or wicked sinners, but He could! Only His mercy accounts for the "exceptional" acts of His judgment, and that mercy will one day draw to a close.

If Jesus was right in this world to drive the money changers out of His Father's house (Matt. 21:12-13), He will be equally right in the next world to exclude unbelievers from that heavenly home!

One's doctrine of the final judgment of the wicked is a direct reflection of one's doctrine of God. Liberals like Ferré and Robinson argue that point and come to universalism — all must be saved for God to be a good God. Now some evangelicals are telling us that the traditional view of God seems like Hitler at his worst!

God's Holy Hatred

We are quite accustomed to the double declaration that "God hates the sin, but loves the sinner." However, is such a declaration biblically accurate? Seventeenth-century universalists (such as Peter Sterry and Jeremiah White) argued that love is God's supreme attribute. His wrath is therefore an aspect of His love, and His wrath is directed not against the sinner but against the sin. "So," they taught, "the sinner's torment in hell will be the agony of enduring God's holy burning love until his sins are burned up and he himself is pure."[33]

Although such universalists appear to affirm God's holiness, they deny the biblical truth that some will not be brought into the kingdom of God because of unbelief. Some sinners will reject the atoning work of Christ, and as P.T. Forsyth once stated, "Christianity is not the religion of love, but of holy and therefore atoning love, which makes it all the more divine as it makes it less promptly popular."

Sam Milolaski declared, "Unless God is angry with sin, let us put a bullet in our collective brain, for the universe is mad." Jonathan Edwards said that the reason we find hell so offensive is because of our insensitivity to sin; we simply don't hate sin as God hates it. Is it possible that the Bible declares in places that God's anger is against the sinner, not just the sin?

R.C. Sproul, commenting on Genesis 2:17, emphasizes the holiness of God:

> "The day that you sin, you shall surely die." Is that unjust? Think about it. Was it evil for God to impose the death penalty for all sin? If you say yes, be careful. If you say yes, you are saying it as an expression of the very fallen, sinful nature that exposes you to the death penalty in the first place. If you say yes, you slander the character of God. If you say yes, you do violence to His holiness.[34]

The fact is, we want a God who is just a little bit more divine than Santa Claus. T.S. Eliot said that if we eliminate the doctrine of final judgment, we convert God into a Santa Claus who declares, "Everybody shall get toys and be glad!"[35]

We want all movies to have happy endings; but alas, life does not always, and eternity will not, end that way. One theological wag said that "God made man in His image and modern man has returned the favor." No individual is immune from imagining what he would like God to be, but that does not make Him so! Even the most arduous Bible-believing follower of Christ must always check his or her doctrine of God with what God has revealed about Himself in the Scriptures. Robert Mounce commented that "all caricatures of God which ignore his intense hatred for sin reveal more about man than about God."[36]

Calvin declared that "we are taught by Scripture to perceive that apart from Christ, God is, so to speak, hostile to us, and his hand is armed for our destruction."[37] He continues, quoting Augustine, that " '[God] loved us even when we practiced enmity toward him and committed wickedness. Thus in a marvelous and divine way he loved us even when he hated us.' "[38] The French Reformer understood reconciliation to mean that "God, to whom we were hateful because of sin, was appeased by the death of his Son to become favorable to us."[39] Seldom do we consider the malevolence of God and almost never preach or hear sermons on God's wrath and justified hatred of sinners.

Concerning the wicked, the psalmist declares that one day God will awake and bring them to judgment: "As a dream when one awakes, so when you arise, O Lord, You will despise them as fantasies" (Ps. 73:20). Psalm 5:5-6 claims: "The arrogant cannot stand in Your presence; you hate all who do wrong. You destroy those who tell lies; bloodthirsty and deceitful men the Lord abhors." Psalm 11:5 states that "The Lord examines the righteous, but the wicked and those who love violence his soul hates." The perverse person is an abomination to the Lord, declares Proverbs 3:32.

We take a statement like "Jacob I have loved, but Esau I have hated" (Mal. 1:3, NKJV) and quickly declare it hyperbole. We (rightfully, I think) compare it to Jesus' challenge that if one is to be His disciple, he must (comparatively speaking) hate his mother and father (Matt. 10:37).

Such a treatment of those two texts seems reasonable. But how does one explain God's declaration to His own people in Leviticus 26:30: "I will destroy your high places, cut down your incense altars, and cast your carcasses on the lifeless forms of your idols; and My soul will abhor you"?

We are all familiar with the story of Job's suffering and the well-intentioned advice of his three friends. A series of sermons could easily be preached on the theology of Job's friends with the title "With Friends Like *These* . . . " Elihu's advice to a suffering Job, for example, leaves a lot to be desired, not the least of which is his declaration that "God is mighty, but does not despise men; he is mighty, and firm in his purpose. He does not keep the wicked alive but gives the afflicted their rights" (Job 36:5-6). But we must respond, the afflicted do not always get their "rights" in this life, the wicked often prosper in inverse proportion to their character, and God does declare that He holds some in contempt.

The fact is, we are extremely uncomfortable with the biblical declaration that "God is angry with the wicked every day" (Ps. 7:11, NKJV). We strongly disagree with Bloesch's statements that

> hell is not outside the compass of God's mercy nor the sphere of his kingdom, and in this sense we call it the last refuge for the sinner . . . Hell will not be seen as an

> evil, but as the place where those who reject Christ are still cared for by Christ – and not simply as Lord and Judge but as Savior and Healer.[40]

The Bible declares that "multitudes who sleep in the dust of the earth will awake: some to everlasting life, others to shame and everlasting *contempt*" (Dan. 12:2, emphasis mine). It certainly sounds as if those sinners who are not covered by the blood of Jesus Christ will be the objects of God's hatred, not His mercy, forever.

There is "a time to love and a time to hate" (Ecc. 3:8). Revelation 2, speaking of the church at Ephesus, records its divine commendation: "you have this in your favor: you hate the practices of the Nicolaitans, which I also hate" (v. 6). God also says that "those who honor me I will honor, but those who despise Me will be disdained" (1 Sam. 2:30). Speaking of the enemies of God's people, the psalmist states in Psalm 53:5 that "God has scattered the bones of him who encamps against you; you have put them to shame, because God has despised them" (NKJV). Psalm 106:40 declares that "the Lord was angry with His people and abhorred His inheritance."

Calvary's Gruesomeness

A few years ago, a respected medical journal featured an article on the physical aspects of Christ's crucifixion. Letters poured in to the editor, decrying that scientific magazine's treatment of a "religious" issue. Such a response is not surprising; the fact of the matter is that by nature we want to turn our eyes away from what happened at Calvary.

We have no problem recognizing the cruelty and abuse of sinful men there, but we must be reminded that Christ was "delivered by the predetermined plan and foreknowledge of God" (Acts 2:23, NASB). Even though people inflicted the physical scourging and the abuse, Isaiah 53:4ff prophesied that God would lay humankind's sins upon the Messiah. Scripture implies that the more severe suffering of Christ was His being forsaken by the Father (cf. His experience in Gethsemane recorded in Luke 22:39-45). The horror of hell and the crime at Calvary seem to stand or fall together.

George Macleod emphasizes that we must not water down the biblical picture of the Cross:

> I simply argue that the cross be raised again at the center of the marketplace as well as on the steeple of the church. I am recovering the claim that Jesus was not crucified in a cathedral between two candles, but on a cross between two thieves; on the town garbage heap; at a crossroad so cosmopolitan that they had to write his title in Hebrew and in Latin and in Greek . . . at the kind of place where cynics talk smut, and thieves curse, and soldiers gamble. Because that is where he died. And that is what he died about. And that is where churchmen ought to be, and what churchmen should be about.[41]

Recently, one of my students was wearing a T-shirt that had an artist's conception of the crucifixion on the front, drawn in excruciating detail. Under the picture were the words: "If I'm OK and you're OK . . . then *explain THIS*!" When people are tempted to edit the biblical picture of the final suffering of the wicked, it appears that they must also clean up the scene at the cross. Christ bore hell there for sinners!

We also want to turn away from Calvary's gruesomeness because we suspect in our souls that what happened there was the *only way* God could deal with sin and righteously provide atonement. Obviously, He could have obliterated us all. But to those who ask God, "Did it have to be Calvary?" we believe He would respond: "If I could have done it another way, I would have."

Is there not a parallel with hell? That is, hell is not some morally unnecessary or arbitrary entertainment for God. If there was no other way in which God could have righteously provided salvation for man other than Calvary (Rom. 3:26; Luke 22:42), is it not reasonable to say that for all who do not receive that work, they go to their graves bearing their own sin, and only hell remains for them?

Leaving Room for Wrath

John Gerstner, the late Reformed church historian, in his book *Repent or Perish*, captures the attitude of many today: "God may not even be," Gerstner hears the unbeliever saying, "but if He is, one thing is sure, He could not send anyone to hell even if He wanted to. His mercy has His hands of holy wrath tied behind his back."[42] The subject of God's wrath has only recently received renewed attention. Psalm 78:49-50 declares that "He unleashed against them His hot anger, His wrath, indignation and hostility — a band of destroying angels. He prepared a path for His anger; He did not spare them from death but gave them over to the plague." The fourth gospel clearly declares that "Whoever believes in the Son has eternal life, but whoever rejects the Son will not see life, for God's wrath remains on him" (John 3:36).

A misunderstanding of the concept of wrath may underlie its relatively minor role in much of evangelical theology. Packer's classic volume *Knowing God* describes God's wrath as "never the capricious, self-indulgent, irritable, morally ignorable thing that human anger so often is. It is, instead, a right and necessary reaction to objective moral evil. God is only angry where anger is called for."[43] Pink defines God's wrath as "His eternal detestation of all unrighteousness and the displeasure and indignation of Divine equity against evil."[44]

Several terms are used for the anger and wrath of God in Paul's writings (e.g. *echthros*, *apobole*, *apotomia*, *orge*). In studying the wrath of God a major question is raised: Is there evidence in Paul's understanding that God's wrath is used to reform or punish the wicked? If the purpose of God's wrath is to punish, then the wicked have no appeal, no hope of reconciliation with God; they are cut off from God's love. If God's wrath reforms, then wrath may be viewed as a function of God's attribute of love, always constructive, ultimately producing good for His creation.

If God is to be viewed primarily as a God of justice, then the eternal loss of vast numbers of His creatures to hell might be considered a victory, argues H.H. Farmer. However, if God is primarily a God of love, then such a loss could only be the most absolute form of defeat.[45] The argument continues that if God's eschatological wrath operates only retributively, then endless retributive wrath (whether it results in annihilation or eternal hell) offers the wicked no recourse and diminishes the picture of God as love.

If, however, wrath is seen not as retributive, but as remedial, as His chastening response to disobedience, then wrath is an element of His love. In this view, "postmortem punishment . . . would be a painful process, but one that would correct, leading to the betterment and purification of souls."[46]

Certainly the view of God's wrath as reformative is much more attractive than the view of God's wrath as retributive. The former view appears to set forth God, some argue, "not [as] a cosmic maniac gleefully extracting retribution from the fallen part of creation for no purpose at all, except perhaps for revenge" but as one who is "above mindless anger, [whose] wrath is good and just, designed to reform and reclaim."[47] But can this view of God's wrath, that it is an aspect of divine love designed to lead rebellious ones to repentance, be sustantiated in the Pauline epistles?

A Love with Limits

This view of God's wrath possessing reformative elements finds no support in Paul's use of the term *orge* ("wrath"). Although believers will be rescued "from the wrath to come" (1 Thes. 1:10; 5:9; cf. Rom. 5:9), unbelievers will be destroyed by the wrath of God (1 Thes. 5:3, 9). This most serious term used by Paul for wrath (*orge*) "expresses the utter hopelessness of the wicked in the face of an angry God."[48] While those other terms allow for hope, *orge* does not: "[Paul] chooses this term to underscore the fact that in the *eschaton* rebellious sinners have no hope of salvation. They will be taken from the presence of God and the righteous and placed, in effect, beyond the pale of God's love. The righteous go the way of life, the wicked the way of death."[49]

Paul's use of *orge* in regard to unbelievers excludes any notion of divine love. As one scholar states, "When [Paul] speaks of wrath, and especially of eschatological wrath, he never hints that it is a manifestation of God's love leading to improvement or repentance. In fact, divine wrath appears to be the opposite of God's love . . . One looks in vain for a remedial use of *orge*."[50] "Wrath," writes Crockett,

> does not function as part of God's love. Rather, it runs parallel to his love. God still loves those with whom he is angry, and when his grace is met with faith, objects of wrath receive the gift of God: salvation. Those under wrath who have no faith but continue in disobedience eventually find themselves under God's eschatological wrath, which in Paul is always final.[51]

One learns from Paul that those who fall under eschatological wrath are forever cut off from God's love. Eschatological *orge* "is genuine anger devoid of love. In Paul's theology eschatological wrath means that after death God no longer loves the wicked, nor is he prepared to act on behalf of the wicked . . . Rather, he separates the righteous from the wicked. There is no meaningful way to say that God loves the wicked after death."[52]

God's love is shown by His merciful acts in history; His love implies action rather than indefinable feelings divorced from deeds. The point is that God is prepared to act on behalf of the nation or individual whom He loves. It is not too much to say that when one refuses God's act of mercy in Christ, only wrath remains.

Wrath and Mercy

This brief look at God's wrath provides another support for the traditional doctrine that death is final, that the unbeliever (one who dies in his or her sins) is lost, and that God's love is not in competition with His holiness.

We are not seeking to take any tone of spiritual superiority in this study. The biblical fact is that all of us deserve God's wrath and judgment. But grace and mercy are being offered to all those who will listen and respond to the Good News about Christ.

The Bible quite clearly declares that all of humanity falls into only two groups: those who believe in the Son and have everlasting life, and those who do not believe in the Son and stand condemned (John 3:18); those who are children of God by rebirth and will be received into the kingdom of God (John 3:5), and those who are by nature objects of wrath (Eph. 2:3) and children of the devil (John 8:44); those who have passed from death to life (John 5:24), and those who still abide in death (1 John 3:14); those for whom Christ is preparing a place (John 14:3), and those who will go to a place originally prepared for the devil and his angels (Matt. 25:41).

We do not rejoice in God's malevolence or His holy hatred or His righteous wrath, but one day we shall declare "true and just are His judgments" (Rev. 19:2). In the in-between time, we rejoice in His grace, and we are thankful for that awful place called Calvary.

The Adequacy of the Traditional View

Be referring to the adequacy of the traditional view of hell, we are arguing that the biblical picture of the destiny of the wicked is one, not many, and that alternative views do not adequately reflect the scriptural data concerning hell. We are not arguing that the eternal conscious punishment view has been exempt from excessive speculation by its defenders. Even such a revolting concept as the righteous looking on the tormented wicked with approval (which seems antithetical to the heart of a Creator who grieves for His creation), appears to have some measure of biblical support (Isa. 66:22-24). If our God takes no pleasure in the death of the wicked, a truth declared three times in the Book of Ezekiel (18:23, 32; 33:11), then, one must ask, how can we?

A word, however, must be said in defense of preacher-theologians such as Jonathan Edwards, whom the universalist Thomas Talbott refers to as "one of the great apostles of fear."[53] His sermon "Sinners in the Hands of an Angry God" should not bring embarrassment to those who profess to believe the Bible, for he connects his homiletical warnings to biblical images, as we saw in chapter 1. Although at least one psychology text cites Edwards' sermons as an example of sadism, the fact is that he believed in the reality of hell and wanted no one to experience that horror. As R.C. Sproul aptly points out: "A sadist who believed in hell would probably be more likely to give assurances to people that they were in no danger of hell, so he could deliciously relish the contemplation of their falling into it."[54]

Is it ever appropriate to speculate about the nature of the wicked's fate? Perhaps it should be pointed out that speculation in and of itself is not necessarily harmful; it becomes harmful when it deviates from scriptural teaching. If hell is so horrific that Jesus had to use terms which seem mutually exclusive (e.g. "fire" and "darkness") and employed the most graphic hyperbole to warn of its danger, then speculation may not be out of place. We should use any words, expressions, or illustrations which keep people from going there!

Pointing out the weaknesses in the three alternative positions to hell does not in itself prove the truth of the traditional eternal conscious punishment view. That view might also be erroneous. Therefore, we will briefly set out four areas in which the traditional position possesses biblical, as well as rational, support.

The Awful Absence of God

Universalism is clearly refuted by a number of biblical statements. All will not be saved, for Jesus declares that some will be disowned by Him (Matt. 10:33). The wicked will be forever separated from the presence of God (Matt. 7:23; 25:41). Some, alas, will be guilty of an "eternal sin" which "will not be forgiven, either in this age or in the age to come" (Matt. 12:32).

God is not required to save all if He is to save some, nor must He redeem all without exception to be a good and holy God.

Annihilationism posits a genuine judgment for the wicked at the end of time, but one is hard pressed to speak of "separation" from the presence of God when annihilationism teaches that the wicked will cease to be. Language such as being cast "outside" the kingdom (Matt. 8:12) and being sent to the place "prepared for the devil and his angels" (Matt. 25:41) implies a continuing existence apart from the fellowship of Christ.

Postmortem conversionism denies the finality of death (as far as one's spiritual condition is concerned) and is clearly contradicted by such texts as Luke 16:19-31 and Hebrews 9:27. Frederick Buechner, in his book *Open Heart*, recounts the experience of Antonio Parr as he stood at the graveside of his twin sister:

> Some stirring of the air or quick movement of squirrel or bird brought me back to myself. And just at that instant . . . I knew that the self I'd been brought back to was some fine day going to be as dead as Miriam . . . Through grace alone I banged right into it – not a lesson this time, a collision.[55]

Death is a collision, not a door opened to spiritual growth and decision, but one which is slammed in the face of unbelievers who die without Christ and of believers who die postponing serious discipleship. Death climactically cuts short opportunities to serve Christ in this world. For both unbelievers and believers, death is an enemy. If there will be opportunities for conversion after death, why does Jesus so sternly warn about casting one's soul upon Him in this life (e.g., John 6:27, 35, 40, 47-51, 54-58, 63-64; 7:37-38; 8:12, 21, 24, 51)?

C.S. Lewis powerfully responds to those who object to hell:

> In the long run the answer to all those who object to the doctrine of Hell is itself a question: "What are you asking

> God to do?" To wipe out the past sins of the damned and, at all costs, to give them a fresh start, smoothing every difficulty and offering every miraculous help? But He has done so, on Calvary. To forgive them? They will not be forgiven. To leave them alone? Alas, I am afraid that is what He does.[56]

Only a society which considers God optional fails to tremble at the prospect of existing eternally separated from His presence. If God is not central to one's life here, He will not forcibly bestow His presence upon the wicked there.[57]

The Catastrophe of Misguided Choice

"Choosing between heaven and hell is the weightiest human concern on earth, and it is with us every day of our lives", argues Harry Blamires.[58] The three alternative positions which we have evaluated fail to do justice to the importance of believing in Christ, and thereby missing hell.

Universalism insists that all without exception will be brought into Christ's kingdom. Of what value, then, one might ask, is human choice? The same question could, of course, be posed about morality. In the seventeenth and eighteenth centuries, when universalism was growing in popularity, one major objection to that viewpoint was the deep-rooted belief that the threat of eternal punishment was a necessary deterrent from immorality during this life. "So weighty was this objection felt to be," writes one scholar, "that some who believed in universal salvation (or even in annihilation) held that this belief must remain an esoteric, secret doctrine for the few, while hell must continue to be preached as a deterrent for the masses."[59]

But the biblical hell is more than a deceitful deterrent. All human beings make poor choices from time to time; however, the Good News of Christ is that one's temporal belief in Him will have everlasting effects. Conversely, those who ignore, postpone, or ridicule the need of responding to the Gospel are playing religious roulette.

Many of us find that the most difficult response to the Gospel today in North America is not the cynicism of the skeptic, nor the competing claims of the cultist, but the disinterested yawn of the Yuppie. As John Gerstner argues, "The fear of hell is the only thing most likely to get worldly people thinking about the Kingdom of God. No rational human being can be convinced that he is in imminent danger of everlasting torment and do nothing about it!"[60]

The most important choice in life lies before each man and woman every day of their existence. Jesus Christ declared that heaven is indeed real. He taught that hell is equally a real place to which unredeemed sinners go forever. If one waits until death to decide about the Gospel, according to Jesus, it is too late!

There are many voices which ridicule the traditional doctrine of hell, implying either that it is not as bad as once thought or that eternity will provide unlimited opportunities to transfer to heaven. One Catholic theologian, for example, even stated that "hell wasn't very full at all and, if there's anyone there, they are not regretting their lives on earth but are looking with disdain and pity at those poor naive folk who have been duped into heaven." This same theologian continues by saying that hell is a type of three-star motel with no room service and a lumpy bed but, once the patrons see the luxury five-star high rises along the beach, they will see what they're missing and move.[61]

Such rhetoric is dangerous not simply because it encourages continued ridicule of hell's reality, but also because it culminates in spiritual ruin. C.S. Lewis again said it best when he emphasized the cruciality of choice: "There are only two kinds of people in the end: those who say to God, 'Thy will be done,' and those to whom God says, in the end, 'Thy will be done.' All that are in Hell choose it. Without that self-choice there could be no Hell. No soul that seriously and constantly desires joy will ever miss it."[62]

A Truthful Theodicy

A number of years ago Rabbi Harold Kushner wrote his book *When Bad Things Happen to Good People.* Grappling with the problem of evil, Kushner concluded that God cares deeply about man, but is unable to solve the problem of evil. Elie Wiesel critiqued Kushner's book and his god by stating, "If that's who God is, why doesn't he get out of the way and let someone more competent take his place?"

Each of the three alternative positions we've examined attempt to provide a defense (theodicy) of God's goodness and justice in the face of the reality of evil. Universalism argues that all must be saved. Robinson, for example, says that a traditional hell would be "the final mockery of God's nature." Barth's principle of universal election suggests that none can be lost, for God's "Yes" outweighs all human "Nos." Ferré argues on the basis of God's attribute of love, insisting that an occupied hell would be an insult to God.

Annihilationism attempts to provide a superior defense of God, claiming that the new heavens and the new earth cannot contain unredeemed sinners forever. Such would be an eternal "plague spot" and therefore they must be put out of existence. Annihilationism fails to account for the biblical teaching concerning future degrees of punishment (Matt. 11:20-24; Luke 12:42-48; Rom. 2:5-9), as well as for the present existence of evil.

Postmortem conversionism, although wanting to provide an answer to the fate of those who have never heard the Gospel, rests on no scriptural basis and compromises the finality of death as well as the importance of missions. Jesus' repeated challenges to commit oneself to Him in this *life* stand especially in opposition to after-death opportunities for redemption.

Each of these three alternatives compromises the holiness and wrath of God. God could have allowed all of us to go to hell. His being is not dependent on His saving all, many, or even a few. To suggest that God had to provide salvation or that it must extend to all is not only not justified biblically, but turns His grace into debt and His mercy into duty.

Universalism particularly suffers from "a reluctance to believe that some of God's truth might be tragic."[63] The popular Christian song, "In Heaven's Eyes, There Are No Losers," is right when understood to be about believers, but dead wrong when applied to the world of lost humanity! There will, unfortunately, be eternal losers.

Stephen Travis, although himself an annihilationist, is right when he argues that "to underplay [divine judgment] is to diminish human significance and to dismantle the gospel."[64] Packer affirms that the biblical picture of judgment (including the concept of eternal conscious punishment) does not raise moral problems; it solves them! It cannot be said, he writes, that the "Bible writers find a moral problem in catastrophic retribution; instead, they see such retribution as solving the moral problem of evil being allowed to run loose in God's good world, because retribution vindicates God's righteousness as judge of all the earth (see Rev. 19:1-5)."[65]

When setting forth a biblical theodicy, one must be careful to reflect the full teaching of the Scriptures on the nature of God. A former missionary friend, who has since moved away from the traditional doctrine of hell, said to me that "God's *penultimate* word to humanity is *wrath*, but His *ultimate* word is *love*." We would have to disagree. Matthew 25:31-46 records Jesus emphasizing that His final words to humanity will be both: some (the sheep) will hear His "inherit the kingdom"; others (the goats) will hear His "depart from Me . . . into the everlasting fire prepared for the devil and his angels" (NKJV).

Every serious student of the Bible must resist the temptation to read all of Scripture from the standpoint of only one of God's attributes. He is not only love; 1 John 4:16's declaration that "God is love" is not meant to be understood as the Bible's final word on the nature of God. The annihilationist could equally choose Hebrews 12:29 ("Our God is a consuming fire.") as the predominant definition of God's nature. The universalist could select the statement that "God may be all in all," as Paul writes in 1 Corinthians 15:28 (so could the pantheist, for that matter!) The totality of Scripture should be our source for our doctrine of God.

Jesus was Himself confronted with the question of theodicy in Luke 13:1-5. In that text He is informed of the brutal death of some of His countrymen at the hands of Pilate (vv. 1-3). They were executed by the Roman governor while apparently worshiping God, their blood being mingled with their sacrifices in a despicable act of desecration. How does Jesus explain such a vicious crime? He does not attack Pilate or suggest that those who were murdered were terrible sinners or deserved their fate. He simply states "unless you repent, you too will all perish" (v. 3).

The Lord Himself raises a second contemporary example of evil in this passage (vv. 4-5). He asks those around Him: "What about the eighteen men who died when the Tower of Siloam fell on them? Were they the worst sinners in Jerusalem?" [He answers His own question and states,] "Not at all! And you too will perish unless you repent." (vv. 4-5, TLB)

Jesus emphasizes in these five verses that the issue is neither the depravity of Pilate's heart nor the gravity of the tower's fall. The issue, according to Jesus, is the need to repent because life is uncertain! "Any of you," He seems to say, "could be next. You could be the victim of a vicious crime or a violent accident. Make sure you're ready for eternity!"

We certainly need to provide the strongest, biblically based theodicy that we can. A pain-plagued, questioning world needs to hear what the Bible says about the problem of evil. But in the final analysis, the issue is not the existence of evil, but its remedy. Jesus states that evil's remedy is repentance and faith in Him. Only such a theodicy, one which takes seriously the Person of Christ and the penalty of sin, does justice to the biblical picture of God.

A Terrible Counterpart

Theologians have often argued whether hell is to be understood as a *state* or as a *place*. Peter Toon concludes that hell is presented in the Bible as both:

> It is a state in which a person has lost all the blessings that are being heaped upon the righteous; and it is a state wherein a person is cursed, condemned, perishing, under God's wrath, being punished and being destroyed. At the same time it is a place which is distinct from the place of the kingdom of God where the righteous receive their rewards; and it is a place like a prison and an abyss where there is everlasting and unquenchable fire and where the inhabitants weep and gnash their teeth.[66]

Toon argues that heaven and hell are not logical equivalents. "The preaching and teaching of Jesus concerning Gehenna, darkness, and damnation," Toon suggests, "were in the context of his proclamation and exposition of the kingdom of God, salvation, and eternal life; they were never proposed as independent topics for reflection and study."[67] Of course, the same might be said of a variety of other biblical topics, for the truths of the Bible stand together. However, when particular doctrinal beliefs are being denied or redefined, a certain amount of individual attention must be given to them.

Toon goes on to say that "to objectify hell and make it into an independent doctrine, a parallel truth, as it were, to that of heaven, is not encouraged by the way in which hell is presented in the New Testament. However, to say this does not mean that we are not to have any doctrine of hell: To warn people to avoid hell means that hell is a reality, or can be a reality."[68]

He admonishes us not to speculate about the nature of hell beyond declaring that it will be characterized by *poena damni* (the pain of the loss of the beatific vision) and possibly *poena sensus* (the pain of sense). We should be satisfied with the minimum of detail "and recognize that we are speaking figuratively."[69]

One must object at this point, however, and ask whether there is stronger support for *poena damni* or for *poena sensus*. We suggested in our last chapter that Luke 16's picture of Dives is certainly that of *poena sensus* and most probably not that of *poena damni* (i.e. Dives seems to have no regret about his unbelief; he seems only concerned to blame God for insufficient warning). Toon takes the opposite position.

Later Toon emphasizes that no one should treat hell as heaven's logical equivalent, nor attempt to predict how many will go to hell. "It may be many, a few, or none. God alone knows," Toon states.[70] Our question to Toon would simply be: Did Dives go to hell (Luke 16:19-31)? How about Jesus' betrayer? Jesus stated concerning Judas that "it would have been better for that man if he had not been born" (Matt. 26:24, RSV). Did Judas go to hell when he committed suicide? Does Jesus not give us a sufficient basis in texts such as Matthew 25:31-46 to declare that indeed some will go to that awful place? Is hell only a hortatory threat which is never realized by anyone? Moreover, if our understanding of man's spiritual nature is correct, and each person who dies goes immediately either to be with Christ (2 Cor. 5:6-9) or to be separated from Him (Luke 16:19-31), then could we not assume that there are some in hell right now?

One is not surprised that Toon later argues that the effort to determine "whether hell means everlasting punishment or annihilation after judgment may be interesting but is both a waste of time and an attempt to know what we cannot know."[71] Of course, we tried to show in chapter 3 that annihilationism compromises biblical doctrine at several points and is not an equally valid view of the fate of the wicked.

Eternal Contrasts

Because some have tried to "de-substantialize" hell, there is merit in setting forth some of the contrasts between heaven and hell. Lewis is right when he says that "To enter heaven is to become more human than you ever succeeded in being in earth; to enter hell, is to be banished from humanity. What is cast (or casts itself) into hell is not a man: it is 'remains.'"[72] But it is nonetheless a real condition of existence. If it is true that "at [God's] right hand are pleasures forevermore" (Ps. 16:11, NKJV), then what must be the condition of those who are separated from Him forever (Luke 13:27)? Would it not be miseries forevermore? For those who are faithful servants, there will be the master's happiness to share (Matt. 25:21, 23); for those who are unfaithful servants, there will be the "weeping and gnashing of teeth" (Matt. 25:30). Heaven will be a place of no tears, no death, no pain (Rev. 21:4); hell will be a place of only weeping, death, and torment (Matt. 8:12; Luke 16:28). Heaven will be a place of light (Rev. 22:5); hell a place of darkness (Matt. 22:13). Heaven will be a place of companionship (1 Cor. 13:12; John 14:3); hell a place of loneliness (Luke 16:26). Heaven will be a place of varying rewards (Eph. 6:8; 1 Cor. 3:14; Rev. 14:13); hell a place of differing punishments (Rev. 2:23; Rom. 2:5-9; 6:23). Finally, heaven will be where Christ is (John 14:3); hell will be where He is not (Matt. 25:41; Rev. 22:14-15).

Is Hell Really Necessary?

The question might be raised, is hell an ontological necessity? That is, some suggest that hell is a cruel and unusual counterpart to heaven. Could God have equally *not* created hell? No biblical text tells us that God had to bring hell into being. Hell is certainly not eternal (i.e. without beginning). In fact, when someone asks the Christian if he believes hell is everlasting, the correct answer probably should be "No, but the lake of fire is everlasting, and hell will be cast into it" (Rev. 20:14).

Jesus declares that the "goats" will be sent into the "eternal fire prepared for the devil and his angels." (Matt. 25:41) We can only assume that for God to be true to His holiness, the preparation of hell for the demonic powers was necessary, not in order that God would conform to some principle outside Himself, but that He would be true to who He is. Revelation 20:7-15 makes it clear that all whose names are not found in the Book of Life are thrown into the lake of fire, the same location to which the devil, the beast, and the false prophet are cast (cf. 20:15, 10).

One theologian said that he would not want to be in heaven with a God who sends people to hell. His preference was to be in hell so that he could live in defiance of such a God. "If such a God exists," he complained, "He is the devil."[73] If God could have omitted hell, creating some less horrendous destiny for the wicked in its place, then hell's existence suggests an unnecessarily and arbitrarily cruel Creator. It appears, however, that to be true to His own holiness, hell was (and is) necessary. He weeps as sinners perish and go there, but He has done all that He can to keep them from that place, short of forcing them into heaven. And that He will not do.

A Nonnegotiable Doctrine

G.K. Chesterton once commented: "Why shouldn't we quarrel about a word? What is the good of words if they aren't important enough to quarrel over?" Our primary intent in this book has not been to quarrel about words, but to ask if the Bible presents a clear, single doctrine of the fate of the wicked.

Such an effort to examine and set forth the biblical material about hell and its nature is understandably resisted. Stephen Travis, for example, argues that "there is little point in asking whether the lost continue to be conscious or are annihilated. It is because later Christians have been more concerned about happiness and misery than about relationship to God that they have persisted in asking such questions."[74]

Theological Unoriginality

But if the Bible has provided sufficient information about the fate of the wicked, we must seek to understand that material, resisting efforts to water down or adapt it to a modern mindset. One suspects that there is an enormous pressure to capitulate to modernism's (or postmodernism's) mindset or to conform or tone down certain unattractive beliefs in Christianity.

Thomas Oden, a former liberal theologian who has returned to what he calls "paleo-orthodoxy," told the Evangelical Theological Society: "I have been passionately dedicated to unoriginality . . . I am doggedly pledged to irrelevance insofar as relevance implies a corrupt indebtedness to modernity. What is deemed most relevant in theology is often moldy in a few days." He then related to us a dream which he had. In his dream he saw his own tombstone on which was the epitaph: "T. Oden. He made no new contribution to theology." Oden says that he then awoke, *relieved*! How scary it would be for some modern evangelicals to wake up, a cold perspiration on their foreheads, and realize that by their denial of the doctrine of hell, they had made not a new contribution to theology, but a subtraction from biblical truth.

Evangelical ***In****essentials*

Clark H. Pinnock, in surveying the differences between theological "Progressives," "Moderates," and "Conservatives," makes a distinction between Christianity's essential and nonessential doctrines. He rightly insists on clarity about the essentials of the Christian faith, and then suggests that "a diversity of interpretation is also possible" on the less-than-essentials. What are some of those "less-than-essentials"? Pinnock lists several questions such as "Is it ever right to call God mother? Does God know all future contingencies? Is hell a place of neverending torment?"[75]

Describing himself as one who wishes "to help reform evangelical thinking,"[76] Pinnock approvingly lists what he considers "changes in the boundaries of [the evangelicals'] faith." A few of these are:

> There is more openness to the humanity of the Bible and to critical methods of explaining it. Simultaneously, there is greater flexibility about the meaning of biblical inerrancy and more hesitation about the usefulness of the term itself.
>
> Evangelicals are now prepared to talk about diversity in the biblical teaching and, consequently, the legitimacy of theological pluralism in their own ranks.
>
> There is an open discussion about the nature of the deity and the possible need to place more emphasis on the openness of God to the temporal process.
>
> Concerning Creation as an event, there is a greater willingness to go beyond fundamentalism and recover the nineteenth-century evangelical model that accepted

evolution as a complementary language for talking about origins.

Regarding salvation, there is a move away from double predestination and a growing tendency to allow for the possibility of the salvation of the unevangelized on the basis of their response to the light they have or to a postmortem encounter. *Some are reconceptualizing hell in terms of fire that consumes rather than fire that torments.*[77]

Bargaining Away the Bad News

We would all agree with Pinnock's challenge that "a missionary theology . . . would insist on being faithful to the gospel and never agree to bargain that away for any reason."[78] But if the Gospel is not just good news, but also very bad news for those who reject Christ, could it not be said that those who bargain away the bad news of the good news have become unfaithful to the Gospel? To be an evangelical means that one is committed to the *euangelion* (Good News). If one denies the good news of the Gospel (for example, saying that good works will bring salvation), he would not be considered an evangelical. However, if the bad news of the good news has also been clearly spelled out in the Scriptures, the denial of that bad news would equally disqualify an individual from the descriptive term "evangelical."

Hell and the Atonement

Leon Morris has well said, "The atonement is the crucial doctrine of the faith. Unless we are right here, it matters little, or so it seems to me, what we are like elsewhere." Evangelical Christianity teaches that the Son of God, the Second Person of the Trinity, the One who knew no sin, became "sin for us" (2 Cor. 5:21). The holy God who is allergic to sin punished Christ in our place.

The Cross is God's infinite response to man's sin. Christ exhausts the punishment due to sinners because He Himself was the infinite and eternal God. Christ did not die for our potential nonexistence, but for our eternal bearing of the wrath of God in a place separated from Him.

One theologian accurately remarks that "A gospel . . . that trades on a diminished view of sin, a modified notion of divine righteousness, and a restructured Atonement is not one that is more appealing . . . but one that is less. It is a gospel that has lost its nerve because it has lost its majesty."[79]

Rather than holding that Christ "descended into Hades" during the three days between His death and resurrection (a view shown in chapter 4 to lack scriptural foundation), the Bible indicates that He was in "Paradise" (Luke 23:43). One of my theology students asked, "Didn't Jesus *have* to go to hell in order to bear our judgment there?" The question is a good one. The cross was the venue where the judgment was borne by the Lamb of God. Jesus' work of atonement was finished on the cross as He Himself declared (John 19:30).

We realize that the atoning work of Christ by which He turned away the wrath of God is to be understood in more than a quantitative fashion. But is there no quantitative dimension to His becoming sin for us? It seems to be consistent with New Testament teaching to say that Christ bore our hell on the cross.

One's view of Christ's work on the Cross is directly related to what one believes will happen both to those who receive that work and to those who reject that work. For the one who believes, everlasting blessedness is promised in the presence of the Savior. For the one who does not believe, only "eternal punishment" awaits that person (Matt. 25:46).

Erosion and the Need to Warn

Who can doubt that there has been and continues to develop an evangelical erosion over the fate of the wicked? To change the metaphor, an editing has taken place. Edith Schaeffer clearly writes:

> The powerful voice of God warns of judgment, and the same voice expresses His compassion for those who come back to Him in His given way. We are to listen with the same intensity of awe we feel when we observe the power

> of water. His spoken truth is not for us to judge or edit; we are to listen, absorb, understand, and bow.[80]

We would add to Edith Schaeffer's last line these words: " . . . and warn!" The world needs to be warned of judgment. Donald Bloesch, himself holding to a less than orthodox view of hell, nevertheless pointedly argues that "We are not called to be the honey of the world but the salt of the earth. Salt stings on an open wound, but it also saves one from gangrene."

Theologian A.A. Hodges once stated: "A man who realizes in any measure the awful force of the words 'eternal hell' won't shut up about it, but will speak with all tenderness."

George Buttrick once stated that "People are driven from the Church not so much by stern truth that makes them uneasy as by weak nothings that make them contemptuous." We would hasten to add that we need to recover the stern truth of hell and carefully include it in our Gospel witness. We must listen to the challenge of D. Martin Lloyd-Jones when he said concerning the church: "This is no age to advocate restraint — The church today does not need to be restrained, but to be aroused, to be awakened, to be filled with the Spirit of glory for she is failing in the modern world."

Of course we Christians would prefer not to speak of hell. Who longs to discuss the most confrontational doctrine imaginable? But Jesus spoke about it, and the servant is not greater than his Master. Peter Cartwright, an early American Methodist pioneer preacher, illustrates this point. Whenever he approached a new town on his preaching circuit, we are told, he would often stand on a hill above the town and those with him would hear him say, "*I smell hell!*" "Such an expression!" comments one writer. "I'm afraid we would stand on the same hill and talk about the beautiful flowers and trees that God has made."[81]

Evangelist Billy Sunday used to say, "If there were more hell preached in our churches, there'd be less hell practiced in our streets!" When was the last time you heard a sermon on hell? One writer rightly emphasizes that "no minister is prepared to preach upon the subject of hell until his soul has been gripped by the poignant fear that some of his audience may make their bed there."[82] A recent book on the Old Testament is entitled: *Loving God and Disturbing Men: Preaching from the Prophets.* That's what we Christians are to do: we are to love God and to disturb people! Some unbelievers need to hear the Gospel from the perspective of the love of God; others need to be told of the wrath of God. If the biblical doctrine of hell (in all its awesomeness as Jesus taught it) won't disturb the second group, nothing will.

Followers of Christ must be prepared to be ridiculed when they refer to God's wrath. We dare not be indifferent to the doctrine of hell; the stakes are too high. "We must remember that indifference," writes William Barclay in another connection, " . . . is a sin, and the worst of all sins, for indifference kills. Indifference does not burn a religion to death; it freezes it to death. It does not behead it; it slowly suffocates the life out of it."[83]

There is indeed an Other Side of the Good News, and it is being ignored, compromised, and redefined. There's an old story about a man who tried to save Sodom from destruction. The city's inhabitants ignored him and asked mockingly: "Why bother everyone? You can't change them." "Maybe I can't change them," the man replied, "but if I still shout and scream, it's to prevent them from changing me!"[84]

The most severe penalty awaits those who reject Christ. "God had to die and suffer the horrors of hell to save us from that dark side," writes Peter Kreeft. We who know Jesus Christ must proclaim both the good and the bad news of the Gospel. Although not writing specifically on the doctrine of hell, Henri Nouwen's challenge to the church deserves to be heeded by all who wish to be faithful to Christ:

> The basic question is whether we ministers of Jesus Christ have not already been so deeply molded by the seductive power of our dark world that we have become blind to our own and other people's fatal state and have lost our power and motivation to swim for our lives.[85]

End Notes

Introduction

1. Clark H. Pinnock, "The Destruction of the Finally Impenitent," *Criswell Theological Review* (Spring 1990), p. 246-47.
2. Pope John Paul II, "General Audience," Wednesday, July 28, 1999, released by the Vatican news Service.
3. "Hell Hath . . . No Fury," *The State* newspaper, July 12, 2002.
4. Chris Stamper, "Authors by the Dozen," *World* magazine, July/August, 2002, p. 53.
5. "Hell Hath . . . No Fury," *The State* newspaper, July 12, 2002.
6. Ibid.
7. James Davison Hunter, *Evangelicalism: The Coming Generation* (Chicago: Univ. of Chicago Pr., 1987), p. 38.
8. Ibid., pp. 38-40.
9. Ibid., p. 183.
10. "Hell's Sober Comeback," *U.S. News & World Report*, 25 March 1991, p. 56.
11. Kenneth S. Kantzer, "Fiddling on the Brink of Hell," *Christianity Today*, 27 May 1991, p. 13.
12. Lance Morrow, "Evil," *Time*, 10 June 1991, p. 49.
13. Frank E. Gaebelein, "The Bible: Both the Source and Setting for Learning," *Christianity Today*, 6 February 1981, p. 23.
14. Frederick Buechner, *A Room Called Remember: Uncollected Pieces* (New York: Harper and Row, 1984), pp. 47-48.

Chapter 1

1. John Bowker, "The Human Imagination of Hell," *Theology* 85 (November 1982), p. 406.
2. Kenneth W. Woodward, "Heaven," *Newsweek*, 27 March 1989, p. 64.

3. Robert H. Schuller, *My Journey* (San Francisco: HarperCollins Publishers, 2001), pp. 127-128.
4. John Thomas, "That Hideous Doctrine," *Moody* magazine, September 1985, p. 91.
5. "The Apocalypse of Peter," in *New Testament Apocrypha*, ed. Edge Hennecke, vol. 3 (Philadelphia: Westminster Press, pp. 672-73).
6. "The Apocalypse of Paul," in *New Testament Apocrypha*, Hennecke, pp. 779-86.
7. Bowker, "Human Imagination of Hell," p. 403.
8. Ibid., p. 405.
9. The quoted material in the following paragraphs is taken from *Select Works of Jonathan Edwards* (London: Banner of Truth Trust, 1959), vol. 2, Sermons, pp. 183-99. See also the article by Bruce W. Davidson, "Reasonable Damnation: How Jonathan Edwards Argued for the Rationality of Hell," *Journal of the Evangelical Theological Society* 38 (March 1995), p. 45.
10. See the article "Hell is not funny," *Current Thoughts & Trends*, July 2002, p. 11. A review of "Speaking Soberly and Sensitively about Hell," by Ligon Duncan, III, in *Modern Reformation*, May/June 2002, Vol. 11, No. 3, pp. 21-24.
11. Quoted in Harry Buis, *The Doctrine of Eternal Punishment* (Philadelphia: Presbyterian and Reformed, 1957), p. 128.
12. Ibid., p. 2.
13. Bishop Newton quoted in Samuel C. Bartlett, *Life and Death Eternal: A Refutation of the Theory of Annihilation* (Boston: American Tract Society, 1866), p. 129.
14. Quoted in Harold B. Kuhn, "Universalism: Pro and Con," *Christianity Today*, 1 March 1963, p. 24.
15. Burnham quoted in Bartlett, *Eternal Punishment*, p. 128.
16. Leadbeater quoted in Buis, *Eternal Punishment*, p. 128.
17. Stanley Haverwas, "On the Production and Reproduction of the Saints," *Reformed Journal* 40 (February 1990), p. 13.
18. Clark H. Pinnock, "The Destruction of the Finally Impenitent," *Criswell Theological Review* 4 (Spring 1990), p. 245.

19. John Thomas, "That Hideous Doctrine," *Moody* magazine, September 1985, p. 91.
20. Charles Colson, *Who Speaks for God?* (Westchester, Ill.: Crossway, 1985), p. 11.
21. H. Richard Niebuhr, *The Kingdom of God in America* (Hamden, Conn: Shoe String Press, 1956), p. 193.

Chapter 2

1. G.C. Berkouwer, "Universalism," *Christianity Today*, 13 May 1957, p. 5.
2. *Seventh-Day Adventists Believe* . . . (Washington, D.C.: Ministerial Association, 1988), pp. 372-73.
3. G.C. Berkouwer, "Universalism," p. 5. For a scholarly treatment of universalism from an Evangelical perspective, see Alan W. Gomes' *Unitarian Universalism* (Grand Rapids: Zondervan, 1998).
4. Clement of Alexandria, "The Stromata, or Miscellanies," vol. 2, bk. 7 in *The Ante Nicene Fathers*, ed. Alexander Roberts and James Donaldson (Grand Rapids: Eerdmans, 1977), pp. 524-25.
5. Quasten quoted in Harry Friesen, "A Critical Analysis of Universalism" (Th.D. diss. Dallas Theological Seminary, 1968), p. 42.
6. Justinian, *Anathematisms against Origen* quoted in Friesen, "Critical Analysis," p. 81.
7. Robert Schnucker, "Origen," in *The New International Dictionary of the Christian Church*, ed. J.D. Douglas (Grand Rapids: Zondervan, 1974), p. 733.
8. Reimensynder quoted in Friesen, "Critical Analysis," p. 44.
9. Plumptre quoted in Friesen, "Critical Analysis," p. 54.
10. "Origen against Celsus," bk. 4, Chap. 8, in *The Ante Nicene Fathers*, vol. 4, p. 502.
11. Reimensynder quoted in Friesen, "Critical Analysis," pp. 48- 49.
12. "Origen De Principiis," bk. 2, chap. 10, in *The Ante Nicene Fathers*, vol. 4, p. 295.

13. Friesen, "A Critical Analysis," p.52. Talbott writes: "All that sinners fear most about God — the wrath and the fearsome punishment associated with his righteous ordinances — was never anything more than a schoolmaster to bring us to Christ and thus to save us from ourselves." (Thomas Talbott, *The Inescapable Love of God* (USA: Universal Publishers, 1999), p. 102).
14. Ibid., p. 68.
15. "Origen De Principiis," bk. 1, chap. 6, 1, in *The Ante Nicene Fathers*, vol. 4, p. 260.
16. Friesen, "Critical Analysis," p. 53.
17. Fisher quoted in Friesen, "Critical Analysis," p. 53.
18. Friesen, "Critical Analysis," p. 52.
19. Rosamond Kent Sprague, ed., *A Matter of Eternity: Selections from the Writings of Dorothy L. Sayers* (Grand Rapids: Eerdmans, 1973), pp. 84-85.
20. Ibid., p. 85.
21. Donald K. McKim, ed., *How Karl Barth Changed My Mind* (Grand Rapids: Eerdmans, 1986), p. ix.
22. Ibid.
23. G.C. Berkouwer, *The Triumph of Grace in the Theology of Karl Barth* (London: Paternoster Press, 1956), p. 265.
24. Gordon R. Lewis and Bruce A. Demarest, *Integrative Theology* vol. 1 (Grand Rapids: Zondervan, 1987), p. 297.
25. Harold B. Kuhn, "Universalism in Today's Theology," *Christianity Today*, 16 September 1957, p. 9.
26. Karl Barth, *Church Dogmatics* (Edinburgh: T. and T. Clark, 1957), vol. 2, part 2, p. 167.
27. Lewis and Demarest, *Integrative Theology*, p. 297.
28. Barth, *Church Dogmatics*, vol. 4, part 1, p. 35.
29. Ibid., p. 57.
30. Ibid., p. 39.
31. Ibid., p. 57.
32. Ibid., p. 66.
33. Ibid., pp. 99-100. In another place Barth writes: "In his own death [Jesus Christ] makes their peace with God — before they themselves have decided for that peace and quite apart

from that decision." (Karl Barth, *Christ and Adam: Man and Humanity in Romans 5*, trans. T.A. Smail (New York: MacMillan, 196), p. 23).
34. Ibid., p. 100.
35. Ibid., p. 11.
36. Barth, *Church Dogmatics*, vol. 2, part 2, p. 57.
37. Ibid., p. 14.
38. Barth quoted in Berkouwer, *The Triumph of Grace*, p. 138.
39. Ibid., p. 362.
40. McKim, *Barth Changed My Mind*, p. 128.
41. Ibid.
42. Ibid.
43. Berkouwer, *The Triumph of Grace*, pp. 138-39.
44. Barth, *Church Dogmatics*, vol. 2, part 2, p. 348.
45. Brunner quoted in Berkouwer, *The Triumph of Grace*, p. 264.
46. Barth, *Church Dogmatics*, vol. 4, part 1, pp. 88-89.
47. Brunner quoted in Berkouwer, *The Triumph of Grace*, p. 264.
48. Ibid., pp. 264-65.
49. Berkouwer, *The Triumph of Grace*, p. 265.
50. Barth, *Church Dogmatics*, vol. 4, part 1, p. 90.
51. Ibid., p.81.
52. Barth, *Church Dogmatics*, vol. 3, part 2, p. 145.
53. Barth, *Church Dogmatics*, vol. 4, part 1, p. 53.
54. Ibid., p. 295.
55. Ibid., p. 43.
56. Berkouwer, *The Triumph of Grace*, p. 265.
57. Barth, *Church Dogmatics*, vol. 4, part 1, p. 104.
58. Ibid., p. 89.
59. Ibid., p. 91.
60. Ibid., p. 77.
61. Ibid., p. 100.
62. Ibid., p. 93.
63. Ibid., pp. 87-88.
64. Ibid., p. 107.
65. Ibid., p. 105.

66. Berkouwer, *The Triumph of Grace*, pp. 292-93.
67. Karl Barth, *The Faith of the Church* (New York: Meridian Bks., 1958), p. 173.
68. Ibid., p. 95.
69. Barth, *Church Dogmatics*, vol. 4, part 3, pp. 477-78. See also Ajith Fernando's discussion of Barth's universalism in his *Crucial Questions about Hell* (Wheaton: Crossway Books, 1991), pp. 121-122.
70. McKim, *Barth Changed My Mind*, p. 130.
71. Ibid., pp. 13-14.
72. Bernard Ramm, *After Fundamentalism: The Future of Evangelical Theology* (San Francisco: Harper & Row, 1983), p. 201.
73. Millard J. Erickson, *Christian Theology* (Grand Rapids: Baker 1983), p. 1017, emphasis mine.
74. C.H. Dodd, *New Testament Studies* (Manchester, England: Manchester University Press, 1953), p. 119.
75. Ibid., p. 123.
76. C.H. Dodd, *The Epistle of Paul to the Romans* (London: Hodder and Stoughton, 1932), p. 183.
77. Ibid., p. 184.
78. Ibid.
79. Ibid., p. 185.
80. C.H. Dodd, *The Authority of the Bible* (London: Nisbet, 1928), p. 207.
81. C.H. Dodd, *The Bible Today* (Cambridge, England: Cambridge University Press, 1960), p. 118.
82. Ibid., p. 119.
83. Dodd, *Authority of the Bible*, p. 208.
84. Dodd, *New Testament*, pp. 125-26.
85. Ibid., pp. 127-28. The German New Testament scholar Ethelbert Stauffer concurs, arguing that in his later epistles Paul came to believe that there will be a "universal homecoming" when all will be saved." (*New Testament Theology*, trans. John Marsh [London: SCM Press, 1955], pp. 222-231).
86. Ibid., p. 128.
87. Dodd, *Epistle to the Romans*, p. 186.

88. Dodd, *Authority of the Bible*, p. 117.
89. Ibid., p. 176.
90. Dodd, *New Testament*, p. 127.
91. John A.T. Robinson, *In the End, God* (London: James Clarke, 1950), p. 102.
92. Ibid., pp. 102-03.
93. Ibid., p. 38.
94. Ibid., p. 31.
95. Ibid., pp. 34-35.
96. John A.T. Robinson, "Universalism: Is It Heretical?" *Scottish Journal of Theology*, 2 (June 1949): pp. 143-44.
97. T.F.Torrance quoted in Friesen, "Critical Analysis," p. 104.
98. Nels F.S. Ferré, *Christ and the Christian* (New York: Harper and Brothers, 1958), pp. 63-64.
99. Ibid., p. 53.
100. DeHass quoted in Friesen, "Critical Analysis," pp. 104-5.
101. Nels F.S. Ferré, *The Sun and the Umbrella* (New York: Harper and Brothers, 1953), p. 79.
102. Nels F.S. Ferré, *The Christian Understanding of God* (London: SCM Press, 1951), p. 237.
103. Ibid., p. 228.
104. Ferré, *Christ and the Christian*, p. 247.
105. Nels F.S. Ferré, *Evil and the Christian Faith* (New York: Harper & Brothers, 1947), p. 118.
106. Ibid., pp. 118-19.
107. Ferré, *Christ and the Christian*, p. 248.
108. Ibid., p. 249.
109. Ferré, *Evil and the Christian*, p. 120.
110. Ferré, *Christ and the Christian*, p. 246.
111. Ibid., p. 245.
112. Ibid.
113. Ferré, *Understanding of God*, p. 241.
114. Ibid., p. 230.
115. Ibid., p. 234.
116. Ibid., p. 237.
117. Ibid.
118. Ibid.

119. Strong quoted in Friesen, "Critical Analysis," pp. 63-64.
120. William Barclay, *The Letters to Timothy, Titus, and Philemon* (Edinburgh: St. Andrew Pr., 1960), p. 195.
121. Ferré, *Understanding of God*, p. 240.
122. Ferré, *Evil and the Christian*, p. 8.
123. Ransom quoted in Friesen, "Critical Analysis," p. 158.
124. Ferré, *Understanding of God*, p. 247.
125. Ibid., p. 179.
126. Ferré, *The Sun*, p. 43.
127. Ibid., p. 47.
128. Ibid., p. 50.
129. Ibid., p. 59.
130. Ibid., p. 60.
131. Nels F.S. Ferré, *Know Your Faith* (New York: Harper and Brothers, 1959), p. 23.
132. Lewis Carroll, "Eternal Punishment," in *The Lewis Carroll Picture Book*, ed. Stuart Dodgson Collingwood (London: T. Fisher Unwon, 1899), pp. 345-355, quoted in the forth-coming *Hell Under Fire*, editors: Chris Morgan and Robert Peterson, Grand Rapids: Zondervan, 2002).
133. Nels F.S. Ferré, *Know Your Faith*, p. 23.
134. Friesen, "Critical Analysis," p. 108.
135. Ferré, *Understanding of God*, p. 179.
136. Friesen, "Critical Analysis," p. 109.
137. Ferré, *Evil and the Christian*, p. 118.
138. Ibid.
139. Friesen, "Critical Analysis," p. 119.
140. Ferré, *Understanding of God*, p. 234.
141. Ibid., p. 234.
142. Ibid., p. 236.
143. Ferré, *Understanding of God*, p. 236.
144. See, for example, Ferré, *Christ and the Christian*, p. 50.
145. Ferré, *Understanding of God*, p. 242.
146. Ibid., p. 243.
147. Ibid.
148. Ibid., p. 245.
149. Ibid., p. 246.

150. Ibid., pp. 245-46.
151. Ibid., p. 246.
152. Ibid., p. 233.
153. Ferré, *Evil and the Christian*, p. 117.
154. Ibid., p. 119.
155. Thomas Talbott, *The Inescapable Love of God* (USA: Universal Publishers, 1999).
156. Ibid., p. 12.
157. Ibid., p. 117.
158. Ibid., p. 37.
159. Ibid., p. 77.
160. Ibid., p. 84
161. Talbott, quoted by Craig in http://www.leaderu.com/offices/billcraig/docs/talbott1.html)
162. Thomas Talbott, *The Inescapable Love of God*, p. 86
163. Ibid., p. 107
164. Other arguments which Talbott makes, for example that the term "punishment" refers only to remedial, not retributive, punishment, should be challenged. He cites the well-respected commentator William Barclay to support his contention but fails to mention that Barclay was himself committed to universalism and that the term "punishment" does sometimes carry the sense of divine retribution and revenge (see William Lane Craig's articles in http://www.leaderu.com/offices/billcraig/docs/talbott1.html.
165. George MacDonald, Unspoken Sermons (Sunrise Centenary Editions of the Works of George MacDonald, 1996.
166. George MacDonald, *Getting to Know Jesus* (New Canaan, Conn.: Shepherd Illustrated Classics, 1980), p. 93.
167. Ibid., p. 126.
168. Ibid., p. 130.
169. Ibid., p. 169.
170. Thomas Talbott, *The Inescapable Love of God*, p. 37.
171. George MacDonald, *Getting to Know Jesus*, p. 57.
172. Ibid., pp. 65-66.
173. Ibid., p. 87.
174. New York: Seabury Press, 1977, p. 97.

175. D.A.Carson, *The Gagging of God: Christianity Confronts Pluralism* (Grand Rapids: Zondervan, 1996), p. 527n. See also the book by Jan Bonda, *The One Purpose of God: An Answer to the Doctrine of Eternal Punishment* (Grand Rapids: Eerdmans, 1998).
176. Barth, *Church Dogmatics*, Ibid., p. 732.
177. Ibid., p. 731.
178. Charles quoted in Maurice Jones, *The Epistle to the Philippians* (London: Methuen and Co., 1918), p. 35.
179. J.B. Lightfoot, *St. Paul's Epistle to the Philippians* (reprint, Grand Rapids: Zondervan, 1953), p. 115.
180. Gerald F. Hawthorne, *Word Biblical Commentary: Philippians* (Waco, Texas: Word Inc., 1983), p. 94.
181. Barth, *Church Dogmatics*, vol. 4, part 1, p. 74.
182. Nels F.S. Ferré, *God's New Age* (New York: Harper & Brothers, 1956), p. 66.
183. Thomas Oden, *Life in the Spirit*, "Systematic Theology," vol. 3 (San Francisco: Harper and Row, 1992), p. 450.
184. Erickson, *Christian Theology* (Grand Rapids: Baker, 1983), p. 1020.
185. Lewis and Demarest, *Integrative Theology*, vol. 2, p. 391.
186. Ibid., p. 407.
187. W.H. Griffith Thomas, *Studies in Colossians and Philemon* (Grand Rapids: Baker, 1973), p. 55.
188. Curtis Baughan, *Bible Study Commentary: Colossians and Philemon* (Grand Rapids: Zondervan, 1973), pp. 46-47.
189. Ramm, *After Fundamentalism*, p. 171.
190. Ibid., p. 172.
191. Barth quoted in Berkouwer, *The Triumph of Grace*, p. 138.
192. H.R. Mackintosh, *Immortality and the Future: The Christian Doctrine of Eternal Life* (New York: George H. Doran, 1917), p. 207.
193. James I. Packer, "'Good Pagans' and God's Kingdom," *Christianity Today*, 17 January 1986, p. 25.
194. J.H. Bernard, *The Pastoral Epistles* (reprint, Grand Rapids: Baker, 1980), p. 41.
195. Lewis and Demarest, *Integrative Theology*, vol. 1, p. 308.

196. Berkouwer, "Universalism," p. 6.
197. Martin Moynihan, ed., *The Latin Letters of C.S. Lewis* (Wheaton, Ill.: Crossway, 1987).
198. Kuhn, "Universalism in Today's Theology," p. 9.
199. Berkouwer, "Universalism," p. 5.
200. Ibid., p. 6.
201. Kuhn, "Universalism in Today's Theology," p. 11.

Chapter 3

1. *The Mystery of Salvation, The Story of God's Gift: A Report by the Doctrine Commission of the General Synod of the Church of England* (London: Church House Publishing, 1995) p. 180. Quoted in Morgan and Peterson, *Hell Under Fire* (Grand Rapids: Zondervan, 2002).
2. *The Nature of Hell: A Report by the Evangelical Alliance Commission on Unity and Truth Among Evangelicals* (London: ACUTE, 2000), p. 128. Quoted in *Hell Under Fire.*
3. Clark H. Pinnock, "The Destruction of the Finally Impenitent," *Criswell Theological Review*, 4.2 (1990), pp. 253-54.
4. Houston: Providential Press, 1982.
5. Downers Grove: InterVarsity, 2000.
6. Ibid., p. 106.
7. Philip Edgcumbe Hughes, *The True Image* (Grand Rapids: Eerdmans, 1989); John Wenham, *The Goodness of God* (Downers Grove, Ill.: InterVarsity Press, 1974); Stephen Travis, *I Believe in the Second Coming of Jesus* (Grand Rapids: Eerdmans, 1982); John R.W Stott and David L. Edwards, *Evangelical Essentials* (London: Hodder and Stoughton, 1988); Clark H. Pinnock, "Fire, Then Nothing," *Christianity Today*, 20 March 1987, pp. 40-41; Clark H. Pinnock and Delwin Brown, *Theological Crossfire: An Evangelical/Liberal Dialogue* (Grand Rapids: Zondervan, 1990), pp. 224-34, 246-49; Pinnock, "The Finally Impenitent," pp. 243-59. In 1991, Wenham defined conditional immortality as the belief "that God created Man only potentially immortal. Immortality is a state gained by grace through faith when the believer receives eternal life and

becomes a partaker of the divine nature, immortality being inherent in God alone." (John Wenham, *Facing Hell: An Autobiography* [London: Paternoster Press, 1998], p. 230. Quoted in Morgan and Peterson, *Hell Under Fire.*)

8. John R. W. Stott, *Culture and the Bible* (Downers Grove, Ill.: InterVarsity Pr., 1979), pp. 33-34.

9. London: Hodder and Stoughton, 1988.

10. Stott and Edwards, *Evangelical Essentials*, pp. 319-20.

11. Ibid., p. 315.

12. Delwin Brown, "Rethinking Authority from the Right: A Critical Review of Clark Pinnock's Scripture Principle," *Christian Scholar's Review* (19 September, 1989) p. 78.

13. Pinnock, "Fire, Then Nothing," p. 41.

14. Ibid., p. 40.

15. Ibid. Pinnock says he is now drawn to a new orientation which sees God as love, away from the view of God as authoritarian and austere Judge. He focuses on love as God's reigning attribute. One wonders what keeps him from moving into full-blown universalism? He states in his *A Wideness in God's Mercy*: "The idea that hell means everlasting conscious punishment contributes much to belief in universal salvation. If the choice is between hell as everlasting torture and universal salvation, who could resist the latter? Sensitive persons would be practically forced to accept it, since they cannot accept that God would subject anyone, even most corrupt sinners, to unending torture in both body and soul as Augustine and Jonathan Edwards taught. If that is what hell means, many will conclude that there should not be a doctrine of hell in Christian theology." (Clark Pinnock, *A Wideness in God's Mercy: The Finality of Jesus Christ in a World of Religions* [Grand Rapids: Zondervan, 1992], p. 157. Quoted in *Hell Under Fire.*)

16. Pinnock and Brown, *Theological Crossfire.*

17. Ibid., p. 220.

18. Ibid., p. 224.

19. Ibid., p. 226.

20. Ibid.

21. Ibid., p. 227.

22. Ibid., p. 229.
23. Ibid., p. 233.
24. Ibid.
25. Ibid., p. 247.
26. Stott and Edwards, *Evangelical Essentials*, p. 315.
27. Pinnock, "The Finally Impenitent," p. 252.
28. Pinnock and Brown, *Theological Crossfire*, pp. 226, 230.
29. Pinnock, "The Finally Impenitent," p. 252.
30. John Calvin, *Institutes of the Christian Religion,* ed. John T. McNeill, (Philadelphia: Westminster Pr., 1977) Bk. 3, chap. 25, 6, cf. bk. 1, chap. 15, p. 6.
31. William Temple quoted in *Seventh-Day Adventists Believe* (Washington, D.C.: Ministerial Association, 1988), pp. 371-72.
32. Alan W. Gomes, "Evangelicals and the Annihilation of Hell, Part One," *Christian Research Journal* (Spring 1991): p. 17.
33. Ibid.
34. Murray J. Harris, "The New Testament View of Life after Death," *Themelios* 11 (Jan. 1986): p. 47.
35. Murray J. Harris, *From Grave to Glory: Resurrection in the New Testament* (Grand Rapids: Zondervan, 1990), pp. 268-69.
36. Ibid., 331, note 15.
37. Ibid., p. 244.
38. Berkhof, *Systematic Theology* (Grand Rapids: Eerdmans, 1939), p. 691.
39. "Whistling Past the Graveyard" by Marvin Olasky, *World* magazine, July/August, 2002.
40. Robert L. Reymond, "Dr. John Stott on Hell," *Presbyterion*, 16 (Spring 1990): p. 50.
41. Stott and Edwards, *Evangelical Essentials*, p. 316.
42. Alan W. , "Evangelicals and the Annihilation of Hell", Part Two, *Christian Research Journal* (Summer 1991): p. 10.
43. Stott and Edwards, *Evangelical Essentials*, p. 315.
44. Reymond, "Stott on Hell," p. 53.
45. William F. Arndt and F. Wilbur Gingrich, *A Greek English Lexicon of the New Testament and Other Early Christian Literature* (Chicago: University of Chicago Press, 1957), *phtheiro*, p. 865.

46. Hodge quoted in Gomes, "Evangelicals and Hell, Part Two," p. 10.
47. Reymond, "Stott on Hell," p. 53.
48. Stott and Edwards, *Evangelical Essentials*, p. 316.
49. Ibid.
50. Reymond, "Stott on Hell," p. 46. See also the article "Unquenchable Fire" in *Encounter* magazine, Spring 1992.
51. Gomes, "Evangelicals and Hell, Part Two," p. 11.
52. Ibid.
53. Reymond, "Stott on Hell," p. 57.
54. C.S. Lewis, *The Problem of Pain* (New York: Macmillan, 1962), p. 125.
55. Pinnock, "The Finally Impenitent," pp. 246-47.
56. Ibid., p. 255. The Socinians had a similar objection.
57. Reymond, "Stott on Hell," p. 57.
58. Gomes, "Evangelicals and Hell, Part Two," p. 9.
59. Ibid.
60. Ibid.
61. Daniel Fuller, *The Unity of the Bible* (Grand Rapids: Zondervan, 1992), pp. 231-32.
62. Ibid., p. 232.
63. Ibid., p. 235.
64. Ibid., p. 236. See also Harry Blamires, *Knowing the Truth about Heaven and Hell* (Ann Arbor: Servant Books, 1988), chapter 1 "Is Punishment Necessary?"
65. Fuller, *Unity of the Bible*, p. 238.
66. Ibid., p. 241.
67. D.A. Carson, *Gagging of God: Christianity Confronts Pluralism* (Grand Rapids: Zondervan, 1996), p. 530.
68. Fuller, *Unity of the Bible*, p. 243.
69. *Two Views of Hell: A Biblical and Theological Dialogue* (Downers Grove: InterVarsity, 2000), p. 142.
70. Ajith Fernando, *Crucial Questions about Hell* (Wheaton: Crossway Books, 1991), p. 43.
71. Fuller, *Unity of the Bible*, p. 246.
72. Ewards quoted in Fuller, *Unity of the Bible*, p. 247.
73. Stott and Edwards, *Evangelical Essentials*, p. 319.

74. Ibid.
75. Ibid.
76. William Barclay, *A Spiritual Autobiography* (Grand Rapids: Eerdmans, 1977), p. 65.
77. Ibid., p. 68.
78. Barclay quoted in Vernon C. Grounds, "The Final State of the Wicked," *Journal of the Evangelical Theological Society* (September 1981), p. 213.
79. Grounds, "The Final State," p. 211.
80. Reymond, "Stott on Hell," p. 59.
81. Stott and Edwards, *Evangelical Essentials*, p. 320.
82. Rene Pache, *The Future Life*, quoted in Ajith Fernando, *Crucial Questions about Hell* (Wheaton: Crossway Books, 1991), p. 46.
83. Pinnock, "The Finally Impenitent," p. 256.
84. Ibid.
85. Ibid., p. 257.
86. Ibid.
87. Ibid., p. 259.
88. Gomes, "Evangelicals and Hell, Part Two," p. 11.
89. Ibid.
90. William G.T. Shedd, *The Doctrine of Endless Punishment* (reprint, Minneapolis: Klock and Mock, 1980), p. 92.
91. Stott and Edwards, *Evangelical Essentials*, p. 317.
92. Gomes, "Evangelicals and Hell, Part Two," p. 11.
93. Ibid.
94. Gomes, "Evangelicals and Hell, Part One," p. 18.
95. Ibid.
96. Pinnock, "Fire, Then Nothing," p. 40.
97. Pinnock, "The Finally Impenitent," p. 257.
98. Gomes, "Evangelicals and Hell, Part Two," p. 12.
99. Gomes, "Evangelicals and Hell, Part One," p. 18.
100. Pinnock, "The Finally Impenitent", p. 257.
101. Gomes, "Evangelicals and Hell, Part Two," p. 12.
102. *The Oxford Dictionary of Quotations*, 3rd ed. (New York: Oxford Univ. Press, 1979), p. 565.
103. Grounds, "The Final State," p. 219.

104. Edward Fudge, *The Fire That Consumes* (Houston: Providential Press, 1982), p. 180.
105. Pinnock, "The Finally Impenitent," p. 249.
106. Clark H. Pinnock, *Three Keys to Spiritual Renewal* (Minneapolis: Bethany Hse., 1985), p. 26.
107. Evángel Publishing House, 2000.
108. Clark H. Pinnock and Robert C. Brow (Contributor), (Downers Grove: InterVarsity, 1994).
109. "The Didsbury Lectures" by Clark H. Pinnock (Baker, 2001).
110. John. R.W. Stott, *Our Guilty Silence* (Downers Grove, Ill.: InterVarsity Pr., 1967), p. 45.
111. Walter Brueggemann quoted in *Christianity Today*, 19 August 1991, p. 36.

Chapter 4

1. Clark H. Pinnock, "Toward an Evangelical Theology of Religions," *Journal of the Evangelical Theological Society* 33, (September 1990): p. 361.
2. Ibid., p. 362.
3. Quoted in John E. Sanders, "Is Belief in Christ Necessary for Salvation?" *Evangelical Quarterly* 60 (1988): p. 241.
4. *Operation World: 21st Century Edition*, Patrick Johnstone and Jason Mandryk with Robyn Johnstone (WEC International, 2001), p. 15.
5. Ronald Blue, "Untold Billions: Are They Really Lost?" *Bibliotheca Sacra* (October-December, 1981), p. 340.
6. Ibid.
7. *Operation World*, p. 7.
8. Sanders, "Is Belief Necessary?" p. 241.
9. Ibid., p. 242.
10. Ibid., p. 246.
11. Evert D. Osburn, "Those Who Have Never Heard: Have They No Hope?" *Journal of the Evangelical Theological Society* 32 (September 1989), p. 368. See also John Lawson, *Introduction to Christian Doctrine* (Grand Rapids: Zondervan, 1980), p. 216.
12. Osburn, "Those Who Have Never Heard," p. 368.

13. Ibid., p. 370.
14. Ibid., p. 372.
15. Anderson quoted in J.I. Packer, "Evangelicals and the Way of Salvation," in *Evangelical Affirmations*, ed. Kenneth S. Kantzer and Carl F.H. Henry (Grand Rapids: Zondervan, 1990), p. 123.
16. Bruce J. Nicholls, "The Salvation and Lostness of Mankind," *Evangelical Review of Theology* 15 (January 1991), p. 20.
17. Blue, "Untold Billions," pp. 342-43.
18. Lindsell quoted in Sanders, "Is Belief Necessary?" p. 243.
19. Blue, "Untold Billions," p. 344.
20. Ibid., p. 345.
21. Ibid.
22. Nicholls, "The Salvation and Lostness of Mankind, p. 15.
23. Ibid.
24. Ibid., p. 17.
25. Pinnock quoted in Blue, "Untold Billions," p. 343.
26. Ibid., p. 347.
27. Ibid., p. 346.
28. Kane quoted in Ibid., p. 348.
29. Osburn, "Those Who Have Never Heard," p. 369.
30. Nicholls, "The Salvation and Lostness," p. 19.
31. Ibid.
32. Packer, "Evangelicals and the Way of Salvation," in Kantzer and Henry, *Evangelical Affirmations*, p. 123.
33. J.I. Packer, "Good Pagans and God's Kingdom," *Christianity Today*, 17 January 1986, p. 25.
34. Nicholls, "The Salvation and Lostness," p. 19.
35. Donald G. Bloesch, *Essentials of Evangelical Theology* Vol. 2: "Life, Ministry, and Hope" (San Francisco: Harper and Row, 1978) p. 226.
36. Ibid., p. 227.
37. Sayers quoted in John Bowker, "The Human Imagination of Hell," *Theology* 85 (November 1982), p. 406.
38. C.S. Lewis, *The Great Divorce* (New York: Macmillan, 1946) p. 8.
39. *World* magazine, July/August, 2002.

40. Ibid., p. 54.
41. Ibid., pp. 56-58.
42. Sanders, "Is Belief Necessary?" p. 245.
43. Robert E. Rasmussen, "Are We Too Worried about the Unsaved?" *Discipleship Journal*, July/August, 1991, p. 59.
44. Lewis, *Great Divorce*, p. 72.
45. Sanders, "Is Belief Necessary?" p. 250.
46. Origen quoted in Bloesch, *Evangelical Theology*, p. 230.
47. Ibid., p. 227.
48. Ibid., p. 186.
49. Sanders, "Is Belief Necessary?" pp. 249-50.
50. Ibid., p. 250.
51. Ibid., p. 252.
52. Ibid.
53. Wayne Grudem, *The First Epistle of Peter* rev. ed., Tyndale Bible Commentaries Series (Grand Rapids: Eerdmans, 1988), p. 204.
54. Ibid., p. 206.
55. Ibid., p. 211.
56. Ibid., p. 220.
57. Ibid., pp. 224-25.
58. Ibid., p. 225.
59. Ibid., p. 229. Other examples of this stylistic phrase are listed here.
60. Ibid., p. 229.
61. Ibid., p. 230.
62. Ibid.
63. Ibid., pp. 230-32.
64. Ibid., p. 232.
65. Ibid.
66. Ibid., p. 238.
67. Ibid., p. 239.
68. L. Berkhof, *Systematic Theology* (Grand Rapids: Eerdmans, 1939), p. 342.
69. Ibid.
70. Ibid.

71. I. Howard Marshall, *New Testament Interpretation* (Grand Rapids: Eerdmans, 1977), p. 272. See also Peter H. Davids, *The First Epistle of Peter* (Grand Rapids: Eerdmans, 1990).
72. Philip Schaff, *History of the Christian Church* Vol. 2: Ante Nicene Christianity (Grand Rapids: Eerdmans, 1910), p. 532.
73. Bloesch, *Evangelical Theology*, p. 227.
74. Berkhof, *Systematic Theology*, p. 341.
75. Packer, "Evangelicals and the Way of Salvation," in Kantzer and Henry, *Evangelical Affirmations*, p. 121.

Chapter 5

1. Ellen G. White, *The Great Controversy* (Washington, D.C.: Review and Herald, 1888), p. 534.
2. Ibid., p. 545.
3. Leon Morris, "The Dreadful Harvest," *Christianity Today*, 27 May 1991, p. 34.
4. Ligon Duncan, "Speaking Soberly and Sensitively about Hell," *Modern Reformation*, May/June 2002, vol. 11, no. 3, pp. 21-24.
5. National Press
6. New Kensington, PA: Whitaker House, 1998.
7. See my discussion of Baxter's book in my *Heaven: Thinking Now about Forever* (Camp Hill, PA: Christian Publications, 2002), pp. 53-64.
8. William Barclay, *The Gospel of Mark* (Philadelphia: Westminster Pr., 1954), p.239.
9. Ibid.
10. C.S. Lewis, *The Great Divorce* (New York: Macmillan, 1946), p. 5.
11. Alfred Edersheim, *The Life and Times of Jesus the Messiah* (MacDonald Pub. Co., n.d.), p. 453.
12. Ibid.
13.Laurence E. Porter, *The International Bible Commentary* (Chicago: John C. Winston, 1928), p. 1216.
14.Richardson quoted in Porter, *International Bible*, p. 107.

15. Alan F. Johnson and Robert E. Webber, *What Christians Believe: A Biblical and Historical Summary* (Grand Rapids: Zondervan, 1989), p. 426.
16. Murray J. Harris, "The New Testament View of Life after Death," *Themelios* 11 (January 1986), p.48.
17. Millard J. Erickson, *Christian Theology* (Grand Rapids: Baker, 1987), pp. 527, 775, 1017.
18. Charles C. Ryrie, *Basic Theology* (Wheaton, Ill.: Victor Bks., 1988), p. 519. See also my *DocTALK: A Fairly Serious Survey of All That Theological Stuff* (Scotland: Christian Focus Publications, 2002).
19. James Oliver Buswell, *A Systematic Theology of the Christian Religion* (Grand Rapids: Zondervan, 1962), p. 305.
20. Ibid., pp. 306-08.
21. L. Berkhof, *Systematic Theology* (Grand Rapids: Eerdmans, 1939), p. 688.
22. Ibid., p. 679.
23. Ibid., p. 689.
24. Ibid., p. 683.
25. Ibid., p. 735.
26. Porter, *International Bible*, p. 1216.
27. Ibid.
28. Edward Fudge, *The Fire That Consumes* (Houston: Providential Press, 1982), p. 208.
29. E.J. Tinsley, *The Gospel According to Luke* (Cambridge: Cambridge University Pr., 1965), p. 162.
30. G. Campbell Morgan, *The Gospel According to Luke* (New York: Fleeting H. Revell, 1931), pp. 190-91.
31. Erickson, *Christian Theology*, p. 1177. The annihilationist Edward Fudge says " . . . the intermediate state has absolutely nothing to do with the nature of final punishment in hell . . ." (*Two Views of Hell: A Biblical and Theological Dialogue* (Downers Grove: InterVarsity, 2000), p. 203).
32. A.T. Robertson, *Word Pictures in the New Testament* (Grand Rapids: Baker, 1930), vol. 2, p. 221.
33. William Barclay, *The Gospel of Luke* (Philadelphia: Westminster Pr., 1953), p. 222.

34. Morgan, *The Gospel According to Luke*, p. 191.
35. Ibid., p. 192.
36. Edersheim, *Life and Times of Jesus*, p. 455.
37. W.E. Vine, *An Expository Dictionary of New Testament Words* (Old Tappan, N.J.: Fleeting H. Revell, 1940), kolpos, pp. 141-42.
38. Edersheim, *Life and Times of Jesus*, p. 455.
39. William F. Arndt and F. Wilbur Gingrich, *A Greek English Lexicon of the New Testament and Other Early Christian Literature* (Chicago: Univ. of Chicago Pr., 1957), sterizo, p.775.
40. Robertson, *Word Pictures*, p. 223.
41. R.C. Trench, *Notes on the Parables of Our Lord* (Grand Rapids: Baker, 1948), p. 162.
42. Ray Summers, *Commentary on Luke* (Waco, Texas: Word Inc., 1972), p. 195.
43. *The New Testament in Modern English*, Touchstone Books, 1996.
44. Trench, *Notes on the Parables*, p. 162.
45. Barclay, *Gospel of Luke*, p. 222.
46. Quoted in Charles S. Mackenzie, *Pascal's Anguish and Joy* (New York: Philosophical Library, 1973), fragments 11-194.
47. Trench, *Notes on the Parables*, p. 169.
48. Edersheim, *Life and Times of Jesus*, p. 456.
49. Robertson, *Word Pictures*, p. 224.
50. Ibid.
51. Ibid.
52. Trench, *Notes on the Parables*, p. 17.
53. Harris, "The New Testament View," p. 48.
54. Ibid.
55. Nels F.S. Ferré, *The Christian Understanding of God* (London: SCM Press, 1951), p. 245.
56. *Carl Henry at His Best*, Steve Halliday and Al Janssen eds. (Portland, Ore.: Multnomah, 1989), p. 130.
57. Peter Toon, *Heaven and Hell: A Biblical and Theological Overview* (Nashville: Thomas Nelson, 1986), p. 3.

58. Quoted in Clyde S. Kilby, *A Mind Awake: An Anthology of C.S. Lewis* (New York: Harcourt, Brace and World, 1968), p. 169.
59. *Webster's New Collegiate Dictionary* (Springfield, Mass.: G. and C. Merriam, 1977), p. 65.
60. Robert L. Reymond, "Dr. John Stott on Hell," *Presbyterian* 16 (Spring 1990), p. 46.
61. John Wenham, *The Enigma of Evil* (Grand Rapids: Zondervan, 1986), p. 27.
62. John H. Gerstner, "Jesus and Hell," *Tabletalk*, July 1990, p. 7.
63. Kantzer quoted in Harry Friesen, "A Critical Analysis of Universalism" (Th.D. diss., Dallas Theological Seminary, 1968), p. 103.

Chapter 6

1. Wicks quoted in Michael Pocock, "The Destiny of the World and the Work of Missions," *Bibliotheca Sacra* 145 (October-December 1988), p. 448.
2. John Bowker, "The Human Imagination of Hell," *Theology* 85 (November 1982), p. 407.
3. Clark H. Pinnock, "The Destruction of the Finally Impenitent," *Criswell Theological Review* 4 (Spring 1990), p. 253.
4. John Lawson, *Introduction to Christian Doctrine* (Grand Rapids: Zondervan, 1980), p. 262. Emphasis mine.
5. Ibid., p. 263.
6. Pinnock, "The Finally Impenitent," p. 253.
7. Jonathan Edwards, "A Treatise Concerning Religious Affections," in *The Works of Jonathan Edwards*, vol. 2, ed. Perry Miller (New Haven: Yale Univ. Press, 1957).
8. John R.W. Stott, *Culture and the Bible* (Downers Grove, Ill.: InterVarsity Pr., 1979), pp. 33-34.
9. Donald G. Bloesch, *Essentials of Evangelical Theology*, Vol. 2 "Life, Ministry, and Hope" (New York: Harper and Row, 1978), p. 225.

10. Quoted by Johan D. Tangelder in his article "The Teaching of Clark Pinnock," http://www.banneroftruth.co.uk/articles/2001/11/teaching.htm.)
11. Clark H. Pinnock, *Tracking the Maze* (New York: Harper and Row, 1990), p. 53.
12. Ibid., p. 161.
13. Ibid.
14. Ibid., p. 168. Emphasis mine.
15. Ibid., p. 175.
16. Ibid.
17. Ibid., p. 176. For Pinnock's doctrine of inspiration, see his *The Scripture Principle* (New York: Harper and Row, 1984).
18. Clark H. Pinnock, *The Scripture Principle* (New York: Harper and Row, 1984), p. 117.
19. Quoted in Leonard Sweet, *Aqua Church* (Loveland, Colorado: Group Publishing, 1999), p. 59. From Pinnock's book *Tracking the Maze* (New York: Harper & Row, 1984), p. 224.
20. Quoted by Johan D. Tangelder in his article "The Teaching of Clark Pinnock," http://www.banneroftruth.co.uk/articles/2001/11/teaching.htm.
21. Clark H. Pinnock and Delwin Brown, *Theological Crossfire: An Evangelical/Liberal Dialogue* (Grand Rapids: Zondervan, 1990), pp. 226-27. Emphasis mine.
22. Ibid., p. 230. Emphasis mine.
23. Ibid. Emphasis mine.
24. J.I. Packer, "Evangelicals and the Way of Salvation," in *Evangelical Affirmations,* ed. Kenneth Kantzer and Carl F.H. Henry (Grand Rapids: Zondervan, 1990), p. 117.
25. Ibid., p. 126.
26. C.S. Lewis, *The Lion, the Witch, and the Wardrobe* (New York: Macmillan, 1950), pp. 75-76.
27. John W. Wenham, *The Enigma of Evil* (Grand Rapids: Zondervan, 1985), p. 26.
28. A.T. Robertson, *Word Pictures in the New Testament* (Grand Rapids: Baker, 1932), vol. 5, p. 386.

29. C.S. Lewis, *The Great Divorce* (New York: Macmillan, 1946), p. 77.
30. Quoted in Clyde S. Kilby, *A Mind Awake: An Anthology of C.S. Lewis* (New York: Harcourt, Brace & World, 1968), p.170.
31. Alfred Edersheim, *The Life and Times of Jesus the Messiah* (MacDonald Pub. Co., n.d.), p. 253.
32. Philip Yancey, *Disappointment with God* (Grand Rapids: Zondervan, 1988), p. 84.
33. Richard J. Bauckham, "Universalism: A Historical Survey," *Evangelical Review of Theology*, 15 (January 1991), p. 27.
34. R.C. Sproul, *The Holiness of God* (Wheaton, Ill.: Tyndale Pubs., 1985), p. 150.
35. Eliot quoted in Bernard Ramm, *After Fundamentalism: The Future of Evangelical Theology* (San Francisco: Harper and Row, 1983), p. 201.
36. Robert Mounce, *The Book of Revelation* (Grand Rapids: Eerdmans, 1977), p. 295. Quoted in Fernando, p. 96.
37. John Calvin, *Institutes of the Christian Religion*, ed. John T. McNeill, (Philadelphia: Westminster Pr., 1977), bk. 2, chap. 16, sec. 2.
38. Ibid., sec. 4.
39. Ibid., chap. 17, sec. 3.
40. Bloesch, *Evangelical Theology*, vol. 2, pp. 227, 229.
41. MacLeod quoted in Edmund Fuller, ed., *Affirmations of God and Man: Writings for Modern Dialogue* (New York: Association Press, 1967), p. 44. John H. Gerstner, *Repent or Perish* (Ligonier, Pa.: Soli Deo Gloria Pub., 1990), p. 16.
42. John H. Gerstner, *Repent or Perish* (Ligonier, Pa: Soli Deo Gloria Pub., 1990), p. 16.
43. J.I. Packer, *Knowing God* (Downers Grove, Ill., InterVarsity Pr., 1973), p. 136.
44. Arthur W. Pink, *The Attributes of God* (Swengel, Pa.: Refiner Publications, 1967), p. 83.
45. Farmer quoted in William V. Crockett, "Wrath That Endures Forever," *Journal of the Evangelical Theological Society* 34 (June 1991), p. 97.
46. Ibid.

47. Ibid., p. 198.
48. Ibid., p. 195.
49. Ibid., p. 196.
50. Ibid., p. 199.
51. Ibid., p. 200.
52. Ibid., p. 201.
53. Thomas Talbott, *The Inescapable Love of God* (Universal Publishers, 1999), p. 34.
54. R.C. Sproul, "The Limits of God's Grace: Jonathan Edwards on Hell", *Tabletalk*, July 1990, 4. See also Bruce W. Davidson's article, "Reasonable Damnation: How Jonathan Edwards Argued for the Rationality of Hell," *Journal of the Evangelical Theological Society* 38 (March 1995), p. 47.
55. Buechner quoted in Timothy K. Jones, "Death in the Mirror," *Christianity Today*, 24 June 1991, p. 30.
56. C.S. Lewis, *The Problem of Pain* (New York: Macmillan, 1962), p. 128.
57. For a discussion on getting ready for heaven, please see my *Heaven: Thinking Now about Forever* (Camp Hill, PA: Christian Publications, 2002).
58. Harry Blamires, *Knowing the Truth about Heaven and Hell: Our Choices and Where They Lead Us* (Ann Arbor: Servant Bks., 1988), p. xii.
59. Bauckham, "Universalism: A Historical Survey," p. 27. See also the article "Can We Be Good Without Hell?" in *Christianity Today*, June 16, 1997.
60. Gerstner, *Repent or Perish*, p. 28.
61. Rollheiser quoted in Rick Bell, "Paying the Price," *Western Report*, 8 July 1991, pp. 42-43.
62. Lewis, *The Great Divorce*, pp. 72-73.
63. J.I. Packer, "Evangelicals and the Way of Salvation," in Kanzter and Henry, *Evangelical Affirmations*, p.117.
64. Stephen H. Travis, "The Problem of Judgment," *Themelios* 11 (January 1986), p. 56.
65. Packer, "Evangelicals and the Way of Salvation," in Kantzer and Henry, *Evangelical Affirmations*, p. 118.

66. Peter Toon, *Heaven and Hell: A Biblical and Theological Overview* (Nashville: Thomas Nelson, 1986), p. 46.
67. Ibid., p. 199.
68. Ibid., p. 200.
69. Ibid., p. 201.
70. Ibid.
71. Ibid.
72. Lewis, *Problem of Pain*, p. 125.
73. Quoted in Erwin W. Lutzer, *Coming to Grips with Hell* (Chicago: Moody Pr., 1990), p. 7.
74. Toon, *Heaven and Hell*, p. 179.
75. Pinnock, *Tracking the Maze*, p. 190. Emphasis mine.
76. Pinnock, *Theological Crossfire*, p. 231.
77. Pinnock, *Tracking the Maze*, pp. 67-68. Emphasis mine.
78. Ibid., p. 7.
79. David F. Wells, "Everlasting Punishment," *Christianity Today*, 20 March 1987, p. 42.
80. Schaeffer quoted in Haddon Robinson, *Biblical Preaching* (Grand Rapids: Baker, 1980), p. 101.
81. Stephen Brown, *No More Mr. Nice Guy: Saying Goodbye to "Doormat" Christianity* (Nashville: Thomas Nelson, 1986), p. 44.
82. Harold B. Kuhn, "Universalism in Today's Theology," *Christianity Today*, 16 September 1957, p. 10.
83. William Barclay, *The Gospel of Matthew* (Philadelphia: Westminster Pr., 1957), vol. 2, p. 14.
84. Quoted in Charles Colson, *Who Speaks for God?* (Westchester, Ill.: Crossway, 1985), p. 68.
85. Henri J.M. Nouwen, *The Way of the Heart* (San Francisco: Harper and Row, 1981), p. 21.

Subject Index

Scripture Index

Other books of interest from Christian Focus Publications

LARRY DIXON

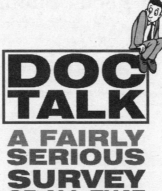

DOC TALK

A FAIRLY SERIOUS SURVEY OF ALL THAT THEOLOGICAL STUFF

Doc-Talk

A Fairly Serious Survey of all that Theological Stuff

Larry Dixon

People ask for the strangest things in Christian books – a *pocket-sized*, large print Bible or a profound leader's guide for *instant* Bible studies! Half a moments thought would make us realise just how silly we can be....does a really interesting book on Christian doctrine come into the same category?

God is the most interesting person you could know, so why did you ever doubt it could be done?

In Today's sitcom-stupid society, wisecracking can sometimes still stab awake people, especially young people, whom anything else would send to sleep. So there is a real job out there for this jokey-sober workbook on Christian Foundations to do.

J.I. Packer,
Regent College, Vancouver, British Columbia

Whenever Larry Dixon writes about doctrine, it's very understandable AND practical. He writes in a way that not only satisfies your intellect, but warms your heart and motivates you to action.

Dr. George W. Murray, President,
Columbia International University, South Carolina, USA

There is a widespread flight from theology in our churches. The result? – a merely 'feel good' Christianity, spiritually flabby, weak as water. We must, must, must, get Christians to study Bible doctrine. We should work hard at getting this book into the hands of family members, giving it to our youth group members, commending it from our pulpits.

Dr Geoffrey Grogan,
Former Principal Emeritus, Glasgow Bible College

Larry Dixon has a marvelous facility with words, making profound concepts appear straightforward. Covering the entire scope of Christian theology as he does, the reader is teased along to richer territories effortlessly. For Christians who want a primer on the basics of Christian theology, this is the book to read.

Derek W. H. Thomas,
Reformed Theological Seminary

Dr. Dixon is a systematic theologian, and his material is well organized. Hence the ease with which a reader makes his way through the book. I recommend the book to Christians who want to know what to believe - and to theologians too!

C. Donald Cole,
Moody Broadcasting Network.

ISBN 1 85792 729 X

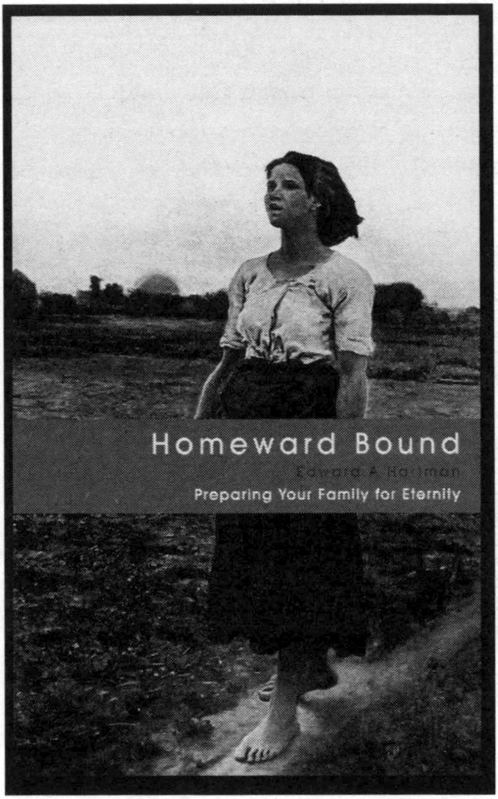
Homeward Bound
Edward A Hartman
Preparing Your Family for Eternity

Homeward Bound

Preparing Your Family for Eternity

Edward A Hartman

Never do anything which you would be afraid to do were it the last hour of your life **Jonathan Edwards (aged 19)**

The concept of dying well has been very real to Ed Hartman since August 1995. Hartman was studying at Westminster Theological Seminary, California and had just discovered a treatise by the Puritan William Perkins on the *'Right Manner Of Dying Well'*.

This discovery was no accident, as it was a matter of minutes later that Ed discovered that his wife, the mother of their 4 children, was not at all well. Amy Hartman was diagnosed with a Brain Tumour, which after 6 months of much prayer, and great heartache, proved to be terminal.

With this traumatic experience behind him, Hartman deals with the topic of preparing your life, and the life of those you love, for death in a practical and thoroughly Christ-centred manner.

Hartman looks at our most important relationships, with God, with our spouses, with our family and with those around us. He shares with us the advice of Perkins and other Puritans, who lived in a time that had a much healthier attitude, and much closer relationship, with death.

He concludes that the primary aim, of those sincerely desiring to die well, must be to have Christ at the centre of everything - and that true devotion to Christ comes only through our relationship with him.

Included in the book is the full Perkins Treatise "*Right Manner of Dying Well*' which became such a comfort to Edward in a time of great trial.

If your heart thirsts not for pious platitudes from the complacent but for real comfort from a brother who has found God faithful in the valley of death's shadow, read this book.

Dennis E. Johnson, Ph.D.,
Professor of Practical Theology,
Westminster Theological Seminary of California

ISBN 1 85792 682 X

Christian Focus Publications

publishes books for all ages

Our mission statement –

STAYING FAITHFUL

In dependence upon God we seek to help make His infallible word, the Bible, relevant. Our aim is to ensure that the Lord Jesus Christ is presented as the only hope to obtain forgiveness of sin, live a useful life and look forward to heaven with Him.

REACHING OUT

Christ's last command requires us to reach out to our world with His gospel. We seek to help fulfill that by publishing books that point people towards Jesus and help them to develop a Christ-like maturity. We aim to equip all levels of readers for life, work, ministry and mission.

Books in our adult range are published in three imprints.

Christian Focus contains popular works including biographies, commentaries, basic doctrine, and Christian living. Our children's books are also published in this imprint.

Mentor focuses on books written at a level suitable for Bible College and seminary students, pastors, and other serious readers. The imprint includes commentaries, doctrinal studies, examination of current issues, and church history.

Christian Heritage contains classic writings from the past.

For a free catalogue of all our titles, please write to

Christian Focus Publications, Ltd
Geanies House, Fearn,
Ross-shire, IV20 1TW, Scotland, United Kingdom
info@christianfocus.com

For details of our titles visit us on our website
www.christianfocus.com